TEACHING SIGN LANGUAGE TO CHIMPANZEES

List of Tables

List of Figures

Contents

Project Washoe was originally supported by grants MH-12154 from the National Institute of Mental Health and GB-7432 from the National Science Foundation. We gratefully acknowledge this support and the support that sign language studies of chimpanzees have received since then, in Reno, from NIH, NSF, the National Geographic Society, the Grant Foundation, the Spencer Foundation, the University of Nevada, and UNR Foundation. At Oklahoma, sign language studies of chimpanzees have been supported by NSF, NIH, and the University of Oklahoma; at Ellensburg, by the Friends of Washoe Foundation, the National Geographic Society, and Central Washington University.

Published by
State University of New York Press, Albany

©1989   State University of New York

For information, address State University of New York
Press, State University Plaza, Albany, N.Y., 12246

Library of Congress Cataloging-in-Publication Data

Teaching sign language to chimpanzees/edited by R. Allen Gardner,
    Beatrix T. Gardner, Thomas E. Van Cantfort.
        p. cm.
    Bibliography: p.
    Includes index.
    ISBN 0-88706-965-7.   ISBN 0-88706-966-5 (pbk.)
    1. Chimpanzees—Psychology.   2. Human-animal communication.
    3. Sign language.   4. Learning in animals.   I. Gardner, R. Allen,
    1930–   . II. Gardner, Beatrix T., 1933–   . III. Van Cantfort,
    Thomas E., 1949–   .
    QL737.P96T42 1989
    599.88′ 440459—dc19   88-18863
                                                                    CIP

TEACHING SIGN LANGUAGE TO CHIMPANZEES

Edited by:

R. Allen Gardner
Beatrix T. Gardner
Thomas E. Van Cantfort

STATE UNIVERSITY OF NEW YORK PRESS

Preface

With the beginning of Project Washoe in 1966, sign language studies of chimpanzees provided a new tool for comparative studies of intelligence and communication. With time, the methodology of the research has developed and the scope of investigation has enlarged. In studies of human children, the narrow interest in syntax, to the exclusion of almost every other aspect of intellectual development, has given way to a much broader view of the role of two-way communication in the development of intelligence and the relation of linguistic development to all aspects of intellectual development. This, in turn, has yielded a broader empirical base for comparisons between human and nonhuman beings, together with empirical results showing the intimate relationship among communicative, intellectual, and social developments. In this volume, investigators who have participated in sign language studies of chimpanzees report the methods and findings of their laboratories, summarize recent developments, and point out future directions in plain language that should make the discussion accessible to a wide range of readers.

Until now, our reports have usually taken the form of relatively short, highly compressed articles in widely scattered professional books and journals with much of the background detail sacrificed to save space. This volume began as a way of collecting earlier reports and publishing them together with the most recent findings in one easily accessible place. Within this format, we found that we could devote whole chapters to detailed descriptions of the unique laboratory procedures developed in this line of research and to explain the rationale for each procedure in more detail and, we hope, more clearly than we ever could do in separate articles. Chapter 1 describes the role of cross-fostering and the role of American Sign Language (ASL), and relates these to the findings that appear in later chapters. Chapter 3 describes how ASL was used in the cross-fostering laboratory in Reno, how we taught signs to the cross-fosterlings, and how each sign looked. We are particularly grateful for the opportunity to publish for the first time in Tables 3.1 and 3.2 comprehensive descriptions of all of the signs in the vocabularies of Washoe, Moja, Tatu, and Dar.

The cross-fosterlings did not lose their voices when they learned to sign, they developed a normal (for their age level) repertoire of chimpanzee vocal behavior. Chapter 2 reports an experiment that compared the voiced and signed responses of Tatu and Dar both to announcements of emotionally charged events and to the events, themselves. The voiced responses were far more stereotyped and more closely bound to the emotionally charged events than were the signed responses, a finding that confirms the rationale for using a signed rather than a spoken language with chimpanzees. To arrive at a suitable list of events to announce in this experiment, we prepared a representative list of daily events and activities and rated each event and activity for its degree of positive and negative charge. Thus, Table 2.1 also provides a valuable inventory of daily life in the cross-fostering laboratory to supplement the description in Chapter 1.

Washoe, Moja, Pili, Tatu, and Dar used the signs of ASL to communicate information. Chapter 4 describes the methods and results of a vocabulary test in which the chimpanzees had to communicate with observers whose only source of information was the signs made by the chimpanzees. All of the trials on these tests were first trials to show that the signs referred to natural language categories, FLOWER for any flower, SHOE for any shoe, DOG for any dog, and so on.

Observations made during formal tests represent only a fraction of the observations of spontaneous conversational signing in the cross-fostering laboratory. Chapters 5 and 6 report systematic samples of the conversational use of signs and compare developmental trends in children and chimpanzees. Human children form appropriate replies to questions before they, themselves, produce well-formed questions. In a sense, the ability to restrict replies to correct sentence constituents is more significant than the ability to memorize sematically correct answers. For example, when someone asked WHO THAT? while indicating Roger Fouts, all semantically correct replies had to include the name sign ROGER (e.g., ROGER, THAT ROGER, GOOD ROGER). Nevertheless, incorrect names such as SUSAN or GREG were still correct in a way that replies such as HAT or BLACK or TICKLE ME were not. Chapter 5 analyzes systematic samples of the replies of Washoe, Moja, Pili, Tatu, and Dar to Wh-questions for developmental trends that parallel the trends found in the development of human children.

Each human language uses a mixture of devices such as markers, inflections, and word order to modulate meaning. English is unusual in its heavy reliance on word order, but ASL is more like other languages that rely heavily on inflectional devices. In the case of human signers, skill at using the inflectional devices of ASL develops throughout childhood. Chapter 6 is a report of the early use of inflectional devices comparing development in children and cross-fostered chimpanzees.

There are other ways to teach sign language and to test for the results. The poor results of Project Nim at Columbia University are puzzling until the methods of Project Nim are compared with the methods of the Reno laboratory. After Nim left Columbia he went to the University of Oklahoma where he found human conversational partners who followed Roger Fouts' procedures rather than the operant rigor and drill of the Columbia laboratory. Chapter 7 reports the results of an experiment that contrasted Fouts' conversational style ✓ with Terrace's operant rigor when used with the same chimpanzee, Nim.

Washoe left Reno for the Institute for Primate Studies in Norman, Oklahoma with Roger Fouts when she was about five years old. Later Moja joined her in Oklahoma. Later still the colony moved to Central Washington State University in Ellensburg with Roger and Deborah Fouts. Eventually, all of the chimpanzees who had been cross-fostered in the Reno laboratory joined the group in Ellensburg.

When he was ten months old, Loulis was adopted by 14-year-old Washoe in Oklahoma shortly after the death of her own newborn infant. To show that Washoe could teach signs to an infant without human intervention, the Foutses introduced a drastic procedure. For five years, all human signing was forbidden when Loulis was present. Chapter 8 reports on the signs that Loulis learned that he could only have learned from Washoe and the other cross-fostered chimpanzees. The Foutses also used remotely operated video cameras to record conversations among the chimpanzees in the Ellensburg laboratory under conditions in which no human beings were present. Chapter 9 reports on Loulis' role as a conversational partner as observed in these records.

Inevitably each new discovery in these sign language studies of chimpanzees has been drawn into one or another of the classical debates about the gap between human and nonhuman, between intelligence and action, between language and communication, between gesture and word, between language and prelanguage. Stimulated by a wave of research and discovery in the linguistics of sign languages, there has been a corresponding increase in controversy over the fundamental continuity between signed and spoken languages. In Chapter 10, William Stokoe discusses the parallel controversies over the continuity between human speech and human sign on the one hand, and between human signing and chimpanzee signing on the other. Stokoe, chief author of the *Dictionary of American Sign Language* (based on linguistic principles), founder of the Linguistics Research Laboratory at Gallaudet College, and founding editor of *Sign Language Studies* (the first international journal devoted to the linguistics of sign languages), writes from his perspective as pioneer and leader in the descriptive linguistics of sign languages.

This volume is written for those who are more interested in what chimpanzees have done and said under these unique laboratory conditions than in what philosophers and theoreticians might conclude on the subject. Truly discontinuous, all-or-none phenomena must be rare in nature. Historically, the great discontinuities have turned out to be conceptual barriers rather than natural phenomena. They have been passed by and abandoned rather than broken through in the course of scientific progress. The sign language studies of chimpanzees described in this volume have neither sought nor discovered a means of breathing humanity into the soul of a beast. They have assumed instead that there is no discontinuity between verbal behavior and the rest of human behavior or between human behavior and the rest of animal behavior—no barrier to be broken, no chasm to be bridged, only unknown territory to be explored.

1. A Cross-Fostering Laboratory

R. Allen Gardner and Beatrix T. Gardner

O n June 21, 1966, an infant chimpanzee arrived in our laboratory. We named her Washoe, for Washoe County, the home of the University of Nevada. To a casual observer Washoe's new home may not have looked very much like a laboratory. In fact, it was the Gardner residence in the suburbs of Reno, purchased as a faculty home some years earlier, a small, one story, brick and wood home with an attached garage and a largish garden in the back. To that same casual observer, Washoe's daily life may not have looked much like laboratory routine, either. It was rather more like the daily life of human children of her age in the same suburban neighborhood.

Washoe was about ten months old when she arrived in Reno, and almost as helpless as a human child of the same age. In the next few years she learned to drink from a cup and to eat at a table with forks and spoons. She also learned to set and clear the table and even to wash the dishes, in a childish way. She learned to dress and undress herself and she learned to use the toilet to the point where she seemed embarrassed when she could not find a toilet on an outing in the woods, eventually using a discarded coffee pot that she found on a hike. She had the usual children's toys and was particularly fond of dolls, kissing them, feeding them, and even bathing them. She was attracted to picturebooks and magazines almost from the first day and she would look through them by herself or with a friend who would name and explain the pictures and tell stories about them. The objects and activities that most attracted her were those that most engaged the grownups. She was fascinated by household tools, eventually acquiring a creditable level of skill with hammers and screwdrivers.

Washoe lived in a used house trailer, parked in a garden behind the house. With a few minor alterations, it was the same trailer that its previous owners had used as a travelling home. It had the same living room and bedroom furniture and the same kitchen and toilet facilities. Someone came in to the trailer to check her each night and all through the night every night someone listened to her by means of an intercom connected to the Gardner home.

1

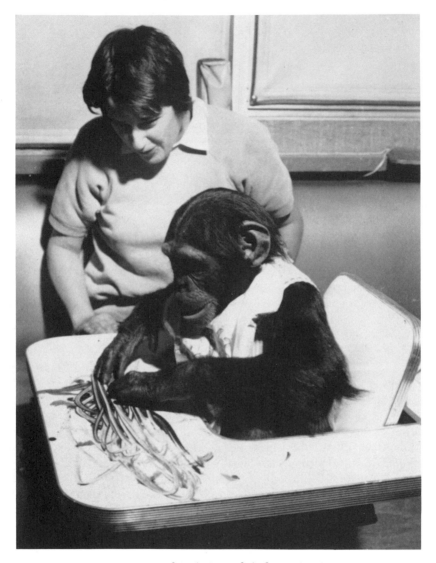

Fig. 1.1 Washoe (27 months): finger-painting.

CROSS-FOSTERING

The first scientist to comment on the Reno laboratory was Winthrop Kellogg (1968), the great pioneer in this field.

Apes as household pets are not uncommon and several books by lay authors attest to the problems involved. . . . But pet behavior is not child behavior, and pet treatment is not child treatment. It is quite another story, therefore, for trained and qualified psychobiologists to observe and measure the reactions of a home-raised pongid amid controlled experimental home surroundings. Such research is difficult, confining, and time-consuming. (p. 423) . . . Although often misunderstood, the scientific rationale for rearing an anthropoid ape in a human household is to find out just how far the ape can go in absorbing the civilizing influences of the environment. To what degree is it capable of responding like a child and to what degree will genetic factors limit its development? (p. 426)

In 1933, Kellogg and Kellogg had outlined the requirements for cross-fostering.

One important consideration upon which we would insist was that the *psychological* as well as the *physical* features of the environment be entirely of a human character. That is, the reactions of all those who came in contact with the subject, and the resulting stimulation which these reactions afforded the subject, should be without exception just such as a normal child might receive. Instances of anthropoid apes which have lived in human households are of course by no means unknown. But in all the cases of which we have any knowledge the "human" treatment accorded the animals was definitely limited by the attitude of the owner and by the degree of his willingness to be put to boundless labor. It is not unreasonable to suppose, if an organism of this kind is kept in cage for a part of each day or night, if it is led about by means of a collar and a chain, or if it is fed from a plate upon the floor, that these things must surely develop responses which are different from those of a human. A child itself, if similarly treated, would most certainly acquire some genuinely *unchildlike* reactions. Again, if the organism is talked to and called like a dog or a cat, if it is consistently petted or scratched behind the ears as these animals are often treated, or if in other ways it is given *pet stimuli* instead of *child stimuli* the resulting behavior may be expected to show the effects of such stimulation.

In this connection it was our earnest purpose to make the training of the ape what might be called *incidental* as opposed to *systematic* or controlled training. What it got from its surroundings it was to pick up by itself just as a growing child acquires new modes of behavior. We wished to avoid deliberately teaching the animal, trial by trial, a series of tricks or stunts which it might go through upon signal or command. The things that it learned were to be its own reactions to the stimuli about it. They were furthermore to be specifically responses to the household situation and not trained-in or meaningless rituals elicited by a sign from a keeper. The spoon-eating training, to take a concrete example, was to be taken up only in a gradual and irregular manner at mealtime, as the subject's muscular coordination fitted it for this sort of manipulation. We would make no attempt to set it down at specified intervals and labor mechanically through a stated number of trials, rewarding or punishing the animal as it might succeed or fail. Such a proposed procedure, it will be readily seen, is loose and uncontrolled in that it precludes the obtaining of quantitative data on the number of trials necessary to learn,

the number of errors made, or the elapsed time per trial. It has the advantage, nevertheless, of being the same sort of training to which the human infant is customarily sub-
jected in the normal course of its upbringing. (pp. 12–13)

It seems as if no form of behavior is so fundamental or so distinctively
species-specific that it is not deeply sensitive to the effects of early experience.
Ducklings, goslings, lambs, and many other young animals learn to follow the
first moving object that they see, whether it is their own mother, a female of
another species, or a shoebox. The mating songs of many birds are so species-
specific that an ornithologist can identify them by their songs alone without
seeing a single feather. Distinctive and species-specific as these songs may be,
they, too, depend upon early experience.

Niko Tinbergen and his students have made the English herring gull one
of the most thoroughly studied of all animals. Normally reared herring gulls
spend the entire year in England. The lesser black-backed gull also breeds on
English shores, but members of this species normally migrate south to spend
the winter on the seacoasts of Spain, Portugal, and northwest Africa. Harris
(1970) arranged for experimental cross-fostering by placing herring gull eggs
in the nests of lesser black-backs and vice versa, banding the chicks after hatch-
ing so that they could be identified as adults. Many cross-fostered herring gulls
were recovered on the coasts of Spain and Portugal, even though few of the
lesser black-backs stayed in England for the winter.

How about our species, how much does our common humanity depend
upon our common experience of a species-typical human childhood? The question is so tantalizing that even alleged but unverified cases of feral children,
such as Itard's (1801/1962) account of Victor, "the wild boy of Aveyron," attract
serious scholarly attention. Many, presumably insurmountable, ethical and
practical difficulties stand in the way of experimentally controlled, or even ver-
ifiable cases of human children cross-fostered by nonhuman beings. The Kelloggs were the first to attempt the logical alternative; a form of cross-fostering
in which the subjects are chimpanzees and the foster parents are human
beings.

Sibling Species

In appearance the close resemblance between humans and chimpanzees
is certainly striking. Recent research reveals closer and deeper biological
similarities of all kinds (Goodall, 1986). In blood chemistry, for example, relationships between species have been measured more precisely than ever before. On this dimension the chimpanzee is not only the closest species to the
human, but the chimpanzee is closer to the human than the chimpanzee is to
the gorilla or to the orangutan (Goodman, 1976; Sarich & Cronin, 1976).

Of particular importance for cross-fostering is the amount of time that it takes for a chimpanzee to grow up. Newborn chimpanzees are quite helpless. In our laboratory, they did not roll over by themselves until they were four to seven weeks old, sit up until they were ten to fifteen weeks old, or creep until they were twelve to fifteen weeks old. In our laboratory, the change from milk teeth to adult dentition begins when they are about five years old. Under natural conditions in Africa, infant chimpanzees are almost completely dependent on their mothers until they are two or three years old and weaning only begins when they are between four and five years old. Menarche occurs when wild females are ten or eleven, and their first infant is born when they are between twelve and fifteen years old (Goodall, 1986, pp. 84–85, 443). Captive chimpanzees have remained vigorously alive, taking tests and solving experimental problems when they were more than fifty verified years old (Maple & Cone, 1981).

Ten-month-old Washoe was very young, indeed, when she arrived in Reno; she did not have her first canines or molars, her eye-hand coordination was rudimentary, she could only crawl about, and she slept a great deal. We spent the first few months making friends with her and adapting her to the daily routines.

Sign Language Only

In 1968, Kellogg reviewed the results of four attempts at cross-fostering that had been undertaken by professional comparative psychologists before Project Washoe. In all four cases, the infant chimpanzees thrived under human rearing conditions, and they resembled human children in almost all aspects of their behavioral development, with one striking exception. In spite of the fact that the human foster parents in these experiments made every effort to speak to their adopted chimpanzees as parents normally speak to hearing children, the chimpanzees hardly acquired any speech at all. In the most successful case, the chimpanzee Viki spoke only four words, "mama", "papa", "cup", and "up", after nearly seven years of intensive exposure to English together with additional sophisticated, thorough, and ingenious attempts at remedial teaching (Hayes & Nissen, 1971).

For decades, the fact that these cross-fostered chimpanzees all failed to speak was cited and recited to support the traditional doctrine of absolute, unbridgeable discontinuity between human and nonhuman. Other scientists, aware of the silent habits of chimpanzees, concluded that speech was an inappropriate medium of communication for the chimpanzee. What was needed was a human language that did not require human speech. This was the innovation of Project Washoe. For the first time, the human foster family used a gestural rather than a vocal language.

With the introduction of sign language, the line of research pioneered by the Kelloggs and the Hayeses moved forward, dramatically. In 51 months,

<u>Washoe acquired at least 132 signs.</u> She asked for goods and services, and she also asked questions about the world of objects and events around her. When Washoe had about eight signs in her expressive vocabulary, she began to combine them into meaningful phrases. YOU ME HIDE, and YOU ME GO OUT HURRY were common. She called her doll, BABY MINE; the sound of a barking dog, LISTEN DOG; the refrigerator, OPEN EAT DRINK; and her potty-chair, DIRTY GOOD. Along with her skill with cups and spoons, and pencils and crayons, her signing developed stage for stage much like the speaking and signing of human children (B. Gardner & Gardner, 1971, 1974; Van Cantfort & Rimpau, 1982).

The sign language that we chose was American Sign Language (ASL), the naturally occurring gestural language of the deaf in North America. Word-for-sign translation between English and ASL is about as difficult as word-for-word translation between English and any other spoken language. English has many common words and idiomatic expressions that have no precise equivalent in ASL, and ASL has its own complement of signs and idioms that have no precise equivalent in English. There are also radical differences in grammar. Where English relies heavily on word order, ASL is like the many other human languages that convey most of the same distinctions through inflection (see Chapter 6 this volume). Where English makes heavy use of auxiliary verbs such as the copula to be, ASL is like the many other human languages that avoid this device entirely.

Attempting to speak good English while simultaneously signing good ASL is about as difficult as attempting to speak good English while simultaneously writing good Russian. Often, teachers and other helping professionals who only learn to sign in order to communicate with deaf clients, attempt to speak and sign simultaneously. Those who have only recently learned to sign soon find that they are speaking English sentences while adding the signs for a few of the key words in each sentence (Bonvillian, Nelson, & Charrow, 1976). When a native speaker of English practices ASL in this way, the effect is roughly the same as practicing Russian by speaking English sentences and saying some of the key words both in English and in Russian. It is obviously not a good way to master a foreign language.

It was clear from the start of Project Washoe that the human foster family would provide a poor model of sign language if they spoke and signed at the same time. <u>Signing to the infant chimpanzee and speaking English among themselves would also have been inappropriate.</u> That would have lowered the status of signs to something suitable for nursery talk, only. In addition, Washoe would have lost the opportunity to observe adult models of conversation, and the human newcomers to sign language would have lost significant opportunities to practice and to learn from each other. Until 1986, the Reno laboratory was the only laboratory that maintained the rule of sign language only.

To a casual observer looking in on Washoe and her foster family the greatest departure from the world of most human children would probably have been the silence. Modern man is a noisy member of the animal kingdom. Old or young, male or female, wherever you find two or more human beings they are usually vocalizing. By contrast, chimpanzees are usually silent. They seldom vocalize unless they are excited (Yerkes, 1929, pp. 301–309; Goodall, 1986, p. 125). Washoe was also very silent and so were her human companions. The only language that we used in her presence was ASL. There were occasional lapses, as when outside workmen or her pediatrician entered the laboratory, but the lapses were brief and rare.

When Washoe was present, all business, all casual conversation was in ASL. Everyone in the foster family had to be fluent enough to make themselves understood under the sometimes hectic conditions of life with this lively youngster. Visits from nonsigners were strictly limited. Some university professors declined to enter the laboratory when they realized that speaking was against the rules. Others discovered within minutes that the discipline was too much for them, "I know I mustn't talk, but . . ." and their visits were shortened accordingly. A few truly social beings invented their own sign language on the spot. Eventually, we hit on the procedure of teaching visitors a few key phrases that they could repeat indefinitely, I VERY HAPPY MEET YOU, YOU PRETTY GIRL, WASHOE SMART GIRL, and so forth.° Visitors from the deaf community who were fluent in ASL were always a welcome relief.

The rule of sign-language-only required some of the isolation of a field expedition. We lived and worked with Washoe on that corner of suburban Reno as if at a lonely outpost in a hostile country. We were always avoiding people who might speak to Washoe. On outings in the woods, we were as stealthy and cautious as Indian scouts. On drives in town, we wove through traffic like undercover agents. We could stop at a Dairy Queen or a McDonald's fast-food restaurant, but only if they had a secluded parking lot in the back. Then one of Washoe's companions could buy the treats while another waited with her in the car. If Washoe was spotted, the car drove off to return later for the missing passenger and the treats, when the coast was clear.

°Here and throughout this volume, English glosses of ASL signs are written in capital letters. Signed utterances are transcribed into word-for-sign English. We adopted this practice because translations into good English would add words and word endings that have no signed equivalents either in the vocabularies of the chimpanzees or in ASL. This mode of transcription makes the utterances appear to be in a crude or pidgin dialect, but the reader should keep in mind the fact that equally literal word-for-word transcriptions between Russian or Japanese and English appear equally crude. See also B. Gardner & Gardner (1980, pp. 350–352) and Chapters 2, 5, & 6 this volume.

Foster Families

Infant chimpanzees are very much like human children. They each have their own favorite foods and favorite toys, favorite games and favorite people—even their own irrational fears. Viki, who grew up in the Hayes family, was afraid of tarpaulins. The Hayeses would hang pieces of tarpaulin on the handle of a closed door and that was enough to keep Viki from entering a room. Canvas never bothered Washoe, but she was afraid of large dust-mops and we could use those to keep her out of forbidden places. Neither canvas nor dust-mops bothered Moja, but she was extremely disturbed by ice-tray dividers. We kept ice-tray dividers hidden in drawers and closets ready to be shown to Moja as a punishment. One day two-and-a-half-year-old Tatu found one of the ice-tray dividers hidden in a playroom and discovered how much it terrified her friend, five-and-a-half-year old Moja. After chasing big Moja around the room by shaking the ice-tray divider at her, Tatu then tried shaking it at her human companions as if testing its powers.

The worst punishment in our armamentarium was to threaten to leave a crossfosterling entirely alone. We only threatened, since truly leaving one alone was against the rules (except at night when they were asleep). But the threat, itself, was a powerful weapon. Perhaps the most distressing events in any day were the times when a favorite person had to leave. It did not seem to matter whether or not the departing companion was leaving the infant with another favorite person, the parting could still be very difficult. This strong, affectionate attachment of infant chimpanzees to particular human beings is one of their most appealing traits.

As critical as a stable family environment may be for a human child, the stability of a human foster family is even more critical for a cross-fostered chimpanzee. Each human member of a foster family had to have a long and thorough acquaintance with the cross-fosterling. This was an essential ingredient of the family environment and an essential requirement if the observers were to respond appropriately and to record observations in their proper context. Some turnover was inevitable, but most of the personnel participated on a long-term basis. During the fourth and last year that she was in Reno, for example, Washoe spent all of her waking hours with one of six individuals in her foster family. Of these six, three had participated from the day that Washoe arrived in Reno. Two others had been members of her family for three years. The sixth individual arrived at the beginning of the fourth year, replacing another individual who had been a member of the family for the first three years. There were also two regular visitors, who each spent about three hours with Washoe each week, but visitors were never left alone with her.

Reveille was at 7:00 AM and lights out at 8:00 PM, and through all of those hours the cross-fosterlings were never left alone. One or more adults had to be there with each one of them every day, seven days a week, every week of the year. We divided each chimpanzee day into overlapping periods of four to eight hours in which one adult was in primary charge. The overlap of at least one hour between periods made it easier to transfer the youngster from one primary caregiver to the next. It was also the time for games and other activities that required more than two players, and the time when adults could converse with each other in sign language. When one adult was assigned a period longer than four hours, there were scheduled visitors to break up the period and to make it more social. Expensive as these overlaps were in personnel costs, they were essential to the method.

In laboratories, infant chimpanzees do survive in cages without the individual attention that Washoe, Moja, Pili, Tatu, and Dar received in Reno, but the mortality rate is far higher and the landmarks of development such as rolling over, sitting up, even creeping unaided are reached many weeks later (Riesen & Kinder, 1952). It is one thing to take a caged infant out for occasional, brief periods of individual play or testing; it would be another matter altogether to try to leave a cross-fostered infant alone in a cage on weekends and holidays.

Second Project

In October, 1970, after 51 months in Reno, when Washoe was about five years old, she went to the University of Oklahoma with Roger Fouts (see Chapter 8 this volume). Then, in 1972 we began a second venture in cross-fostering. The objectives were essentially the same, but there were several improvements in method. For example, Washoe was nearly one year old when she arrived in Reno. A newborn subject would have been more appropriate, but newborn chimpanzees are very scarce and none were offered to us at the time. After Project Washoe, it was easier for us to obtain newborn chimpanzees from laboratories. Chimpanzee Moja, a female, was born at the Laboratory for Experimental Medicine and Surgery in Primates, New York, on November 18, 1972, and arrived in our laboratory in Reno on the following day. Chimpanzee Pili, a male, was born at the Yerkes Regional Primate Research Center, Georgia, on October 30, 1973, and arrived in our laboratory on November 1, 1973. (Pili died of leukemia on October 20, 1975, so that his records cover less than two years.) Chimpanzee Tatu, a female, was born at the Institute for Primate Studies, Oklahoma, on December 30, 1975, and arrived in our laboratory on January 2, 1976. Finally, chimpanzee Dar, a male, was born at Albany Medical College, Holloman AFB, New Mexico, on August 2, 1976, and arrived in our laboratory on August 6, 1976.

We had to replicate the procedure and results of Project Washoe with several other subjects. At the same time, the chimpanzees of the second project could interact with each other and this, in itself, added a new dimension to the cross-fostering. In a human household, children help in the care of their

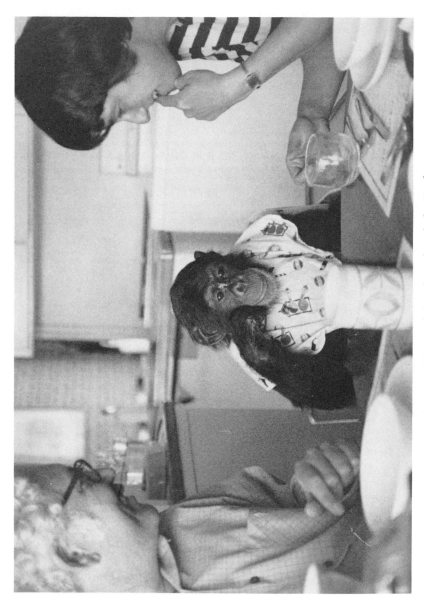

Fig. 1.2 Moja (30 months): at brunch with the Gardners.

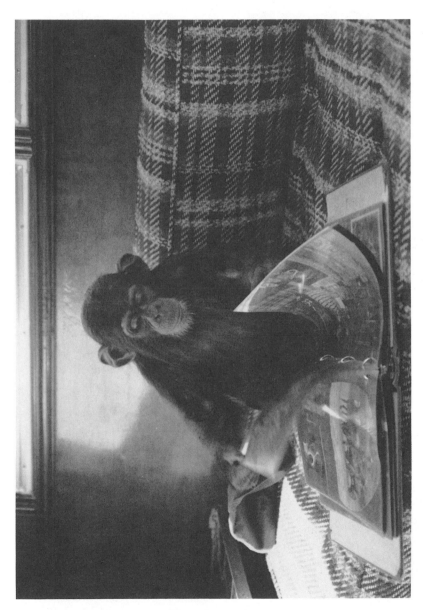

Fig. 1.3 Pili (17 months): looking through a picture book.

Fig. 1.4 Tatu (62 months): feeding B.T. Gardner.

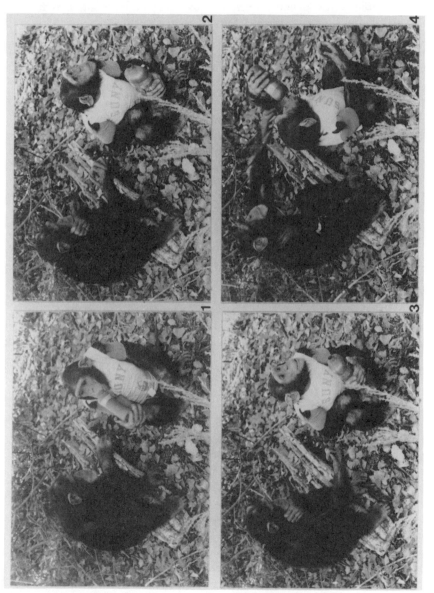

Fig. 1.5 Dar (51 months) evading the request of Tatu (58 months), GIMME DRINK.

younger siblings who, in their turn, learn a great deal from older siblings. Sibling relationships are also a common feature of the family life of wild chimpanzees (Goodall, 1986, pp. 74, 176–177, 337). At Gombe, older offspring stay with their mothers while their younger siblings are growing up and they share in the care of their little brothers and sisters. Close bonds are established among the older and younger members of the same family who remain allies for life. Equally significant, from our point of view, are the ways in which the younger siblings follow and imitate their big sisters and big brothers. Seven-year-old Flint followed and imitated his young adult brother, Faben, in a way that would certainly be described as hero worship if they had been human brothers. Faben was partially paralyzed as an aftereffect of polio and had a peculiar and striking way of supporting his lame arm with one foot while he scratched the lame arm with the good arm. During our 1971 visit to Gombe, we ourselves, observed how Flint copied even this peculiar scratching posture of his brother Faben.

In order to capitalize on the relationships between older and younger foster siblings, we started them newborn, but at intervals, so that there would be age differences. Starting the subjects at intervals in this way also had the practical advantage of allowing us to add human participants to the project more gradually. In each family group there was always a core of experienced human participants for the new recruits to consult as well as a stock of records and films to study. This helped us achieve the necessary stability and continuity in the foster families. Fifteen years after the start of Project Washoe there were still five human participants who had been long-term members of Washoe's original foster family.

The second project became a fairly extensive enterprise by the time there were three chimpanzee subjects. At that point, we moved from the original suburban home to a secluded site that used to be a guest ranch. The chimpanzees lived in the cabins that formerly housed ranch hands. Many of the human family members lived in the guest apartments and the rancher's quarters. The humans' bedrooms were wired to intercoms in the chimpanzees' cabins so that each of the cross-fosterlings could be monitored by at least one human adult throughout each night. There were great old trees and pastures, corrals and barns to play in. There were also special rooms for observation and testing as well as office and shop facilities. The place was designed to keep the subjects under cross-fostering conditions until they were nearly grown up, perhaps long enough for them to begin to care for their own offspring.

At all times in the second project, there were several human members of the family who were deaf, themselves, or who were the offspring of deaf parents, and still others who had learned ASL and used it extensively with members of the deaf community. With the deaf participants it was sign-language-only all of the time, whether or not there were chimpanzees present. The native signers were the best models of ASL, for the human participants who were learning ASL as a second language as well as for the chimpanzees who were learning it as a first language. The native signers were also better observers because it was easier for them to recognize babyish forms of ASL. Along with their own fluency they had a background of experience with human infants who were learning their first signs of ASL.

After Project Washoe, prospective human participants usually began corresponding with us well before they joined the project. In this way, they could begin to prepare themselves months and years before they arrived in Reno. They arrived with a serviceable command of ASL as well as training in experimental psychology, primatology, and related fields. Many had made friends in their local deaf community and had even acquired firsthand experience with deaf children. News of the success of Project Washoe had been warmly received in the deaf community. There were enthusiastic articles in *The Deaf American*, the most widely circulated publication in the deaf community at that time (e.g., Swain, 1968, 1970). When we lectured at Gallaudet College (the national college of the deaf in Washington, D.C.) in 1970, we were told that our audience was the largest that had ever turned out for a lecture in the history of the college up to that time. Valuable channels of communication had been opened for us for consultation, advice, and recruitment.

TEACHING

The procedures that we used to teach signs were modelled after the procedures commonly used in human homes with human children. Most of all, we signed to each other and to the cross-fosterlings throughout the day the way human parents model speech and sign for human children. We used a very simple and repetitious register of ASL. We made frequent comments on common objects and events in short, simple redundant sentences. We amplified and expanded on their fragmentary utterances (e.g., Tatu: BLACK/ Naomi: THAT BLACK COW/). We asked known-answer questions (e.g., WHAT THAT? WHAT YOUR NAME? WHAT I DO?). We attempted to comply with requests and praised correct, well-formed utterances. All of these devices are common in human households (de Villiers & de Villiers, 1978; Moerk, 1983; Snow, 1972). Parents throughout the world seem to speak to their children as if they had very similar notions of the best way to teach languages such as English or Japanese to a young primate (Snow & Ferguson, 1977).

The first descriptions of mothers' speech to young children were undertaken in the late sixties in order to refute the prevailing view that language acquisition was largely innate and occurred almost independently of the language environment. The results of those mothers' speech studies may have contributed to the widespread abandonment of this hypothesis about language acquisition but a general shift from syntactic to semantic-cognitive aspects of language acquisition would probably have caused it to lose its central place as a tenet of research in any case. (Snow, 1977, p. 31) . . . all language learning children, even those raised by fathers or older siblings, have access to a simplified speech register. No one has to learn to talk from a confused, error-ridden garble of opaque structure. Many of the characteristics of mothers' speech have been seen as ways of making grammatical structure transparent, and others have been seen as attention-getters and probes as to the effectiveness of communication. (Snow, 1977, p. 38)

Natural Gestures and Operant Conditioning

Just as the words of English are made with natural human sounds so the signs of ASL are made with natural human movements. The handshapes and movements of ASL had to be part of the natural behavior of chimpanzees or they could never learn to make the signs in the first place. All that anyone can teach a child or a chimpanzee is to use words or signs in their appropriate contexts.

At first, it seemed prudent to include as much of the technique of operant conditioning as might be compatible with the overall objective of raising an infant chimpanzee like a human child (B. Gardner & Gardner, 1971, pp. 129–140). After all, a popular notion in 1966 was that human families must use variants of operant conditioning every day without realizing that they are doing so—hence in an inefficient, amateurish way. We began by building on the spontaneous gestures that we saw every day.

Some chimpanzee gestures seem to be primate universals. Almost from the first, Washoe had a begging gesture—an extension of her open hand, palm up. She seemed to make this gesture in situations in which she wanted us to come to her and in situations in which a companion was holding some object that she wanted. We only needed to get her to add a beckoning motion of the wrist or fingers to make this approximate ASL for GIVE or COME (listed as COME/GIMME in Table 3.2). HURRY is another sign of this type. When waiting for a treat, the cross-fosterlings often shook one open hand vigorously at the wrist in an impatient flourish. The result is a good approximation of the ASL sign HURRY (see Table 3.2). In the early days, Washoe was likely to shake one or both hands this way after signing OPEN. Washoe, Moja, Pili, Tatu, and Dar all made this sign at times that indicated meaningful usage, as when urging themselves to hurry—for example, when rushing to the toilet.

Anyone who watches wild or cross-fostered chimpanzees soon discovers their passion for being tickled. In the early months of Project Washoe, when we paused in our tickling, Washoe would take our hands and place them against her ribs or around her neck. Her meaning was unmistakable without ASL. During a bout of tickling, she often brought her arms together, defensively, at the place being tickled. The ASL sign for MORE consists of bringing the hands together so that the fingertips touch (see Table 3.2). If we stopped tickling and then pulled Washoe's hands apart and away from her body, she tended to bring them back together again. If she brought them back together at all, we would tickle her again. From time to time, we would stop tickling and wait for her to put her hands together by herself. At first any approximation of MORE, however crude, was rewarded with a tickle. Later we required closer approxima-tions and sometimes prompted her by making good MORE signs ourselves for her to imitate. Soon Washoe was signing MORE on her own, but the sign was specifically tied to the tickling situation.

In the sixth month of Project Washoe, we were able to elicit MORE for swift rides across the kitchen floor in a laundry basket. At first, we elicited the sign by making it ourselves. When she signed MORE we sent her sailing across the room in the basket. Before long, Washoe was starting basket rides herself by signing MORE without any prompts at all, except for questions such as, WHAT NOW? or, WHAT YOU WANT? Soon after MORE became a spontane-ous and reliable part of the laundry basket game, it began to appear as a request for more swinging (by the arms)—again, after we elicited it by signing MORE, ourselves, at first. From then on Washoe transferred her MORE sign to all ac-tivities, in one new situation after another, without any hints from us, except for occasional questions. In many new situations we, ourselves, did not know that Washoe wanted "more" until she signed to us. She could tell us something that we only knew from her signs.

The sign OPEN had a similar history. When Washoe wanted us to open a door in those days, she would often hold up both hands and pound on the door with her palms or her knuckles.This is fairly close to the ASL sign OPEN which consists of holding the hands palm down and parallel and then lifting them apart (see Table 3.2). We would wait for her to place her hands on the door and then lift them away, and we also modelled good OPEN signs, ourselves, in this and similar situations. We started with three particular doors that she used every day. But soon, Washoe was using her OPEN sign for all doors; then con-tainers, such as the refrigerator, cupboards, drawers, briefcases, boxes, jars, and eventually—an invention of Washoe's—she used it to ask us to turn on water faucets (see R. Gardner & Gardner, 1973, for filmed examples of Washoe's early use of MORE and OPEN).

Modelling and Molding

In principle, it should be possible to add arbitrarily many signs to a vocabu-lary by what operant conditioners call *shaping* as in the case of MORE and OPEN. In practice, however, it should be clear to most readers, as it soon be-came clear to us, that the step by step procedures we have described here for teaching MORE and OPEN were too laborious and too time-consuming to be practical. The first few words or signs of human infants are sometimes called the "trick" vocabulary because they seem to be acquired by operant shaping the way Washoe acquired MORE and OPEN. Perhaps this is a critical stage in which the infant first learns the instrumental value of verbal behavior. As plaus-ible as this conjecture may be with respect to the first few words or signs, how-ever, the process of operant shaping is entirely too slow and too inefficient to account for the rapid growth and productive use of vocabulary that we see in the next stage of development of children and chimpanzees.

Fortunately, both children and chimpanzees can learn by procedures that tell them directly, "This is an X" or "You are (or I am) now Xing." Modelling words and signs in this way is a natural part of nursery life. For example, our cross-fosterlings had to brush their teeth after every meal. At first, Washoe resisted this routine. Gradually she came to submit with less and less fussing, and within the first year, she started to help and even to brush her teeth for herself. Usually, after having finished her meal, she would try to leave her highchair. We would restrain her, signing, FIRST TOOTHBRUSH, THEN YOU CAN GO.

One day, in the tenth month of the project, Washoe was visiting the Gardner home and found her way into the bathroom. She climbed up on the counter, looked at our mug full of toothbrushes, and signed TOOTHBRUSH. At the time, we believed that Washoe understood the sign TOOTHBRUSH, but we had never seen her use it. She had no reason to ask for the toothbrushes in the Gardner bathroom, because they were well within her reach; and it is very unlikely that she was asking to have her teeth brushed. This was one of the earliest examples of a situation in which Washoe named an object with no obvious motive other than communication.

Washoe was affected by the importance that adults seemed to attach to the routine objects and events of everyday life. In the 1960s several members of Washoe's foster family were smokers. She must have watched them asking each other for cigarettes and matches over and over again, although she, herself, was not allowed to smoke cigarettes or play with matches. One day, during the 30th month of Project Washoe, Naomi (a nonsmoker) needed to light the stove for cooking, but could not find any matches. Washoe watched the search intently. By way of explanation, Naomi held up an empty box of matches. And Washoe replied, SMOKE. After this first observation, we discovered that Washoe signed SMOKE to name both cigarettes and matches or their familiar containers.

One way to tell a chimpanzee or a child that "This is the sign for X" is to take their hands and mold them into the sign while putting them through the movement. We call this procedure molding (cf. Fouts, 1972). Parents and teachers of deaf human children use it often to teach signs (Bonvillian & Nelson, 1978, pp. 191, 199; Maestas y Moores, 1980, pp. 5-6), and variants of molding are used in teaching all sorts of motor skills to human children and to human adults, also. The sixth sign that Washoe acquired, and the first that she acquired by molding, was TICKLE.

Whether the method was modelling or molding, success depended heavily on the attention-getting value of the referent. Tickling commands attention on its own. Toothbrushing and smoking commanded attention because the adults treated them so seriously. Some balance is necessary, of course, since an excited youngster can become too distracted to learn. Thus, DOG was an early sign for all of our chimpanzees, but live dogs were too distracting to use as exemplars. The youngsters chased them, patted them, tickled them, and pulled their tails; but they were usually just too excited to sign about them. We had to use drawings and pictures to teach this sign. Once they had mastered it they could use it to name live dogs, also, and even to comment on the barking of an unseen dog.

When excitement and attention are well balanced, acquisition can be rapid. DOG is signed by patting the thigh with an open hand. When she was 24 months old, Moja and her family invented a game in which she signed DOG on a friend's thigh (an inflected form, see Chapter 6 this volume), then the friend would bark like a dog. The dog imitation of her human companion might be quite dramatic, even including getting down on all fours and jumping over furniture. It was one of Moja's favorite games. When he was 16 months old, Pili had already started to sign DOG to name pictures of dogs, but progress was slow until he learned the dog game from Moja. After one incident of watching Moja play it with a mutual friend it became a favorite game of his, also. With the dog game added to the list of appropriate contexts, his DOG sign quickly passed the criterion of reliability (see Chapter 3 this volume).

Food and sweets can be powerful distractors. We soon learned that one of the worst times to teach anything was at the beginning of mealtime. The hungrier the chimpanzee and the more attractive the food, the more the teaching session would dissolve into a frenzy of begging (cf. R. Gardner & Gardner, 1988).

Operant conditioning was impractical as a method of teaching signs. Once a sign had been introduced into the vocabulary by whatever method, it was equally impractical to attempt to reward all appropriate usage by prompt and consistent delivery of appropriate goods and services. Even in those few cases where prompt and consistent rewards might be practical, all that we could hope to teach in this way would be a set of requests. Meanwhile, all connected discourse or conversation would certainly be disrupted by such a procedure. For the objectives of cross-fostering, the only practical way to proceed was to treat Washoe, Moja, Pili, Tatu, and Dar as if they had an intrinsic motive to communicate with us, the way human parents treat human children.

Obviously, as their verbal skills improved, the cross-fostered chimpanzees were more successful in making their wishes known, and, presumably, more successful in getting what they wanted. But, the same can be said for human children—or human adults for that matter. We also showed our approval or disapproval of signing by smiling or frowning, by nodding or shaking our heads, and by praising or scolding the youngsters in ASL, just as human adults normally respond to the verbal behavior of human children.

Communication and Motive

Normal human children learn to speak as if they were born with a powerful motive to communicate; no other incentive seems to be necessary. In modern times, of course, we recognize that there are many inborn motives rather than a few basic ones, such as hunger and thirst, that give rise to the rest through a process of conditioning. Moreover, other inborn and unlearned motives can be more powerful determinants of behavior than hunger and thirst. Harry Harlow's experiments on contact comfort with infant monkeys come immediately to mind (Harlow, 1958). Many other species behave as if they were born with a powerful motive to communicate; communication is by no means a uniquely human motive (Tinbergen, 1953). Inborn motives such as contact comfort and communication have obvious selective advantages. To the modern mind, the existence of many such inborn motives seems rather more compatible with Darwinism than the elaborate process of conditioning based on hunger and thirst that was formerly posited.

Chimpanzees are among the many species that behave as if they were born with a powerful motive to communicate (Goodall, 1986). Captive chimpanzees are similar to wild chimpanzees in this respect (Kellogg, 1968) unless their conditions of captivity are so severe that normal behavior is suppressed. On the basis of our own early observations (B. Gardner & Gardner, 1971, p. 141), and reports of Viki (Hayes and Nissen, 1971, which was written in 1957 and made available to us in draft form in the early days of Project Washoe), we learned to avoid drill and *quid pro quo* rewards. Occasionally we failed to observe this rule, as for example, when we rewarded Tatu and Dar with treats for obedient test-taking behavior, but the extrinsic rewards usually had to be discontinued because their main effect was to interfere with the intrinsically motivated task at hand (see Chapter 4 this volume). In those cases we found ourselves rediscovering the lessons reported by Hayes and Nissen.

. . . one hot summer day [Viki] brought a magazine illustration of a glass of iced tea to a human friend. Tapping it, she said "Cup! Cup!" and ran to the refrigerator, pulling him along with her. It occurred to us that pictures might be used to signify needs more explicitly than had been possible with words . . .

A set of cards was prepared showing magazine illustrations in natural color of those things she solicited most frequently. [For four days Viki consistently used the picture-cards for requests, but on the fifth day]. . . suddenly she acted as if imposed upon, tremendously. She had to be coaxed to cooperate and then used the pictures in a completely random way.

[After seven months of erratic performance] . . . the technique which had seemed so promising was dropped, pending revision. Spring weather, plus a new car, gave Viki a wanderlust so that no matter what situation sent her to the picture-communication pack, when she came upon a car picture she made happy noises and prepared to go for a ride. We eliminated all car pictures from the pack, but it was too late. Long afterwards Viki was tearing pictures of automobiles from magazines and offering them as tickets for rides. (1971, pp. 107–108)

Negative effects of reward are commonly seen in teaching and training situations of all kinds (Levine & Fasnacht, 1974). Freehand drawing, for example, is one of the favorite activities of children in a nursery school. Yet, Lepper, Greene, and Nisbett (1973) found that drawing in the nursery school was suppressed by response contingent reward. Freehand drawing is also a favorite activity of young chimpanzees. When Desmond Morris (1962) tried rewarding a young chimpanzee for his artwork the results were very similar.

The outcome of this experiment was most revealing. The ape quickly learnt to associate drawing with getting the reward but as soon as this condition had been established the animal took less and less interest in the lines it was drawing. Any old scribble would do and then it would immediately hold out its hand for the reward. The careful attention the animal had paid previously to design, rhythm, balance and composition was gone and the worst kind of commercial art was born! (pp. 158–159)

It is, perhaps, a tribute to the success of the cross-fostering studies that so many operant behaviorists have insisted that the results were "established in chimps through rigorous application of conditioning principles" (Schwartz, 1978, p. 374). We began early and explicitly to describe our departures from the prescriptions of operant behaviorism (B. Gardner and Gardner, 1971, pp. 123–140), but the extent of the departure seems to come out more clearly in films and tapes (e.g., R. Gardner & Gardner, 1973). In a letter that we received from B. F. Skinner following a public television show, for example, positive results are attributed to operant conditioning, while obvious departures from his operant prescriptions are attributed to lapses in discipline.

I recently saw your Nova program and want to congratulate you. I have done enough of that sort of thing myself to know how difficult it is. . . [however] I was quite unhappy about your new recruits—the young people working with the new chimps. They were not arranging effective contingencies of reinforcement. Indeed, they were treating the subjects very much like spoiled children. A first course in behavior modification might save a good deal of time and lead more directly to results. (Personal Communication, May 24, 1974)

Eventually, a prominent student of B. F. Skinner fielded a rigorously operant version of Project Washoe, with the chimpanzee Nim (Terrace, 1979). This was carried to the point where research assistants were forbidden to treat Nim like a child (p. 118). They were even forbidden to comfort him if he cried out in the night (p. 71). Training sessions were conducted in a small room designed to simulate an operant conditioning chamber (p. 49). Mostly, training sessions consisted of demonstrating signs for Nim to imitate and showing him things to name, then rewarding correct responses promptly with the requested object or with some other treat (see Terrace, Petitto, Sanders, & Bever, 1980, pp. 377–378 for detailed description). It can hardly be surprising that video-tape records of these training sessions showed Nim mostly imitating the trainer's signs and begging for treats (Terrace, 1979; Sanders, 1985).

Terrace concluded that Nim lacked,

the motivation needed to sign about things other than requests. . . . Can one instill a greater motivation to sign than we managed to instill in Nim? . . .

The ease with which a child learns language may be less a consequence of superior intellectual machinery than of a child's willingness to inhibit its impulses to grab and to use words instead. In contrast to a child, a chimpanzee seems less disposed to inhibit its impulses, preferring to operate upon the world in a physical, as opposed to a verbal, manner. To get a chimpanzee into the habit of signing, it would help to begin instruction in sign language at an age at which its physical coordination is limited. During the chimpanzee's first year, it is essentially as helpless as a human infant: its locomotion is rather limited, and it is quite uncoordinated in its attempts to grasp things. . . . While Nim was quite helpless, I should have required him to sign, or a least attempt to sign, for anything he wanted. (Terrace, 1979, p. 223)

It seems more likely that Nim grabbed so much because his trainers provided conditions that evoked grabbing rather than communication. Nim's signs were usually requests because his trainers taught him to use signs for requests rather than for communication. The relentless application of extrinsic incentives evoked the extrinsic responses that stifled communication. Human children are not born with some mysterious "willingness to inhibit impulses to grab," they are, instead, reared in an environment that evokes communication rather than grabbing. Even in the case of Nim very different results were obtained when, after leaving Terrace's laboratory, Nim found himself among conversational partners rather than operant conditioners (see Chapter 7 this volume).

Approaching the problem in much the same way as Terrace, Rumbaugh and his associates taught the chimpanzee, Lana, to use a multiple-choice response panel to obtain a variety of goods and services (mostly foods and drinks) under conditions closely patterned after the operant conditioning chamber for pigeons.

With regard to the intensity of training, it was decided that Lana would live in the language environment 24 hours a day. There, her linguistic expressions would provide repeated, reinforcing engagement with the system, since she would have to obtain all of her necessities and social interactions by making appropriate requests of it. (Gill & Rumbaugh, 1977, p. 158)

A striking result of these conditions was the great difficulty that Rumbaugh and his associates had in transferring Lana from one problem to the next. She often required extensive retraining to master new sequences even though she had used the same responses correctly for tens of thousands of requests in other sequences (Gill & Rumbaugh, 1974).

Later, Savage-Rumbaugh and her associates used a similar multiple-choice response panel with the chimpanzees Sherman and Austin. The second project concentrated on naming rather than pressing keys in specific sequences, and trainers handed rewards to the chimpanzees directly rather than relying on automatic dispensers. The greater social interaction between experimenters and chimpanzees and the relaxation of some of the operant rigor of reward delivery seemed to help Sherman and Austin. But, the Rumbaughs taught Sherman and Austin to use the panel step by step according to the same Skinnerian model of language-learning as before. Each step in the conditioning program consisted of a still more elaborate way to ask for food rewards (Savage-Rumbaugh, 1984, pp. 230–247).

By contrast Washoe, Moja, Pili, Tatu, and Dar both learned and used the signs of ASL in an environment modelled after the living and learning conditions of a human household. We did not have to tempt them with treats or ply them with questions to get them to sign to us. They initiated conversations on their own, and they commonly named objects and pictures of objects in situations in which we were unlikely to reward them.

Washoe often signed to herself in play, particularly in places that afforded her privacy, i.e., when she was high in the tree or alone in her bedroom before going to sleep. . . . Washoe also signed to herself when leafing through magazines and picture books, and she resented our attempts to join in this activity. If we did try to join her or if we watched her too closely, she often abandoned the magazine or picked it up and moved away. Our records show that Washoe not only named pictures to herself in this situation, but that she also corrected herself. On one occasion, she indicated a certain advertisement, signed THAT FOOD, then looked at her hand closely and changed the phrase to THAT DRINK, which was correct.

Washoe also signed to herself about her own ongoing or impending actions. We have often seen Washoe moving stealthily to a forbidden part of the yard signing QUIET to herself, or running pell-mell for the potty chair while signing HURRY. (B. Gardner & Gardner, 1974, p. 20)

The lack of spontaneity and communication and the difficulties that the Rumbaughs had in transferring Lana, Sherman, and Austin from step to step in their program of "language-learning" are typical of the successes and failures of other rigorous applications of operant behaviorism. Where they relaxed operant rigor as in the case of the pigmy chimpanzee, Kanzi, the Rumbaughs themselves obtained dramatically more advanced results.

Because pigmy chimpanzees are such rare and precious specimens, the laboratory regime was somewhat relaxed from the start. Thus, the Rumbaughs' first pigmy subject, Matata, was allowed to keep the nursing infant, Kanzi, clinging to her while she worked at a response panel under the same operant procedures formerly used with Sherman and Austin. Matata was poor at this task, but one day the infant Kanzi began to operate the response panel on his own and, indeed, seemed to have learned some of the relations between real objects and the keys on the panel by observing his mother at her lessons (Savage-Rumbaugh, Rumbaugh, & McDonald, 1985).

To their great credit, the Rumbaughs abandoned the operant conditioning program that had been the foundation of their laboratory for so long and that they had defended so eloquently and so often in print, and proceeded to communicate with Kanzi as they would with a child—within the limits that their personnel, laboratory facilities, and response panel would permit. Most important of all, they stopped tying communicative behavior to food reward or to demands in general (Savage-Rumbaugh, McDonald, Sevcik, Hopkins, & Rubert, 1986). Even the fragmentary results that have appeared so far stand in dramatic contrast to the results obtained by the same experimenters in the same laboratory using the same "Yerkish lexigrams" with Lana, Sherman, and Austin.

A ROBUST PHENOMENON

Washoe, Moja, Pili, Tatu, and Dar signed to friends and to strangers. They signed to each other and to themselves, to dogs and to cats, toys, tools, even to trees. Along with their skill with cups and spoons, pencils and crayons, their signing developed stage for stage much like the speaking and signing of human children (Van Cantfort & Rimpau, 1982; Chapter 5 this volume). They also used the elementary sorts of sign language inflections that deaf children use to modulate the meaning of signs (R. Gardner & Gardner, 1978, pp. 56–58; Chapter 6 this volume). Cross-fostered chimpanzees converse among themselves, even when there is no human being present and the conversations must be recorded with remotely controlled cameras. The infant Loulis, adopted by Washoe when he was about a year old, learned more than 50 signs of ASL that he could only have learned from other chimpanzees (Fouts, Hirsch, & Fouts, 1982).

In 1989, nineteen years after she left Reno, Washoe was still signing, not only to humans but to other chimpanzees whether or not there were any human beings in sight (see Chapter 9 this volume). This is more remarkable when we consider the procedure of Project Loulis. When Loulis was ten months old he was adopted by 14-year-old Washoe, shortly after she lost her own newborn infant. To show that Washoe could teach signs to an infant without human intervention, Roger Fouts introduced a drastic procedure. All human signing was forbidden when Loulis was present. Since Loulis and Washoe were almost inseparable for the first few years, this meant that Washoe lost almost all her input from human signers. It was a deprivation procedure for Washoe. Later, Moja joined the group in Oklahoma, and still later Tatu and Dar joined the group in Ellensburg, Washington. The signing chimpanzees were allowed to sign to each other; indeed, there was no way to stop them. They became part of Loulis' input.

As Loulis grew older and moved freely by himself from room to room in the laboratory, there were more opportunities for the human beings to sign to the other chimpanzees when Loulis was not in sight. As expected, however, the rule against signing to Loulis had a generally negative effect on all human signing. There was very little incentive for the research assistants to become fluent in ASL, and only a few of the most senior personnel acquired any signing facility. Thus, whether or not Loulis was in sight, there was very little human signing to be seen. Human signing was almost completely withdrawn for five years. It was a deprivation experiment for the cross-fostered chimpanzees.

Washoe, Moja, Tatu, and Dar continued to sign to each other and also attempted to engage human beings in conversation throughout the period of deprivation. Washoe modelled signs for Loulis in ways that could only be described as explicit teaching; and she also molded his hands the way we had molded hers (Fouts, Hirsch, & Fouts, 1982; Chapter 8 this volume). Loulis learned more than 50 signs from the cross-fostered chimpanzees during the five years in which they were his only models and tutors. Meanwhile, Washoe, herself, learned some new signs from Moja, Tatu, and Dar.

Once introduced, sign language is robust and self-supporting, unlike the systems that depend on special apparatuses such as the Rumbaugh keyboards or the Premack plastic tokens. At this writing, Lana, Sherman, and Austin are no longer operating their keyboards; their trainers have abandoned the special apparatus in favor of simpler tasks (Rumbaugh, 1986). A similar condition seems to have overtaken chimpanzee Sarah, the subject of Premack's early studies (Premack, 1986). The regimen that the Foutses enforced to demonstrate that the infant Loulis could learn signs from Washoe, Moja, Tatu, and Dar was a drastic procedure for the cross-fosterlings. It slowed the growth of their sign language, but it certainly demonstrated that the sign language acquired by the cross-fostered chimpanzees becomes a permanent and robust aspect of their behavior.

References

Bonvillian, J. D., & Nelson, K. E. (1978). Development of sign language in autistic children and other language-handicapped individuals. In P. Siple (Ed.), *Understanding language through sign language research*, (pp. 187–209). New York: Academic Press.

Bonvillian, J.D., Nelson, K.E., & Charrow, V.D. (1976). Language and language-related skills in deaf and hearing children. *Sign Language Studies*, *12*, 211–250.

de Villiers, J., & de Villiers, P.A. (1978). *Language acquisition*. Cambridge, MA: Harvard University Press.

Fouts, R.S. (1972). Use of guidance in teaching sign language to a chimpanzee. *Journal of Comparative and Physiological Psychology, 80*, 515–522.

Fouts, R.S., Hirsch, A.D., & Fouts, D.H. (1982). Cultural transmission of a human language in a chimpanzee mother-infant relationship. In H.E. Fitzgerald, J.A. Mullins & P. Page (Eds.), *Psychobiological perspectives: Child nurturance*, (Vol. 3, pp. 159–193). New York: Plenum Press.

Gardner, B.T., & Gardner, R.A. (1971). Two-way communication with an infant chimpanzee. In A. Schrier & F. Stollnitz (Eds.), *Behavior of nonhuman primates*, (Vol. 4, pp. 117-184). New York: Academic Press.

Gardner, B.T., & Gardner, R.A. (1974). Comparing the early utterances of child and chimpanzee. In A. Pick (Ed.), *Minnesota symposium on child psychology*, (Vol. 8, pp. 3–23). Minneapolis: University of Minnesota Press.

Gardner, R.A., & Gardner, B.T. (1973). Teaching sign language to the chimpanzee, Washoe. (16-mm sound film). State College, PA: Psychological Cinema Register.

Gardner, R.A., & Gardner, B.T. (1978). Comparative psychology and language acquisition. *Annals of the New York Academy of Sciences, 309*, 37–76.

Gill, T.V., & Rumbaugh, D.M. (1974). Mastery of naming skills by a chimpanzee. *Journal of Human Evolution, 3*, 483–492.

Gill, T.V., & Rumbaugh, D.M. (1977). Training strategy and tactics. In D.M. Rumbaugh (Ed.), *Language learning by a chimpanzee*, (pp. 157–162). New York: Academic Press.

Goodall, J. (1986). *The chimpanzees of Gombe*. Cambridge, MA: Harvard University Press.

Goodman, M. (1976). Toward a geneological description of the primates. In M. Goodman & R.E. Tashian (Eds.), *Molecular anthropology*, (pp. 321–353). New York: Plenum Press.

Harlow, H.F. (1958). The nature of love. *American Psychologist, 13*, 673–685.

Harris, M.P. (1970). Abnormal migration and hybridization of *Larus argentatus* and *L. fuscus* after interspecies fostering experiments. *Ibis, 112*, 488–498.

Hayes, K.J., & Nissen, C.H. (1971). Higher mental functions of a home-raised chimpanzee. In A.M. Schrier & F. Stollnitz (Eds.), *Behavior of nonhuman primates*, (Vol. 4, pp. 59–115). New York: Academic Press.

Itard, Jean-Marc-Gaspard. (1801/1962). *The wild boy of Aveyron* (G. & M. Humphrey, Trans.). New York: Appleton-Century-Crofts.

Kellogg, W.N. (1968). Communication and language in the home-raised chimpanzee. *Science, 162*, 423–427.

Kellogg, W.N., & Kellogg, L.A. (1933). *The ape and the child.* New York: Hafner Publishing Co.

Lepper, M.R., Greene, D., & Nisbett, R.E. (1973). Undermining children's intrinsic interest with extrinsic rewards. *Journal of Personality and Social Psychology, 28*, 129–137.

Levine, F., & Fasnacht, G. (1974). Token rewards may lead to token learning. *American Psychologist, 29*, 816–820.

Maestas y Moores, J. (1980). Early linguistic environment: Interactions of deaf parents with their infants. *Sign Language Studies, 26*, 1–13.

Maple, T.L., & Cone, S.G. (1981). Aged apes at the Yerkes Regional Primate Research Center. *Laboratory Primate Newsletter, 20*, 10–12.

Moerk, E.L. (1983). *The mother of Eve—as a first language teacher.* Norwood, NJ: ABLEX Publishing Corporation.

Morris, D. (1962). *The biology of art.* New York: Alfred A. Knopf.

Premack, D. (1986). *Gavagai!* Cambridge, MA: MIT Press.

Riesen, A.H., & Kinder, E.F. (1952). *Postural development of infant chimpanzees: A comparative and normative study based on the Gesell behavioral examination.* New Haven: Yale University Press.

Rumbaugh, D.M. (1986). Implications of current and future research on chimpanzee intellect. Paper presented at Understanding Chimpanzees: Symposium and International Forum, Chicago Academy of Sciences, Chicago, IL.

Sanders, R.J. (1985). Teaching apes to ape language: Explaining the imitative and nonimitative signing of a chimpanzee. *Journal of Comparative Psychology, 99*, 197–210.

Sarich, V.M., & Cronin, J.E. (1976). Molecular systematics of the primates. In M. Goodman & R.E. Tashian (Eds.), *Molecular anthropology*, (pp. 141–170). New York: Plenum Press.

Savage-Rumbaugh, E.S. (1984). Verbal behavior at a procedural level in the chimpanzee. *Journal of the Experimental Analysis of Behavior, 41*, 223–250.

Savage-Rumbaugh, E.S., Rumbaugh, D.M., & McDonald, K. (1985). Language learning in two species of apes. *Neuroscience & Behavioral Reviews, 9*, 653–665.

Savage-Rumbaugh, E.S., McDonald, K., Sevcik, R.A., Hopkins, W.D., &

Rubert, E. (1986). Spontaneous symbol acquisition and communicative use by pigmy chimpanzees. *Journal of Experimental Psychology: General, 115,* 211–235.

Schwartz, B. (1978). *Psychology of learning and behavior.* New York: W.W. Norton.

Snow, C. (1972). Mother's speech to children learning language. *Child Development, 43,* 549–565.

Snow, C. (1977). Mother's speech research: From input to interaction. In C. Snow & C. Ferguson (Eds.), *Talking to children,* (pp. 31–49). Cambridge: Cambridge University Press.

Snow, C.E., & Ferguson, C.A. (Eds.) (1977). *Talking to children.* Cambridge: Cambridge University Press.

Swain, R.L. (1968). Why the language of signs is being taught to a chimpanzee at the University of Nevada. *The Deaf American, 21,* 5–7.

Swain, R.L. (1970). Washoe's advanced training in the language of signs. *The Deaf American, 22,* 9–12.

Terrace, H.S. (1979). *Nim.* New York: Alfred A. Knopf.

Terrace, H.S., Petitto, L., Sanders, R.J., & Bever, T.G. (1980). On the grammatical capacity of apes. In K.E. Nelson (Ed.), *Children's language,* (Vol. 2, pp. 371-495). New York: Gardner Press.

Tinbergen, N. (1953). *Social behaviour in animals.* New York: John Wiley & Sons.

Van Cantfort, T.E., & Rimpau, J.B. (1982). Sign language studies with children and chimpanzees. *Sign Language Studies, 34,* 15–72.

Yerkes, R.M., & Yerkes, A.W. (1929). *The great apes: A study of anthropoid life.* New Haven: Yale University Press.

Chi square:
Compares data for correlation —

2. Voiced and Signed Responses of Cross-Fostered Chimpanzees

R. Allen Gardner, Beatrix T. Gardner
and Patrick Drumm

Human beings are noisy animals. There is a hubbub of voices at almost every social gathering; a great din at the most peaceful cocktail party or restaurant dining room. It is a mark of discipline and respect when an audience settles down in silence to listen to a single speaker. In the rest of the animal kingdom there are very few creatures, perhaps only some of the birds, whales, and dolphins, that make nearly so much vocal racket when they are otherwise undisturbed.

Chimpanzees are silent animals most of the time. A group of ten wild chimpanzees of assorted ages and sexes feeding peacefully in a fig tree at Gombe may make so little sound that an inexperienced observer passing below can altogether fail to detect them. As late as 1971, Tanzanian tourist guidebooks described chimpanzees as noisy, because the amateur observer rarely noticed wild chimpanzees in the forest unless they happened to be excited and noisy. Since the time of the Tarzan films, chimpanzee movie stars have appeared to chatter incessantly on the screen. The effect is created by harassing the chimpanzees when they are off-camera, and then dubbing their cries of distress onto the sound track. To those who are familiar with the natural vocal repertoire of chimpanzees the result is irritating and distracting. The voice on the sound track clashes with the facial expressions and the postures on the screen, and it is easy to imagine the unpleasant scenes that actually evoked those high-pitched, nattering cries. When chimpanzees use their voices they are usually too excited to engage in casual conversation. Their vocal habits, much more than the design of their vocal apparatus, are what keep them from learning to speak.

Even under the most favorable conditions, as in the cross-fostering experiments before Project Washoe, attempts to teach chimpanzees to speak were doomed to failure. As obvious as this may seem now, in those early days influential comparative psychologists still argued that almost anything could be taught to almost any animal by the force of operant conditioning. The early experiments, particularly the seven-year, thoroughgoing, and highly professional cross-fostering experiment of the Hayeses with Viki, was a necessary preliminary to Project Washoe. Before the definitive work of the Hayeses it would have been much more difficult to abandon spoken language in favor of sign language.

Washoe, Moja, Pili, Tatu, and Dar were as silent as wild chimpanzees, when they were calm and undisturbed. When they vocalized, they were excited. In the case of these cross-fostered chimpanzees, however, there was a small group of trained observers who knew each chimpanzee intimately over a long period of time. The observers knew the life histories, the vocal repertoires and the vocabulary of signs, the likes and dislikes, and the events that were most likely to evoke the emotional responses of each of these young chimpanzees. Under these conditions we conducted the following systematic study of the relationship between vocal and gestural responses to emotionally charged stimuli.

METHOD

Subjects

Tatu, a female, was 64 months old and Dar, a male, was 56 months old when they participated in this experiment. Both had been placed under the cross-fostering conditions described in Chapter 1 of this volume within a few days of their birth and maintained under those conditions continuously up to and including the period of this experiment.

Experimenters

The nine human members of Tatu's foster family and eight human members of Dar's foster family represented an overlapping group of 13 individuals. In this group, the median amount of cross-fostering experience was 4.7 years. Seven members of this group had been part of Tatu's or Dar's foster family from the day that the cross-fostered chimpanzee arrived in Reno as a newborn, and all but three had participated for more than one year. Of the ten who had participated for more than one year, three who were primarily members of Tatu's foster family, three who were primarily members of Dar's foster family, and one who participated equally in both foster families were selected to serve as experimenters. These seven were selected because their schedules of participation fitted the requirements of the experimental schedule. In addition, all seven had met the following criterion of ability to identify vocalizations.

Examples of pant-hoots, rough-grunts, laughter, whimpers, and screams were taped from the sound track of Marler and Goodall (1971), the film and sound record of a study of the vocalizations of free-living wild chimpanzees at Gombe. A single example of each of these five types of vocalization was selected for the qualifying test by eliminating those cases in which more than one chimpanzee was vocalizing at the same time. The test tapes contained three repeated presentations of each type of vocalization, and were played to a group of prospective experimenters who attempted to identify the vocalizations on individual written response sheets. The seven experimenters were chosen from those who identified all five vocalizations on this test correctly.

The preparation of the experimenters included discussion of the purpose of each step of the procedure, supervised practice in such procedures as signing the announcements and timing the events, and discussion of Marler and Tenaza's (1977) catalog of chimpanzee vocalizations. Extra copies of Marler and Tenaza's catalog were available for reference during trials.

Events

The daily activities of Tatu and Dar contained a wide spectrum of events that were routinely announced in sign language. Master lists of events that might be suitable for this experiment were drawn up in consultation with the long-term members of the foster families of Tatu and Dar. Independent, written ratings were obtained from current members of the human foster family of each subject, all nine for Tatu and five for Dar. The ratings were made on a scale of 1 (most negative affect) to 7 (most positive affect).

The list of rated events together with the median and range of the ratings appears in Table 2.1. While not an exhaustive list of possible events it is a generous sample and offers a useful picture of the life of a cross-fostered chimpanzee in this laboratory. As might be expected the bulk of the events were common to both Tatu and Dar. In general, there was also a high correlation between the cross-fosterlings with respect to the positive and negative affective charge of each event. Arrivals of friends, social play, snacks, and outdoor activities were distinctly favored. Chores, toiletting, and dressing were neutral events. The opposites of the positive events, departures of companions or taking away of toys, were rated as negative events.

Their preferences were highly correlated, but there were also clear differences. Carrots and milk were favorite foods for Tatu, but Dar could take them or leave them. Both subjects often played with Halloween masks, but masks were much more positive for Tatu, while Dar was particularly fond of "fun-flowers," a cloth, flower-shaped type of child's toy. Tatu had never had any particular interest in fun-flowers so she did not own any and this item was not rated for her. Tatu was attracted to water; washing, bathing, and being squirted with a water gun were all more positive for her. Indeed, of the five cross-fostered chimpanzees in this laboratory, Tatu played with water the most, and was the only one who voluntarily waded in streams. In most respects, however, Tatu was more timid than Dar, which is reflected in less positive ratings for such activities as pretend fights with the bogeydog (see Chapter 3 this volume,

Table 2.1
Affective Ratings of Events in the Daily Routines of Tatu and Dar

Events	Tatu	Dar	Events	Tatu	Dar
Toys/playthings			*Play*		
Wig, bring out	5/4–6	6/5–6	HC gives C		
Wig, put away	4/3–5	3/2–4	Hug	5/4–7	5/5–6
Balloon, bring out	6/4–6	6/5–6	Kiss	5/4–7	4/4–5
Balloon, put away	4/3–5	3/3	Ride in wagon/sled	7/5–7	6/5–6
Cow, bring out	5/4–7	6/5–6	Swing	6/5–7	6.5/6–7
Cow, put away	4/3–4	3/3–4	Peek through outside	6/4–7	5/4–6
Mask, bring out	7/6–7	5/5–6	window		
Mask, put away	2/1–3	3/3–4	Peek through shop	6/5–7	na
Doll, bring out	5/4–6	5/5–6	window (to see		
Doll, put away	4/3–5	3/3–4	handyman work)		
Fun-flower, bring out	na	7/6–7	HC agent		
Fun-flower, put away	na	2/1–3	Hides objects	5/4–6	6/3–6
(Dar's favorite toy)			Hides self	5/2–6	6/3–6
Black hose, bring out	2/1–4	na	Chases C	7/6–7	7/7
Black hose, put away	6/4–6	na	Chases C with toy	6/4–7	7/5–7
(Object feared by Tatu)			Tickles C	7/6–7	7/6–7
TV set, bring out	4/3–6	na	Tickles C with toy	6/4–7	7/6–7
TV set, turn on	5/4–6	na	Squirts C with watergun	5/1–7	1.5/1–2
TV set, put away	4/4–6	na	Gives drink with	6/5–7	6/6–7
HC gives own			watergun		
possessions			Pretends to fight	3.5/1–6	6/1–6
Eyeglasses	6/4–7	6.5/6–7	with imaginary		
Belt	6/5–7	6/5–6	bogeydog		
Shoes	6/5–7	6/5–7	C agent		
Watch	7/6–7	6/6–7	Hides from HC	5/4–7	6/5–7
Open closet or cupboard			Chases HC	6/4–7	6/6–7
C to select a toy	6/5–7	6/6–7	Tickles HC	5.5/4–6	6/6
C to play inside	6/5–7	6/6–7			
			Going out		
School			Preparations (put on	6/2–7	6/5–6
HC presents			outdoor clothes, etc.)		
Building blocks	4/3–6	5/2–5	Going outdoors	7/7	7/6–7
Picture book	5/5–7	5/5–6	Drive to wildlife area	7/5–7	5/3–6
Tools and wood	6/5–7	6/5–7	Return from drive	4.5/2–7	4/2–4
Paper and pen/pencil	5/3–7	5/3–5	Drive with other chimp	6.5/6–7	7/7
Lesson in ASL	3.5/3–6	3/2–3	Meet other chimp	7/6–7	7/6–7
Go to testing room	5/3–7	3.5/1–5	Part from other chimp	2.5/2–4	2.5/2–3
Leave testing room	5/4–7	6/5–6	Return home	1/1–6	4/3–4

Table 2.1 (continued)

Events	Median/Range		Events	Median/Range	
	Tatu	Dar		Tatu	Dar
Mealtime			*Arrivals and Departures*		
Preparations (put out	6/4–7	6/6	AG arrives	7/6–7	7/6–7
utensils, light stove)			AG departs	2/1–4	2/1–3
Seat C at table	3/1–7	4/3–5	BG arrives	7/6–7	7/6–7
Put on bib	4/3–7	3/3–5	BG departs	2/1–4	1.5/1–2
Serve			BP arrives	6/5–7	na
Vegetables	5/4–7	4/3–5	BP departs	2/1–4	na
Cereal	4.5/3–5	6/5–6	CL arrives	4/2–6	na
Fruit	6/5–7	5/5–7	CL departs	4/2–4	na
Milk	6/6–7	4.5/3–5	DC arrives	na	5/4–6
Dessert (pudding/	6/5–7	7/6–7	DC departs	na	2/2
jello, as last course			JF arrives	4/2–6	na
of meal)			JF departs	4/2–5	na
			JP arrives	na	5.5/5–6
Snacks between meals			JP departs	na	3/2–4
Ice cream	7/5–7	7/6–7	JR arrives	na	6/6
Cookies	6/3–7	7/6–7	JR departs	na	3/2–4
Carrots	6/5–7	4/3–5	NR arrives	6/6–7	na
Raisins or grapes	6/6–7	6/6–7	NR departs	2/1–4	na
Nuts	6/5–7	6/5–6	PD arrives	6/6–7	6/6–7
Soda pop	6/5–7	6/6–7	PD departs	4/1–5	2/1–4
C's choice from	6/5–7	6/6–7	SN arrives	6/5–7	5.5/4–6
refrigerator			SN departs	3/1–4	3/2–4
HC's food	6/4–7	5/5–6	VC arrives	5/4–6	6/5–7
HC's drink	6/5–7	6/5–7	VC departs	4/2–6	3/1–4
(HC's often brought			HC departs (feint only	2/1–3	1/1–2
food for own			e.g., gathers belong-		
consumption)			ings, turns doorknob)		
Chores					
HC and/or C					
Wash dishes	4/4–7	5/3–5	*Bedtime and naptime*		
Put up window	4/4–6	4/3–4	Blankets, bring out	7/5–7	4.5/4–6
curtains			Blankets, put away	3/1–5	4/3–4
Remove window	5/4–7	5.5/5–6	Put C to bed	6/5–7	5/5–6
curtains			Sit on bed with C	5/4–7	5/4–5
Put trash in trash can	4/2–5	4/4–5	Say good night	5/3–7	na
Clean up spills/	4/3–6	4/3–5	Turn lights out	5/3–7	4/3–6
sink/tub			Get C up from nap	4/1–6	6/4–6
HC only					
Writes in log	4/3–7	3/3–4			
Vacuums floor/sofa	3/2–5	6/5–7			
Signs with another HC	3/2–7	3/2–5			

Table 2.1 (continued)

Events	Median/Range		Events	Median/Range	
	Tatu	Dar		Tatu	Dar
Dressing			*Hygiene/grooming*		
Pants, put on	4.5/4–5	5/5	Prepare for bath	5/2–7	3/2–4
Pants, take off	4/4–7	4.5/4–5	Finish bath	5/3–7	5/5–6
Shirt, put on	3/1–7	5/5–6	Towel dry after bath	5/3–7	4/2–5
Shirt, take off	5/4–7	5/4–5	Wash bottom	4/2–6	3/2–4
Coat, put on	4/2–7	5/3–6	Wash face	3/2–5	2/2–4
Coat, take off	4.5/4–7	5/4–5	Wash hands	4/3–6	2/2–4
Nightie, put on	5/4–7	3/3–4	Lotion hands/feet	5/4–7	4/3–4
Nightie, take off	5/4–7	5/4–5	Brush teeth	5/3–7	5/5
Give/apply medicine			Groom skin/hair	6/4–7	6/5-7
			Swab ears/nose	4/3–7	4/4–5
Oral medicine	6/4–7	6/5–6	Comb hair	5/4–7	5/5–6
Topical medicine	3/2–7	3/2–6	Brush hair	6/4–7	5/5–6
Vitamins	5.5/4–7	5/3–6	Bring to toilet	4/2–6	4/3–5
Take temperature/ pulse	3.5/3–7	3/2–4	Allow to leave toilet	5/4–7	5/4–5

Note: 7 = most positive, 1 = most negative rating; 9 Tatu raters, 5 Dar raters; HC = Human companion, C = Chimpanzee

p. 65). For the most part, these individual differences were stable, long-term characteristics. For example, Dar's first fun-flower was a favorite toy when he was only six months old, and 50 months later he usually kept his latest fun-flower with him, carried in his hand or tucked into his clothes, when he went outdoors.

Only those human companions who were regular members of both foster families were rated (with respect to arrivals and departures) for both chimpanzees. In general, variations in the positive ratings for arrival and the negative ratings for departure are related to tenure of the human companions in the foster families. Tatu and Dar liked their oldest friends the best. As pointed out in Chapter 1, Tatu and Dar always had at least one human companion from reveille in the morning to lights-out at night and, more dependent than human children, the cross-fostered chimpanzees reacted negatively to all departures, even though one friend always remained. The chimpanzees did misbehave, and when particularly exasperated, a human companion sometimes threatened to leave the cross-fosterling entirely alone. This is the event indicated by "HC departs" in Table 2.1.

Clearly negative events were defined as those rated 1–3 by 100% of the raters, neutral as those rated 3–5 by 100%, and positive as those rated 5–7 by 100%. The predominance of positive items in the list reflects the predominantly positive nature of the laboratory conditions, but this made it difficult to find a sufficient number of clearly neutral and clearly negative events. It was an easy matter to select ten clearly positive events from those listed in Table 2.1, but the original criterion was too stringent to yield an equal number of neutral and negative events. Even when the number of events was lowered to five, and the percent of ratings within the appropriate range was lowered to 75% (for 3 of Tatu's neutral items, and 2 of her negative items), there were still too few negative items on the list.

Additional negative items were solicited at a meeting of the raters and three items were selected that received unanimous negative ratings. As a neutral item to balance the positive arrival of R. A. Gardner (A.G.), we added the arrival of the handyman, who was familiar to both chimpanzees, yet not a member of either foster family. The raters agreed unanimously that the arrival of the handyman was a clearly neutral event. The final list of events that was used in the experiment consisted of 20 events for each of the two subjects, 10 positive, 5 neutral, and 5 negative, and a list of these appears in Table 2.2.

Announcements

An integral feature of the cross-fostering procedure in this laboratory was to announce routine events in advance in sign language. Announcements of this kind served as a primary teaching device, as they normally do for human children (Moerk, 1972; Snow, 1977, p. 40). For the purposes of this experiment, two announcements were constructed for each event; one in the form of a statement, and one in the form of a question. These announcements were constructed in such a way that positive, neutral, and negative announcements, whether in statement or in question form, would be similar in length and complexity. Thus, the frames TIME ____ and TIME ____ NOW could accommodate a variety of positive, neutral, and negative statements such as, TIME COOK FOOD NOW, TIME ME COVER WINDOW, and TIME B.P. LEAVE NOW. Similarly, the frames YOU WANT ____? and YOU WANT ____ NOW? could accommodate a variety of positive, neutral, and negative questions such as, YOU WANT OUT NOW?, YOU WANT WORKMAN COME NOW?, YOU WANT A.G. LEAVE NOW?*

---

*Here and throughout this volume, signed utterances are transcribed into word-for-sign English. We adopted this practice because translations into good English would add words and word endings that have no signed equivalents either in the vocabularies of the chimpanzees or in ASL. This mode of transcription makes the utterances appear to be in a crude or pidgin dialect, but the reader should keep in mind the fact that equally literal word-for-word transcriptions between Russian or Japanese and English appear equally crude.

Table 2.2
Events and Announcements Presented to Tatu and Dar

Tatu	Dar	Events	Announcements
P	P	Dessert served	S: TIME SWEET NOW Q: YOU WANT SWEET NOW?
P	P	E goes outdoors with C	S: TIME OUT NOW Q: YOU WANT OUT NOW?
P	P	R.A. Gardner arrives	S: R.A.G. COME NOW Q: YOU WANT R.A.G. COME NOW?
P	P	Ice cream served	S: TIME ICECREAM NOW Q: YOU WANT ICECREAM?
P	P	Refrigerator opened for C's choice	S: YOU CHOOSE THERE Q: YOU WANT CHOOSE THERE?
—	P	Fun-flower brought out	S: ME GET FLOWER Q: YOU WANT FLOWER?
P	—	Mask brought out	S: ME GET PEEKABOO Q: YOU WANT PEEKABOO?
—	P	Cookies served	S: ME GIVE-YOU COOKIE Q: YOU WANT COOKIE?
P	—	Milk served	S: TIME MILK NOW Q: YOU WANT MILK NOW?
—	P	Vacuum cleaning begins	S: ME VACUUM NOW Q: YOU WANT ME VACUUM?
P	—	Blanket brought out	S: ME GET BLANKET Q: YOU WANT BLANKET?
—	P	Meal preparations begin	S: TIME COOK FOOD NOW Q: YOU WANT ME COOK FOOD NOW?
P	—	Gets ride in wagon	S: YOU RIDE THERE Q: YOU WANT RIDE THERE?
—	P	Closet opened for play inside	S: YOU PLAY THERE Q: YOU WANT PLAY THERE?
P	O	Carrots served	S: ME GIVE-YOU CARROT Q: YOU WANT CARROT?

Table 2.2 (continued)

Tatu	Dar	Events	Announcements
O	—	Given trash to put in trash can	S: THAT PUT-IN GARBAGE Q: YOU WANT THAT PUT-IN GARBAGE?
—	O	Brought to toilet	S: YOU GO-THERE POTTY Q: YOU WANT GO-THERE POTTY?
O	—	Doll put away	S: ME PUT-THERE BABY Q: YOU WANT ME PUT-THERE BABY?
—	O	Given rag to clean up spill	S: YOU CLEAN THERE Q: YOU WANT CLEAN THERE?
O	—	TV brought out	S: ME GET TV Q: YOU WANT ME GET TV?
O	O	Curtains put up	S: TIME ME COVER WINDOW Q: YOU WANT ME COVER WINDOW?
O	O	Handyman arrives[a]	S: WORK MAN COME NOW Q: YOU WANT WORK MAN COME NOW?
N	N	E pretends to leave	S: ME LEAVE Q: WANT ME LEAVE?
N	N	E stays, other HC leaves	S: TIME ___ LEAVE NOW Q: YOU WANT ___ LEAVE NOW?
N	—	Mask put away	S: TIME PEEKABOO PUT-THERE Q: YOU WANT PEEKABOO PUT-THERE?
—	N	Fun-flower put away	S: ME PUT-THERE FLOWER Q: YOU WANT ME PUT-THERE FLOWER?
N	—	Kept seated at table after meal[a]	S: YOU STAY SIT Q: YOU WANT STAY SIT?
—	N	Preferred food taken away[a]	S: THAT ___ ME PUT-THERE Q: YOU WANT THAT ___ PUT-THERE?
N	—	Feared black hose brought out	S: BIG BLACK DOG COME Q: YOU WANT BIG BLACK DOG COME?
—	N	Tight shirt put on[a]	S: YOU PUT-ON SHIRT Q: YOU WANT PUT-ON SHIRT?

[a]Events added to list after rating of events in Table 2.1 (see text).
Note: P = positive; O = neutral; N = negative; HC = Human companion, C = Chimpanzee.

The final list of announcements and events is shown in Table 2.2. On each day of his or her participation in the experiment, each experimenter received a list of scripts that specified the signing of each announcement for that day. The experimenters were instructed to practice their scripts before a mirror in advance of testing.

Procedure

Trials. Trials were conducted indoors, either in the subject's home quarters or in one of the other enclosed play areas on the laboratory grounds. For each day in which an experimenter participated in the testing, he or she received a data sheet which listed the announcements for that day in the prescripted form with appropriately labeled spaces for recording responses. Each trial was conducted as follows: (1) The experimenter (E) established eye contact with the subject (S). (2) Immediately after establishing eye contact, E presented the announcement in sign language. (3) E observed S's responses for 10 sec. (In pilot trials, 10 sec. was the longest latency observed for vocalization after an announcement—except, of course, for infinitely long latencies that were scored as no response). (4) E presented the event. (5) E observed S's responses for 10 sec. (6) At the next possible opportunity, E recorded the vocalization and signing observed during (3) and (5) together with other relevant information.

Reliability Sample. As a check on reliability, a second observer witnessed 10% of the trials (usually through a window in the experimental room) and independently recorded S's responses on a second data sheet.

Design. Tatu and Dar each received two trials from each of four experimenters with each of the 20 announcement-event sequences shown in Table 2.2. On one of the two trials the announcement was made in statement form and on the other trial it was made in question form. The complete set of 40 trials was replicated four times with each of the two subjects, once with each of the four experimenters assigned to that subject. Four trials were lost for each subject because of experimenter errors. The errors were discovered when it was too late to make up the lost trials, so that the total number of trials analyzed was 156 for each subject rather than 160. The lost trials were evenly distributed among the conditions of the experiment.

Six of the experimenters conducted 4 or 5 trials on each day that they participated. The seventh experimenter conducted 8 trials with Dar on each day that he participated. The prescribed announcements assigned to each experimenter for each day were designed to balance the appearance of statements and questions as well as positive, neutral, and negative trials over the course of the day and throughout the period of 62 days during which trials were conducted. The order in which an experimenter conducted the assigned trials for a day's testing was partly determined by the normal occurrence of the events, because many of the routine events, such as mealtime events and bedtime

events, occurred at particular times of day. Apart from the timing that was prescribed by the laboratory schedule, the experimenters were allowed to announce and present events at conveniently spaced intervals throughout the day.

RESULTS

Vocal and Signed Responses Compared

Reliability. For the reliability sample, the interobserver agreement as to
presence vs. absence of vocal responses was 94% and agreement as to presence
vs. absence of signed responses was 93%. Thus, reports of the presence or absence of vocal and signed responses were reliable enough to support further
analyses of the frequencies of those responses.

Statements vs. Questions. Announcements in the form of questions
were somewhat more likely to evoke both vocal and signed responses, but the
effect was weak. Since other evidence (Lovass-Nagy, Gardner, & Gardner,
1989) from this laboratory indicates that Tatu and Dar did respond differently
to the different conversational styles of their human interlocutors, we suspect
that the lack of significance here had to do with the overriding effects of the
announcement style. In context, pairs such as TIME ICECREAM NOW vs.
YOU WANT ICECREAM? or YOU CLEAN THERE vs. YOU WANT CLEAN
THERE? (see Table 2.2) seem to have been marginally different ways of saying
the same thing.

When McNemar's chi-square test for the difference between correlated
frequencies (McNemar, 1949, pp. 204–207) was used to compare the two forms
of announcements, this difference was not statistically significant ($p > .05$)
either for Tatu or for Dar, for all announcements, or for announcements of
positive, neutral, and negative events considered separately. Therefore, the
data for statements and for questions were pooled in all subsequent analyses.

Occurrence and Co-occurrence. Across all of the conditions of this experiment, signed responses were more likely than vocal responses and the frequencies of the two types of response were highly correlated. In order to establish this finding, the announcement and event phases of each trial were tabulated separately and the frequencies of signed and vocal response ($S+/V+$),
signed but not vocal response ($S+/Vo$), vocal but not signed response ($So/V+$),
and neither response (So/Vo), are presented in Table 2.3.

In Table 2.3, most of the chi-squares for the contingency between signing
and vocalization for Tatu and Dar considered separately, and all of the summed
chi-squares (Snedecor, 1956, pp. 212–216), were highly significant. The same
tabulation showed that signed responses were much more frequent than vocal
responses. McNemar's chi-square test for differences takes the correlation between signing and vocalization into account. In Table 2.3, the critical values for
the McNemar test of the difference between signing and vocalization are the
cells for $S+/Vo$ and $So/V+$. The higher values for $S+/Vo$, as compared with

So/V+ in each case, indicate that signed responses were more likely than vocal responses. The last column of Table 2.3 shows that all of the chi-squares for this contrast are highly significant.

Announcements vs. Events. Across all of the conditions of this experiment, signed responses were more likely to be evoked by announcements of events, while vocal responses were more likely to be evoked by the events, themselves. In order to establish this finding, signed and vocal responses on each trial were tabulated separately. First, each trial was tabulated according to whether signed responses occurred in both phases of the trial (A+/E+), in the announcement but not the event phase (A+/Eo), in the event phase but not the announcement phase (Ao/E+), or in neither phase (Ao/Eo). Next, each trial was tabulated in the same way for vocal responses. The results of these tabulations and of the McNemar test for the difference between correlated frequencies are shown in Table 2.4. Here, the critical values for the McNemar test are the differences between A+/Eo and Ao/E+. The last column of Table 2.4 shows that most of the chi-squares for Tatu and Dar considered separately and all of the summed chi-squares were significant.

Table 2.3
Co-occurrence of Signing and Vocalization

Announcement Phase					
	Frequency				*Chi-squares*	
	S+V+	S+Vo	SoV+	SoVo	*Contingency*	*McNemar*
Tatu	26	62	7	61	8.5**	43.8**
Dar	14	77	9	56	0.1	53.8**
Sum					8.6*	97.6**
Event Phase					
	Frequency				*Chi-squares*	
	S+V+	S+Vo	SoV+	SoVo	Contingency	McNemar
Tatu	34	31	13	78	26.0**	7.4**
Dar	23	33	12	88	17.4**	9.8**
Sum					43.5**	17.2**

Notes:
   S+ = signed response observed; So = signed response not observed; V+ = vocal response observed; Vo = vocal response not observed

Summed chi-squares have 2 *df*
   *p < .05; **p < .01

Table 2.4
Frequency of Responses During Both Announcement and
Event Phases of the Same Trial

Signed Responses					
	Frequency				McNemar
	A₊E₊	A₊Eo	AoE₊	AoEo	Chi-square
Tatu	48	40	17	51	9.3**
Dar	41	50	15	50	18.8**
Sum					28.1**
Vocal Responses					
	Frequency				McNemar
	A₊E₊	A₊Eo	AoE₊	AoEo	Chi-Square
Tatu	23	10	24	99	5.8*
Dar	5	18	30	103	3.0
Sum					8.8*

Notes:

A_+ = response observed during announcement phase; Ao = response not observed during announcement phase; E_+ = response observed during event phase; Eo = response not observed during event phase

Summed chi-squares have 2 *df*

*p < .05; **p < .01

Affect. The frequencies of signed and vocal responses depended upon the affective values of the events. In Table 2.5 the frequencies have been converted to percentages to facilitate comparison because there were twice as many trials with positive events as there were trials with neutral or negative events. The last column of Table 2.5 shows that all of the chi-squares for contingency were highly significant.

The results shown in Tables 2.3, 2.4, and 2.5 are summarized in Figure 2.1. Signed responses were more likely than vocal responses under all conditions. Affectively charged events evoked more response than affectively neutral events, whether the affective charge was positive or negative, and this pattern was true whether we consider vocal response or signed response. There was also more signed response to the announcement of affectively charged events, whether positively or negatively charged, than there was to the announcement

Table 2.5

Percent of Positive (P), Neutral (O), and Negative (N) Announcements and Events That Evoked Signed and Vocal Responses

		Signed Response			
		P	O	N	*Chi-square*
Announcements	Tatu	71	32	51	16.7**
	Dar	71	36	56	12.9*
	Sum				29.6**
Events	Tatu	52	21	41	10.1*
	Dar	35	18	56	12.7*
	Sum				22.7**
		Vocal Response			
		P	O	N	*Chi-square*
Announcements	Tatu	33	11	8	13.4*
	Dar	24	3	8	11.9*
	Sum				25.2**
Events	Tatu	43	3	31	19.9**
	Dar	22	3	44	18.9**
	Sum				38.8**

Summed chi-squares have 4 *df*

*$p < .01$; **$p < .001$

of affectively neutral events. Although there was more vocal response to affectively charged stimuli than to neutral stimuli, the vocal response to negative announcements was very low, nearly as low as the response to neutral announcements. With respect to the vocal response to the events themselves, however, the response to negative events was slightly higher than response to positive events. This pattern of vocal response is related to the different types of vocal response that were evoked under the different conditions of the experiment, as shown in the next section.

Types of Vocal Response

Reliability. The bulk of the vocal responses that were reported were classified either as pants, grunts, or whimpers. Only one bark was reported, and other vocalizations, such as laughter, squeaks, screams, waa barks, coughs, and

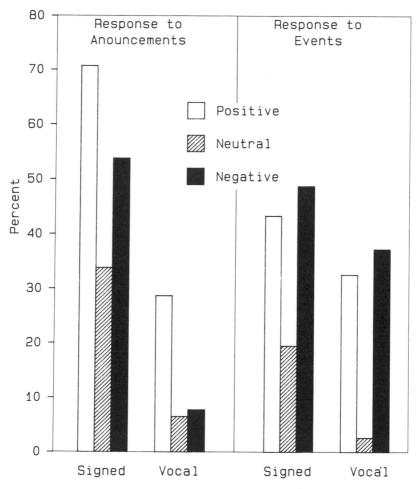

Fig. 2.1 Signed and vocal responses to positive, neutral, and negative announcements and events.

wraa calls (Marler & Tenaza, 1977) were not reported in the present experimental sample (although all had been observed in other situations in this cross-fostering laboratory). The observers reported three different types of grunts—soft grunt, rough grunt, and [plain] grunt—but interobserver agreement was unacceptably low for this distinction. When all of the reports of grunts were classified as a single type, interobserver agreement with respect to types of vocalization was 92%. Because only five pant-hoots were reported, these were combined with pants into a single pant category and the remaining analyses were performed on the reports of pants, grunts, and whimpers. There was only one case in which more than one type of vocal response was reported for the same phase of the same trial; when Dar grunted and then panted at the event, "A.G. arrives."

Table 2.6
Frequency of Pants, Grunts, and Whimpers in Response to Positive (P), Neutral (O), and Negative (N) Announcements and Events

		Pants		
		P	O	N
Announcements	Tatu	14	4	0
	Dar	9	0	0
Events	Tatu	9	1	0
	Dar	1	0	0
		Grunts		
		P	O	N
Announcements	Tatu	12	0	0
	Dar	10	1	1
Events	Tatu	25	0	0
	Dar	16	0	0
		Whimpers		
		P	O	N
Announcements	Tatu	0	0	3
	Dar	0	0	2
Events	Tatu	0	0	12
	Dar	0	0	17

Affect. Table 2.6 shows how the appearance of pants, grunts, and whimpers depended upon whether the events were positive, neutral, or negative. Nearly all of the pants and grunts were evoked by positive announcements or events and virtually no pants or grunts were evoked by negative announcements or events. At the same time, whimpers were only evoked by negative announcements or events. The likelihood of each type of vocalization also depended on whether the stimulus was an announcement or an event. To illustrate this pattern of vocal response, the data of Table 2.6 were recast into Table

Table 2.7
Frequency of Pants, Grunts, and Whimpers During the Announcement and Event Phases of the Same Trial

Pants					
	Frequency				McNemar
	A+E+	A+Eo	AoE+	AoEo	Chi-square
Tatu	8	10	2	136	5.3*
Dar	0	9	1	146	6.4*
Sum					11.7**

Grunts					
	Frequency				McNemar
	A+E+	A+Eo	AoE+	AoEo	Chi-square
Tatu	9	3	16	128	8.9**
Dar	0	12	16	128	0.6
Sum					9.5**

Whimpers					
	Frequency				McNemar
	A+E+	A+Eo	AoE+	AoEo	Chi-square
Tatu	3	0	9	144	9.0**
Dar	2	0	15	139	15.0**
Sum					24.0**

Notes:
   A+ = response observed during announcement phase; Ao = response not observed during announcement phase; E+ = response observed during event phase; Eo = response not observed during event phase

Summed chi-squares have 2 *df*
   *p < .05; **p < .01

2.7 in which pants, grunts, and whimpers are tabulated separately according to whether the vocal response occurred in both phases of a trial (A+/E+), the announcement but not the event phase (A+/Eo), the event phase but not the announcement phase (Ao/E+), or neither phase (Ao/Eo). As Table 2.7 shows, pants were more likely to be evoked by announcements than by events, while grunts and whimpers were more likely to be evoked by events than by announcements. Once again, the McNemar test for correlated frequencies was used to evaluate these results, and the critical values are the differences be-

Table 2.8

Frequency of Incorporation and Reiteration in Signed Replies to Positive (P) vs. Pooled Neutral (O) and Negative Announcements (N)

Reiteration					
	P		**O + N**		
	R+	Ro	R+	Ro	*Chi-square*
Tatu	16	40	3	29	4.4*
Dar	15	40	7	29	0.7
Sum					5.2
Incorporation					
	P		**O + N**		
	I+	Io	I+	Io	*Chi-square*
Tatu	40	16	6	26	22.7**
Dar	42	13	20	16	4.3*
Sum					27.0**
Reiterated Incorporation					
	P		**O + N**		
	RI	RO	RI	RO	*Chi-square*
Tatu	12	4	1	2	2.0
Dar	14	1	4	3	4.2*
Sum					6.2*

Notes:

R+ = signed response with reiteration; Ro = signed response without reiteration; I+ = signed response with incorporation; Io = signed response with incorporation; RI = reiteration of incorporated signs; RO = reiteration of other signs

Summed chi-squares have 2 *df*
*p < .05; **p < .01

tween A+/Eo and Ao/E+. The last column of Table 2.7 shows that most of the chi-squares for Tatu and Dar considered separately and all of the summed chi-squares were significant.

Types of Signed Response

Reliability. Interobserver agreement with respect to the identity of the individual signs in the responses was scored by the following rules: (1) score agreement on sign X; (2) go to the next sign in the record that is different from X, and score that sign; or, (3) go to the next trial record. The purpose of rule 2 was to avoid scoring for reiteration at this juncture. The interobserver agreement for the identity of individual signs was 78%. This figure compares favorably with interobserver agreement on vocalization when we consider that: (1) there were only 12 types of vocalization that could be identified, but the expressive vocabularies of Tatu and Dar contained 141 signs and 122 signs, respectively; (2) the agreement is on 28 different signs observed during the reliability sample as opposed to 5 different types of vocal response within the same sample; and (3) the agreement score includes agreement on the sequence of signs within an utterance. Hence, agreement on sign identification was much farther from chance than agreement on vocal responses. Research designed to evaluate interobserver agreement on sign identification is reported in R. Gardner & Gardner (1984) and Chapter 4 in this volume.

Incorporation and Reiteration. Like human children (Brinton & Fujiki, 1984; Keenan, 1977; Keenan & Klein, 1975), Tatu and Dar often incorporated in their replies a sign that had appeared in the immediately preceding utterance of their human companion. During this experiment, for example, in response to the question, YOU WANT ICECREAM? Dar signed, ICECREAM HURRY GIMME. Also like human children (e.g., Keenan, 1977; Nelson, 1980; and Scollon, 1979, working with hearing children; and Hoffmeister, Moores, & Ellenberger, 1975, p. 123, working with signing children), Tatu and Dar often reiterated a sign within an utterance. In response to the statement YOU PLAY THERE (indicating a cupboard), for example, Dar signed OPEN OPEN. And, again like human children, Tatu and Dar often reiterated an incorporated sign. In response to the statement TIME ICECREAM NOW, Tatu signed ICECREAM ICECREAM ICECREAM ICECREAM ICECREAM ICECREAM. When similar examples occur in samples of child speech, Keenan (1977) and Keenan and Klein (1975) suggest that reiteration and incorporation should be interpreted as pragmatic devices indicating assent or emphasis.°

Keenan (1977) and Keenan and Klein (1975) give examples of cases in which incorporations, reiterations, and reiterations of incorporations in the speech of children can be interpreted as pragmatic devices indicating positive

---

°When used in this context, the term repetition leads to confusion since it is also used to refer to incorporation (Keenan, 1977, p. 125). This confusion is compounded by the practice of classifying some incorporations as repetitions and some as imitations, depending upon adult inferences about the intention of the child. Terminological confusion is still further compounded by the widespread disagreement as to the criteria that might distinguish repetition from imitation in children's replies (Keenan, 1977, pp. 125–129). It is for this reason that we recommend the terms *incorporation*, for items also found in the preceding utterance of an interlocutor, and *reiteration*, for items that recur within a single utterance.

response. To test the hypothesis that these were also positive responses for Tatu and Dar, we tabulated the frequencies of these three devices in the signed responses of Tatu and Dar to announcements.

Since announcements were prescripted, interobserver agreement on incorporations was, of course, the same as interobserver agreement on sign identification. Interobserver agreement on reiteration was scored according to the following rules: (1) score whether agreed sign X is repeated; (2) go to the next agreed sign in the record that is different from sign X and score whether that sign is repeated; or, (3) go to the next trial record. The interobserver agreement for this measure of agreement was 92%. Table 2.8 shows how all three devices, incorporation, reiteration, and reiteration of incorporation, were more likely to occur in response to positive announcements than to neutral and negative announcements.

DISCUSSION
Arbitrary Experience vs. Obligatory Responses

The human participants in this experiment had extensive firsthand experience with the vocalizations of cross-fostered chimpanzees in the Reno laboratory. This experience plus their study of the descriptions of field observations of wild chimpanzees permitted them to identify the vocalizations of wild chimpanzees with the labels assigned by Goodall (1968) and Marler and Tenaza (1977). This was, of course, the qualifying test that these experimenters all passed under blind conditions. The same experimenters agreed closely when they assigned the same labels to the vocalizations of Tatu and Dar during the course of the reliability sample of this experiment.

Taken together, the results of the qualifying test and the reliability sample demonstrate that wild and cross-fostered chimpanzees emit the same vocal responses. These vocalizations are obligatory for chimpanzees in the sense that the same vocal responses are emitted by chimpanzees with very different life histories. In addition, positive stimuli evoke pants and grunts while negative stimuli evoke whimpers both in wild and in cross-fostered chimpanzees. Thus, there is an obligatory connection between the affective values of stimuli and specific types of vocal response. The same affective values evoke the same types of vocalization in both wild and cross-fostered chimpanzees.

Under the systematically varied conditions of this experiment, pants were more likely to be evoked by announcements than by events while grunts and whimpers were more likely to be evoked by events than by announcements. Thus, pants were anticipatory responses evoked by signals of events to come, while grunts and whimpers were evoked by the events, themselves. But, the element of anticipation is relative. The different stimulus events that evoked grunts or whimpers were, themselves, only signals of exciting events still to come. The sight of an ice cream cone only predicts the taste treat. Moreover, to be recognized as positive, even the sight of foods such as cookies or ice cream had to be familiar from past experience. And certainly, the emotional response evoked by the arrival of a favorite human friend depended upon previous experience with that particular person. Thus, whether they were responses to announcements or to events and whether they were vocal responses or gestural responses, all of the responses in this experiment were to some degree anticipatory responses that were arbitrarily connected with particular stimuli as a result of past experience.

Human beings also display obligatory patterns of emotional response to affective stimuli. Ekman (1973), for example, showed that there is an obligatory repertoire of human facial expressions and specific facial expressions are evoked by specific affective stimuli. The same expressions of anger, disgust, happiness and sadness are associated with the same types of affective stimuli, but the particular stimuli that evoke each type of response, the stimulus events as well as the language in which the events are described, depend upon cultural experience. The stimulus-response pairs, as well as the social conditions in which some responses are suppressed and others counterfeited, depend upon social learning. The key to the discoveries of Ekman and his associates was their sophisticated and precise identification of emotions and facial expressions. An essential step, however, was the identification of the different texts and contexts that evoke emotions such as anger and happiness in the different cultures. The affective charge that is associated with particular utterances or particular events varies from culture to culture. It is the arbitrary result of past experience.

Lieberman (1984, pp. 256–286) has proposed that chimpanzees cannot learn English because they cannot form the phonemes of human speech; that the impediment is in the design of their vocal tract. But human beings can speak intelligibly even when they must overcome severe injury to their vocal tract. In our view, it is the obligatory attachment of vocal behavior to emotional state that makes it so difficult, perhaps impossible, for chimpanzees to speak English words. They can, however, use their hands in the arbitrary connections between signs and referents.

Under the conditions of the experiment described in this chapter, vocalization and signing were positively correlated. Whether the stimuli were announcements or events, positive or negative, the stimuli that were more likely to evoke signs were also more likely to evoke vocal responses (see Tables 2.3 and 2.5 and Figure 2.1). But signed responses were much more likely than vocal responses. Overall, Tatu and Dar signed about twice as often as they vocalized under the conditions of this experiment. This finding is all the more impressive when we consider that the positive and negative events were chosen for their relatively high affective charge. In the course of an average day, the preponderance of signing over vocalization was even greater. Taken together with Goodall's (1986) descriptions of the silent habits of wild chimpanzees and with our own observations throughout the cross-fostering research, these experimental results confirm the basic premise of the sign language studies of chimpanzees: chimpanzees use their hands much more readily than they use their voices.

Although they were more likely to sign than to vocalize under all of the conditions of this experiment, Tatu and Dar were more likely to sign in response to announcements than to events, but more likely to vocalize in response to events than to announcements. This confirms the second basic premise of the sign language studies of chimpanzees: signing can be more anticipatory, more independent of the stimuli most closely associated with emotional arousal.

Pragmatics

The meaning of an utterance depends only partly on the arbitrary semantic values of words or signs. Human speakers and signers use syntactic devices such as word or sign orders, inflections, and markers to modulate the meaning of an utterance. Evidence that cross-fostered chimpanzees can use syntactic devices of ASL in appropriate situations is discussed in detail in R. Gardner & Gardner (1978, pp. 57–58), Van Cantfort and Rimpau (1982) and Chapter 6 in this volume. The information in human face-to-face conversation is also modulated by pragmatic devices, such as intonation, stress, and facial gestures. Subtle changes in the intonation or stress of a single word, or momentary changes in the tilt of the head or the height of the eyebrows, often have far more powerful effects than gross changes in word order—that is, when the effect of the utterance is judged by the response of the listener (Argyle, 1972; Bolinger, 1975, pp. 18–22, 603–610; Stokoe, 1978, pp. 69–80).

Until recently, pragmatic devices were virtually ignored in studies of the linguistic development of human children. Early work in this field was narrowly focused on syntax. Meanwhile, pragmatic devices such as reiteration were treated as a kind of random noise in the records. The early workers literally edited reiteration out of their transcripts before analysis because it seemed irrelevant to syntax (cf. Bloom, 1970, p. 70; Hoffmeister et al., 1975, p. 123; Scollon, 1979, p. 226). Apparently, this has led some secondary sources to conclude that reiteration is rare or absent in the speech and signing of human children. "In children's utterances, in contrast, the repetition of a word, or a sequence of words, is a rare event." (Terrace, Petitto, Sanders & Bever, 1979, p. 894).

Commenting on this misunderstanding, Nelson (1980) remarked,

It must be borne in mind that when researchers have analyzed children's utterances, as when in the past they have analyzed chimps' utterances, repetitions do not count. This is true both for words and for whole sentences. Thus many of Nim's productions as reported [here] would not be recorded as 4, 5, or 16 word utterances but as 2 or 3 word utterances with repetitions. That repetitions don't count doesn't mean that they don't exist. My transcripts are full of false starts, repeated words, repeated phrases . . . Anyone who claims that children don't repeat has led a sheltered library existence. (p. 4)

The view of language that omitted so much of the evidence was characteristic of the period in which a concentration on syntax, narrowly defined, dominated psycholinguistics. More recently, there has been a resurgence of interest in broader aspects of verbal behavior (Bates, 1976, pp. 1–41; Bruner, 1978, pp. vii–viii) and studies of children's speech have appeared that are directly concerned with pragmatic devices such as reiteration (e.g., Ervin-Tripp & Mitchell-Kernan, 1977; Garvey, 1984; Lock, 1978; Ochs & Schieffelin, 1979). Thus, Keenan (1977) shows how examples of reiteration, incorporation, and reiteration of incorporation are best understood in context as pragmatic devices indicating agreement or assent. In the present experiment with Tatu and Dar, affective values were systematically varied under controlled conditions. Under these conditions, Tatu and Dar responded the way human children do; reiteration, incorporation, and reiteration of incorporation were more likely to appear in responses to the announcement of positive as compared with neutral or negative events. Once again, observations of cross-fostered chimpanzees and children yield comparable results when based on comparable analyses and comparable rules of evidence (cf. Van Cantfort & Rimpau, 1982).

Methodological Note

This experiment was part of an overall program of research that combined cross-fostering, naturalistic observation, and systematic experiments. True cross-fostering was vital to the special purposes of the research program, and naturalistic observation was required for comparison with currently available studies of human children. The insights gained in this way must also be tested by systematic, controlled, experimental manipulation of independent variables, such as responses to Wh-questions (B. Gardner & Gardner, 1975; Chapter 5 this volume), Piagetian tests of object permanence (Wood, Moriarty, Gardner, & Gardner, 1980), and double-blind vocabulary tests (R. Gardner & Gardner, 1984; Chapter 4 this volume), as well as voiced and signed responses to announcements and events. Fortunately, providing infant chimpanzees with a rich, human-like environment does not preclude systematic experimentation. In fact, the cross-fostering conditions contributed to the quality of these experiments. The usual conditions of caged subjects, or caged subjects that are occasionally treated as pets, would not have yielded the variety of routine events sampled in Tables 2.1 and 2.2 and in similar procedures of the other experiments. Short-term laboratory technicians would not have had the rich, intimate, stable familiarity with their subjects' lives and the language they were using, nor would they have had the professional commitment of the raters, observers, and experimenters in these experiments.

References

Argyle, M. (1972). Non-verbal communication in human social interaction. In R.A. Hinde (Ed.), *Non-verbal communication*, (pp. 243–269). Cambridge: Cambridge University Press.

Bates, E. (1976). *Language and context: The acquisition of pragmatics*. New York: Academic Press.

Bloom, L. (1970). *Language development: Form and function in emerging grammars*. Cambridge, MA: MIT Press.

Bolinger, D. (1975). *Aspects of language*. New York: Harcourt Brace Jovanovich.

Brinton, B., & Fujiki, M. (1984). Development of topic manipulation skills in discourse. *Journal of Speech and Hearing Research, 27*, 350–358.

Bruner, J. (1978). Foreword to A. Lock (Ed.), *Action, gesture and symbol: The emergence of language*, (pp. vii–viii). New York: Academic Press.

Ekman, P. (1973). Cross-cultural studies of facial expression. In P. Ekman (Ed.), *Darwin and facial expression*, (pp. 169–222). New York: Academic Press.

Ervin-Tripp, S., & Mitchell-Kernan, C. (1977). *Child discourse*. New York: Academic Press.

Gardner, B. T., & Gardner, R. A. (1975). Evidence for sentence constituents in the early utterances of child and chimpanzee. *Journal of Experimental Psychology: General, 104*, 244–267.

Gardner, B. T., & Gardner, R. A. (1980). Two comparative psychologists look at language acquisition. In K. E. Nelson (Ed.), *Children's language*, (Vol. 2, pp. 331–369). New York: Gardner Press.

Gardner, R. A., & Gardner, B. T. (1978). Comparative psychology and language acquisition. *Annals of the New York Academy of Sciences, 309*, 37–76.

Gardner, R. A., & Gardner, B.T. (1984). A vocabulary test for chimpanzees. *Journal of Comparative Psychology, 98*, 381–404.

Garvey, C. (1984). *Children's talk*. Cambridge, MA: Harvard University Press.

Goodall, J. van Lawick (1968). A preliminary report on expressive movements and communication in the Gombe Stream chimpanzees. In P. C. Jay (Ed.), *Primates: Studies in adaptation and variability*, (pp. 313–374). New York: Hold, Rinehart and Winston.

Goodall, J. (1986). *The chimpanzees of Gombe*. Cambridge, MA: Harvard University Press.

Hoffmeister, R. J., Moores, D. F., & Ellenberger, R. L. (1975). Some pro-cedural guidelines for the study of the acquisition of sign languages. *Sign Language Studies, 7,* 121–137.

Keenan, E. Ochs (1977). Making it last: Repetition in children's discourse. In S. Ervin-Tripp and C. Mitchell-Kernan (Eds.), *Child discourse,* (pp. 125–138). New York: Academic Press.

Keenan, E. & Klein, E. (1975). Coherency in children's discourse. *Journal of Psycholinguistic Research, 4,* 365–380.

Lieberman, P. (1984). *The biology and evolution of language.* Cambridge, MA: Harvard University Press.

Lock, A. (1978). The emergence of language. In A. Lock (Ed.), *Action, gesture and symbol: The emergence of language,* (pp. 3–18). New York: Academic Press.

Lovass-Nagy, C., Gardner, B., & Gardner, R. A. (1989). Conversational styles in children and chimpanzees. Paper presented at the joint annual convention of the Western Psychological Association and Rocky Mountain Psycho-logical Association, Reno, NV.

Marler, P., & Tenaza, R. (1977). Signaling behavior of apes with special refer-ence to vocalization. In T. Sebeok (Ed.), *How animals communicate,* (pp. 965–1033). Bloomington: Indiana University Press.

Marler, P., & Goodall, J. van Lawick (1971). Vocalizations of wild chimpanzees. (16-mm film). New York: The Rockefeller University.

McNemar, Q. (1949). *Psychological statistics.* New York: John Wiley & Sons.

Moerk, E. (1972). Principles of dyadic interaction in language learning. *Mer-rill-Palmer Quarterly, 18,* 229–257.

Nelson, K. (March, 1980). First words of the chimp and child. Paper presented at the Southeastern Psychological Association Symposium on Apes and Language.

Ochs, E., & Schieffelin, B. B. (1979). *Developmental pragmatics.* New York: Academic Press.

Scollon, R. (1979). A real early stage: An unzipped condensation of a disserta-tion on child language. In E. Ochs & B.B. Schieffelin (Ed.), *Developmen-tal pragmatics,* (pp. 215–227). New York: Academic Press.

Snedecor, G. W. (1956). *Statistical methods.* Ames: Iowa State University Press.

Snow, C. (1977). Mother's speech research: From input to interaction. In C. Snow & C. Ferguson (Eds.), *Talking to children,* (pp. 31–49). Cambridge: Cambridge University Press.

Stokoe, W. C. (1978). *Sign language structure,* revised edition. Silver Spring, MD: Linstok Press.

Terrace, H. S., Petitto, L., Sanders, R. J., & Bever, T. G. (1979). Can an ape create a sentence? *Science, 206,* 891–902.

Van Cantfort, T. E., & Rimpau, J. B. (1982). Sign language studies with children and chimpanzees. *Sign Language Studies, 34*, 15–72.

Wood, S., Moriarty, K. M., Gardner, B. T., & Gardner, R. A. (1980). Object permanence in child and chimpanzee. *Animal Learning & Behavior, 8*, 3–9.

3. The Shapes and Uses of Signs in a Cross-Fostering Laboratory

Beatrix T. Gardner, R. Allen Gardner
and Susan G. Nichols

The English glosses that we have used throughout this volume to transcribe ASL signs only approximate the usage of the signs by the chimpanzee subjects. Meanwhile, the glosses provide no information about the form of the signs; GLASS, for example, bears no resemblance to GLASSES, nor does ICE occur as a part of ICECREAM. Along with the shapes of the signs, the procedures that we used to document observations of signs are also unfamiliar to most readers. In this chapter we will describe and illustrate these procedures, concentrating on the documentation of individual signs in the vocabularies of the cross-fostered chimpanzees.

Because most readers tend to be unfamiliar with ASL, this discussion begins at an elementary level. The object is to explain where the signs came from, what they looked like when made by the chimpanzees and when modelled by their teachers, and how these forms were related to signing that one might see among grownups and toddlers in the deaf community outside of the cross-fostering laboratory. We hope that many readers will enjoy, as we have, the discovery of a language that seems so different from spoken languages on the surface and yet so very like spoken languages in fundamentals. In any event, the material in this chapter is required reading for those who demand to know how we recorded the uses and shapes of individual signs.

SIGNS OF ASL

Sign language should not be confused with finger-spelling. The signs of ASL, like the words of English, represent whole concepts. Finger-spelling is based on a manual alphabet in which each letter of a written language is represented by a particular configuration of the fingers. It is a code in which messages of a written language can be spelled out in the air. Literate signers mix finger-spelling with sign language as a way of referring to seldom used proper names and technical terms, and we used finger-spelling for this purpose in the

Fig. 3.1   Similarity between chimpanzee and human signers: Washoe (27months) and B.T. Gardner sign DRINK.

Reno laboratory. We also used finger-spelling from time to time as a code to prevent understanding, the way human parents commonly spell out messages that they want to keep secrets from their children. In general, we avoided finger-spelling because our still-illiterate subjects could not understand or copy it, and also because too much finger-spelling could easily lapse into manual English and thus defeat the objective of presenting the best possible model of ASL.

Contrary to popular belief, ASL is not an artificial system recently invented by the hearing for use by the deaf. American Sign Language existed in the United States more than one hundred years before Project Washoe (Stokoe, 1960, pp. 8–19). Its roots in European sign languages can be traced back for hundreds of years. Outsiders have sometimes invented artificial gestural systems and taught them to their deaf clients. Within the deaf community, however, artificial sign languages have never competed successfully with the indigenous sign languages developed by the deaf, themselves, over the centuries.

Contrary to another popular belief, ASL does not consist of a set of iconic gestures that are universally understood by all normal human beings. Instead, ASL is one of many, mutually unintelligible sign languages that have developed among the separate deaf communities around the world (Battison & Jordan, 1976; Jordan & Battison, 1976). International meetings of the deaf require simultaneous translators (see Figure 3.2).

Fig. 3.2 A plenary session of the International Congress of the Deaf in Copenhagen in 1977. Seated and facing the audience are six sign language interpreters simultaneously translating the words of the speaker into six different sign languages. The signer who is standing at the central podium is addressing the audience in Gestuno, the Esperanto of sign languages, which he was promoting at the Congress. Since very few members of the audience were fluent in Gestuno, the speaker standing at the podium to the right is translating the signs of Gestuno into English, and it is her speech that the simultaneous translators are rendering into the six official sign languages of the Congress.

Fig. 3.3 Similarity between chimpanzee signers: (top) TREE made by Moja (33 months) and (bottom) TREE made by Washoe (58 months).

Fig. 3.4 Similarity of signs across contexts: Washoe (58 months) signs HAT, for three different hats.

In manuals written for beginners, signs are often described in terms of vivid analogies, e.g., MAN, as if tipping an imaginary hat, FLOWER, as if sniffing an imaginary flower. This tends to reinforce the popular belief that signs are simple, holistic forms. Nevertheless, just as the words of English can be analyzed into phonemes, so the signs of ASL can be analyzed into a relatively small set of distinctive features, meaningless in themselves, that can be combined to form morphemes or signs. Stokoe (1960, p. 30) called these distinctive features cheremes, to emphasize the parallel with the phonemes of spoken languages. The number of legitimate ASL signs that can be formed by combining and recombining cheremic units is virtually unlimited.

New signs are continually introduced into ASL and old signs drop out, just as in spoken languages. Historically, the shapes of the signs of ASL have changed continuously, moving toward simplicity and smoothness of articulation in ways that parallel historical trends in the sounds of spoken languages (Frishberg, 1975; Woodward, 1976). There are procedures for coining new terms in ASL as technical and social needs arise. Fluent signers tend to create the same new coinages for the same concepts, independently, and they tend to agree also on the relative appropriateness of suggested candidates for the same concepts (Bornstein, Hamilton, & Kannapell, 1969). This is what we would expect if there are structural rules that determine the class of gesture that qualifies as a legitimate sign of ASL.

Proper names in ASL can be assigned by combining the initial letter of the name, taken from the manual alphabet, with a sign or gesture indicating some prominent characteristic of the person named. Thus, WASHOE is a "W" hand flicking against one ear, literally, "Washoe big-ears." Technical terms are constructed in a similar way. Thus, LANGUAGE is the ASL sign for SENTENCE made with the "L" hands of the manual alphabet.

Source of Signs

Apart from name signs for the members of the foster families we avoided inventing signs altogether. The one exception is PEEKABOO, made by covering the eyes with one or both open hands, a gesture that Washoe used, irrepressibly, to invite games of hide-and-seek (we used the ASL sign HIDE in the same contexts). Even though Washoe used PEEKABOO in phrases (e.g., YOU ME GO PEEKABOO) as well as in single-sign utterances, we omitted PEEKABOO from our last comprehensive list of Washoe's vocabulary (B. Gardner & Gardner, 1975), because we could not find this sign described in any published dictionary of ASL. Later, Moja, Tatu, and Dar each reinvented this sign for hide-and-seek. Tatu and Dar also used it to refer to masks, which were among their favorite toys, and even to invite human and chimpanzee friends to put on masks. Inevitably, their human playmates fell into the habit of using PEEKABOO rather than HIDE, themselves. In view of all of these observations we decided to add PEEKABOO to the vocabulary lists.

We took some pains to honor the rule against invented signs. Early in Project Washoe, our contacts with the deaf community were sporadic and limited. Available dictionaries at that time were chiefly designed for helping professionals and others who wished to communicate with adult signers. It was difficult to find signs for the common objects in a nursery environment. Rather than invent new signs in such cases, we used signs with closely related meanings that we could find in manuals and dictionaries.

When we failed to find a sign for the English word "bib," for example, we substituted a sign that was glossed as NAPKIN in available sources. This sign is made by rubbing the palm of an open hand over the lips and chin. A prominent ritual at the beginning of each meal consisted of arranging a bib around Washoe's neck and over her chest. As usual, actions were accompanied by simple comments and simple questions. Washoe got fed whether or not she joined in the conversation, of course. One evening in the 18th month of Project Washoe, just before serving dinner, we held up her bib and asked Washoe, WHAT THIS? Washoe replied PLEASE GIMME PLEASE GIMME . . . GIMME . . . and then, with the index fingers of both hands, she drew the outline of a bib, starting from behind her neck where a bib would be tied, down along the outer edge of her chest, bringing her fingers together again at her midriff. It struck us immediately that this was an excellent way of signing BIB, really better than the one we were using—which was glossed as NAPKIN rather than BIB in our best source, anyway.

At the next weekly meeting of the human participants we considered the possibility of adopting Washoe's invented sign for BIB. The outcome of a heated debate was that—however apt Washoe's BIB looked to us, however easy it was for us to understand her when she used it—human children have to learn the language they find in the adult community, and so should a properly cross-fostered chimpanzee. Equally important, the link with native signers depended on known signs of ASL. NAPKIN was a known sign of ASL, so we stuck to it and soon the NAPKIN sign became Washoe's reliable name for bibs as well as for tissues and washcloths. Five months later, on a visit to the California School for the Deaf in Berkeley, we showed films of the early results of Project Washoe to an audience of faculty and students. When we showed the sign that we were using for BIB, native signers in the audience were quick to tell us that the ASL sign for BIB was made by indicating the outline of a bib on the chest—very much like the sign that Washoe had invented for herself.

This observation suggests that Washoe had absorbed enough sign language so that she could coin legitimate signs on her own. It remains an isolated incident, however, because we had more direct sources of nursery signs as our circle of informants in the deaf community widened. During the second project with Moja, Pili, Tatu, and Dar, many native signers, as well as fluent signers who had had extensive contact with the deaf community, were members of the foster families. At the same time, published dictionaries and manuals of sign language continued to improve. Soon, the adult models always had rich vocabularies of authentic nursery signs and they could always keep ahead of chimpanzee inventions. With the exception of PEEKABOO, we corrected the cross-fosterlings when they offered their own nonstandard coinages, just as parents correct human children in similar cases.

Childish Diction

In the early stages, the speech and sign of human children are immature versions of the language of the adults around them. We could only expect the cross-fostered chimpanzees to begin with immature versions of the signs that we modelled for them. The speech of very young children tends to be poorly articulated. Often, only members of their immediate family—sometimes only their own mothers—claim to understand the toddlers. The articulation of very young signers is also much less clear than the articulation of adults and contains typical childish variants. Toddlers, for example, tend to reduce the configuration of the signing hand to a simple pointing index finger and to enlarge or exaggerate the signing area. Thus, DADDY in ASL is made by adults and older children with a thumb extended from a spread hand, tip of the thumb contacting the brow. But toddlers often reduce the configuration to a pointing index and may exaggerate the signing area by contacting the top of their heads. And very young signers often turn signs back toward themselves as Washoe, Moja and Tatu pointed their BIRD signs toward rather than away from themselves.

Given a small vocabularly and many contextual clues, members of the immediate family can still read childish forms of words and signs. Moja, Pili, Tatu, and Dar had a distinct advantage over Washoe because their foster families always included many fluent signers who had experience with the first signs of human children. In this laboratory, however, we had to show that chimpanzee signing was intelligible to strangers as well as to familiars under double-blind conditions, without the aid of contextual cues (R. Gardner & Gardner, 1984; Chapter 4 this volume). Consequently we were more concerned with good diction than the average human parent might be with the diction of the average human child. Nevertheless, when the cross-fosterlings were very young we tolerated a certain amount of baby talk lest we stifle early, stumbling attempts at communication.

FLOWER, for example, is made with a tapered hand, fingertips brought first to one nostril then to the other, as if sniffing a flower. During Washoe's second summer with us, we took advantage of her interest in flowers by discussing the flowers she found in her own garden and by bringing her fresh flowers from outside. In September, 1967, which was the 15th month of the project, we observed Washoe's first FLOWER signs. With typical childish diction, she only touched one index finger to one nostril. We corrected her by signing precise versions of the standard form to her until, gradually, Washoe began to touch both nostrils with her index finger when naming flowers, and eventually to touch both nostrils with the fingertips of her curved hand.

USAGE AND CONTEXT

For a technical description of an unknown dialect linguists can go into the field to interrogate native speakers. Young children are much more difficult to interrogate about their childish versions of adult languages. Thus, when Berko-Gleason (1958) asked little children questions such as, "Why is Thanksgiving Day called Thanksgiving Day?" she got answers such as, "Because we eat lots of turkey." Plainly, it is a mistake to attribute adult meanings to childish words, as the early students of child language often did (cf. Nelson, 1973, pp. 13–15). All we know is what we can observe of the contexts in which they use their childish vocabularies.

Spontaneous and Appropriate Usage

As we pointed out in Chapter 1, we did not teach the chimpanzees to make the signs, we only taught them to associate different signs with different objects and activities. In each context, we made appropriate signs, ourselves. We molded their hands into the correct configurations. We touched or pointed at their hands or at the places where they should put them. In teaching, we prompted the chimpanzees the way teachers commonly prompt human children and human adults (cf. Aiken & Lau, 1967). As with human children their wishes were often denied, but they were more likely to get what they wanted if they could make themselves understood.

After the first year, most of the signed exchanges between the chimpanzees and the human beings in the cross-fostering laboratory were initiated by the chimpanzees, themselves. Thousands upon thousands of incidents of signing appear in the records and in more than half, usually much more than half, of the incidents in any random sample, the signing was initiated by the chimpanzee. It is the spontaneity illustrated in films, video tapes, and written records that most clearly shows that the young cross-fosterlings had made the signs their own and were using them the way human children use words and signs. Nevertheless, most of the hard evidence that we have reported in this volume and elsewhere is based on signing that was evoked by specific questions in specific contexts.

Often the signs in a spontaneous utterance were plainly appropriate to the context in which they appeared. Thus, in a child's picture book or in one of the special scrapbooks that we prepared for the chimpanzee subjects, there might be only one kind of object on a page. If Moja, for example, signed FLOWER when, indeed, the object in the picture was a flower, then the sign was plainly appropriate. And, if she signed TREE in such a context, then the sign would be plainly inappropriate. Again, if Moja signed THAT BLACK DOG indicating a particular object in a more complicated picture, then it was also easy to decide whether the signs in her utterance were appropriate or inappropriate.

The trouble with adventitious observations is that they occur under uncontrolled conditions. When Dar signed BIRD while gazing out the window, his human companion could report that the sign was appropriate if there was, indeed, a bird in sight. But suppose that the human observer failed to see any bird through the window, what then? Perhaps the bird that Dar saw had flown away unnoticed by the human observer. Perhaps Dar had momentarily mistaken a fluttering leaf for a bird. Meanwhile, these chimpanzees were quite capable of signing about objects that were out of sight. Driving home with Washoe, for example, we often drove past a yard where a dog usually rushed to the fence and barked at our car. Several times with no dog in sight, Washoe signed DOG as we passed that yard as if commenting on the absent dog. Perhaps in the incident of the absent bird, Dar was remembering a bird that he saw in that spot earlier in the day or earlier in the week, or perhaps something now in the field of view reminded him of a bird that he had seen some other time and somewhere else entirely.

In all ambiguous cases, the human observers had to record the signing as inappropriate unless they had additional evidence to report. By recording and reviewing details of inappropriate contexts, however, we often discovered unexpected patterns of usage. Still, all such adventitiously discovered patterns remained in doubt until they were verified under conditions in which the verbal and nonverbal contexts had been specified in advance (see Chapter 4 this volume). This is why so much of the evidence must be based on answers to specific questions.

As vocabularies grew, particularly when they included modifiers such as BLACK and RED, MINE and YOURS, LARGE and SMALL, questions had to be more specific. Moja, for example, had a favorite red, transparent, drinking cup which she quite correctly called either DRINK, CUP, RED, GLASS, or SEE (for looking through it), or some combinations of these terms at different times. Sometimes her bandana was a HANKY and at other times it was a BLINDFOLD. In the days before electric watches became more common than windup watches, all of the cross-fosterlings began by calling a watch a LISTEN. As they learned a separate WRISTWATCH sign, we could explain, THAT NAME WRISTWATCH, and THAT MAKE LISTEN, and ask WHAT NAME THAT? and WHAT THAT DO? to evoke different answers. Different types of Wh-questions call for answers that contain different types of signs (see B. Gardner & Gardner, 1975; Chapter 5 this volume).

Creating appropriate contexts for some signs required a fair amount of ingenuity. In Project Washoe, for example, we had a great deal of difficulty with NO. At first we tried to provoke NO in response to clearly unreasonable demands, such as ordering Washoe to bed in the middle of afternoon play or offering her a bowl of rocks at mealtime. This strategy failed, partly because of Washoe's good nature (she sometimes allowed herself to be marched off to bed or tried to lick the rocks) and partly because she could evade difficult situations without saying anything at all (she sometimes climbed a tree or spilled the rocks on the floor). Eventually, we hit on a stratagem that capitalized on Washoe's good faith. We told her a variety of tales of which the following is typical.

It is late in the day, and getting dark outside. Washoe and Roger Fouts are inside her house trailer. Roger peers out the window, comes back, and tells Washoe about the big black dog that he sees out there and how the big black dog has long teeth and eats baby chimpanzees.

Roger: WANT GO OUT NOW?/
Washoe: NO/ (prolonged and emphatic)
Roger: YOU BIRD/(equivalent of "you're chicken")
(Washoe goes to the next room where she finds college football lineman Linn)
Washoe: YOU BIRD/ (to Linn)

Scary tales of this sort were popular with all of the cross-fosterlings and the bogeydog became a familiar phantom in Washoe's young life. We often got her to come inside in the evening by spotting the BIG BLACK DOG coming. The bogeydog reappeared early in the second project with Moja, Pili, Tatu, and Dar. It was rated as highly negative for the experiment on announcements of affectively charged events reported in Chapter 2 of this volume (see Table 2.1) and it appeared in one of the announcement frames of that experiment as BIG BLACK DOG COME and YOU WANT BIG BLACK DOG COME? (see Table 2.2).

Table 3.1: Contexts and Uses

Examples of context descriptions from the field records are presented in Table 3.1, where the signs in the vocabularies of Washoe, Moja, Tatu, and Dar are grouped according to major categories. For one representative sign from each category in Table 3.1 there is a summary description of contexts together with typical questions that evoked that sign and examples of verbal exchanges and phrases in which it appeared. Because their usage is both more complex and more significant, each of the signs in the category that we have called "markers and traits" is described separately. The examples and the summaries were all taken from the formal field records described in the next section.

Table 3.1.
The Contexts and Uses of the Signs

Names, chimpanzees		In response to:	Used in such phrases as:
DAR, MOJA, TATU, WASHOE	e.g., DAR—Chimpanzee Dar; pictures of Dar	WHO THAT?/WHO YOU?/ WHAT YOUR NAME?/ WHO CHASE?/ (During breakfast) John:WHO DRINK MILK?/ Dar:MILK DAR/ (Indoors before playtime with Dar) R.A.G.:WHO MEET?/ Tatu:OUT GO DAR/	CHASE DAR/ DRINK DAR/ MILK DAR/ GOOD DAR/
Names, humans		*In response to:*	*Used in phrase such as:*
ARLENE K., GREG G., LINN A., NAOMI R., R.A.G., SUSAN N., TOMV.; see other names at end of Table 3.2	e.g., NAOMI R.—Naomi Rhodes a human companion; picture of Naomi	WHO THAT?/WHO ME?/ WHO TICKLE NOW?/ (Looking at photos) Tatu:THAT WHO?/ Betty:THAT TOM, WHO THAT?/ Tatu:NAOMI/	YOU NAOMI/ NAOMI TICKLE/ NAOMI COME/ NAOMI GOOD/
Names, generic		*In response to:*	*Used in phrases such as:*
BOY, FRIEND, GIRL	e.g., BOY—Males, especially male strangers or familiar males who do not have name signs; pictures of men in magazines	WHO THAT?/WHICH-SEX THAT?/WHICH-SEX ME?/ WHAT THAT?/ (During lessons in ASL) Susan: WHICH-SEX YOU?/ Dar: BOY DAR/	THAT BOY/ GOOD DAR BOY/ R.A.G. BOY/ BIRD BOY/ (eagle and man on coin)

			Used in phrases such as:
Pronouns		(Of magazine picture of man) Susan: WHAT THAT?/ Dar: BOY/	
		In response to:	*Used in phrases such as:*
ME, WE, YOU	e.g., YOU—The addressee during food-sharing, games with turns such as tickle and hide and other activities	WHO TICKLE?/WHO EAT?/ WHO OUT?/ (Sharing sodapop) Dar: SODAPOP DAR/ Susan: AND WHO OTHER?/ Dar: YOU/	YOU JIM/ YOU PEEKABOO/ YOU TICKLE ME WASHOE/
Nouns, animates		*In response to:*	*Used in phrases such as:*
BABY, BEAR, BIRD, BUG, BUTTERFLY, CAT, COW, DOG, HORSE	e.g., BIRD—Sparrows, ducks, pigeons, and other species of birds; toy birds; pictures of birds; bird calls and human renditions of bird calls	WHAT THAT?/WHO SAY "quack quack"?/NAME THAT/ (Of hidden bird, calling) Pat: WHAT THERE YOU HEAR?/ Dar: HEAR/ Pat: NAME/ Dar: BIRD/	THAT BIRD/ RED BIRD/ LISTEN BIRD/

Table 3.1 (continued)

Nouns, edibles		In response to:	Used in phrases such as:
APPLE, BANANA, BERRY, BREAD, CANDY, CARROT, CEREAL, CHEESE, COFFEE, COOKIE, CORN, CRACKER, CUCUMBER, GRAPES GUM, ICE, ICECREAM, MEAT, MEDICINE, MILK, NUT, ONION, ORANGE, PEA/BEAN, PEACH, SANDWICH, SODA-POP, TOMATO, WATER	e.g., COFFEE—Coffee or tea in mugs, cups, thermos flasks; instant coffee in jars; pictures of cups of coffee	WHAT THAT?/WHAT NAME THAT?/WHAT WANT?/ (Of cup of coffee) Tatu: DRINK/ Betty: WHAT THAT DRINK?/ Tatu: COFFEE/	COFFEE DRINK/ THAT COFFEE/ BABY DRINK MORE COFFEE/ (when Susan pretended to give coffee to doll)
Nouns, inanimate objects		In response to:	Used in phrases such as:
AIRPLANE, BALL, BELT, BIB, BLANKET, BOOK, CLOTHES, COAT, CUP, DIAPER, EARRING, FLOOR, FLOWER, FORK, GARBAGE, GLASSES, GLOVE, GRASS, HAMMER, HANDS, HAT, HOLE, HOSE, HOUSE, HURT, KEY, KNIFE, LEAF, LIPSTICK, LOCK, MIRROR, PANTS, PIN, PURSE, RING, ROCK, SHIRT, SHOE, SPOON, STAMP, STRING, SWAB, TABLE, TELEPHONE, TOOTHPASTE, TREE, WINDOW, WIPER, WRISTWATCH	e.g., WRISTWATCH—Wristwatches, alone or on wrist; pictures of wristwatches	WHAT THAT?/WHAT NAME THAT?/ NAME THAT/ (Of Naomi's watch) Tatu: THAT BLACK/ Naomi: BLACK WHAT?/ Tatu: WRISTWATCH/	THAT WRISTWATCH/ WRISTWATCH GIMME/ WRISTWATCH BLACK/

		In response to:	Used in phrases such as:
Noun/Verbs			
BATH, BED, BLINDFOLD, BLOW, BRUSH, CAR, CHAIR, CLEAN, CLIMB, COMB, COVER/BLANKET, DRINK, FOOD/EAT, HANKY, HEAR/LISTEN, LIGHT OIL, PEEKA-BOO, PEN/WRITE, PIPE, POTTY, RIDE, SCHOOL, SEE, SMELL, SMOKE, SWING, TOOTHBRUSH, VACUUM	e.g., TOOTHBRUSH—Toothbrushes, pictures of toothbrushes; brushing teeth	WHAT THAT?/WHAT NOW?/ WHAT DO?/ (Susan brushes a doll's teeth) Dar: BABY/ Susan: WHAT DO?/ Dar: TOOTHBRUSH BABY/ (At end of meal) Betty: WANT THAT?/ Tatu: TOOTHBRUSH TOOTHBRUSH/	TOOTHBRUSH THAT/ TIME TOOTHBRUSH/ TOOTHBRUSH DAR/
Verbs		In response to:	Used in phrases such as:
BITE, BREAK, CATCH, CHASE, CRY, GO, GROOM, HUG, KISS, LAUGH, OPEN, QUIET, RUN, SLEEP, SPIN, SWALLOW, TICKLE, WRESTLE	e.g., CHASE—Chasing and being chased in play	WHAT WANT?/WHAT DO?/ WHAT PLAY?/ (During chase game) Moja: CHASE/ Tim: WHO CHASE?/ Moja: CHASE ME/	CHASE DAR/ TATU CHASE/ YOU CHASE/
Locatives		In response to:	Used in phrases such as:
DOWN, HOME, IN/ENTER, OUT, THAT/THERE, UP	e.g., OUT—Requesting change in location, as going outdoors or removing an object from a container; designation of location of a person or an object	WHERE GO?/WHERE DAR?/ WHAT WE DO?/WHAT NOW?/ (Near closed door) Moja: OUT OUT/ Tim: SORRY CAN'T NOW/	YOU ME OUT/ CAN'T OUT OUT/ PLEASE BLANKET OUT/ (at blanket in cupboard OUT HOME MILK DAR/ (when in playroom)

Table 3.1 (continued)

Modifiers, colors		In response to:	Used in phrases such as:
BLACK, GREEN, ORANGE, RED, WHITE	e.g., BLACK—Purse, dog, shoe and other items that are black; indicating the part of a multicolored item that is black	WHAT COLOR THAT?/ NAME COLOR THAT/ WHAT COLOR HAT?/ (During lesson in ASL) Ken: WHAT COLOR YOU?/ Moja: BLACK/	THAT BLACK/ SHOE BLACK/ BLACK BERRY/ (raisin)
Modifiers, possessives		In response to:	Used in phrases such as:
MINE, YOURS	e.g., YOURS—Watches, shoes, coffee and other belongings of the companion	WHOSE THAT?/WHOSE SHOE?/WHOSE LISTEN?/ (Of Betty's can of soda) Betty: WHOSE DRINK?/ Tatu: MINE/ Betty: NO, NO/ Tatu: YOURS/	HAT YOURS/ CANDY YOURS/ SUSAN YOURS/
Modifiers, materials		In response to:	Used in phrases such as:
GLASS, METAL, WOOD	e.g., METAL—Pans, pliers, spoons and other items made of metal	WHAT THAT MAKE FROM?/ (Of key Dar found) Pat: WHAT THAT?/ Dar: KEY/ Pat: WHAT THAT MAKE FROM?/ Dar: METAL/	THAT METAL/ METAL HOT/ (cigarette lighter) METAL CUP DRINK COFFEE/ (thermos flask

		Used in phrases such as
Modifiers, materials	*In response to:*	
ONE, TWO	HOW MANY?/ HOW MANY NUT?/HOW MANY CANDY?/ (Of grapes in icebox) Chris: HOW MANY GRAPE WANT EAT?/ Tatu: ONE ONE/	ONE BLACK/ ONE NUT/ ONE GUM/
e.g., ONE—When single items such as a nut, a match, a glove are displayed		
Modifiers, comparatives	*In response to:*	*Used in phrases such as:*
BIG, DIFFERENT, SAME, SMALL	WHAT SIZE THAT?/THAT SMALL, WHAT THAT?/ (Of two toy horses) Jim: THIS SMALL HORSE, WHAT THAT?/ Moja: BIG/	BIG BALL/ BIG HORSE/ BIG SPOON/
e.g., BIG—When pairs of items that differ in size are displayed such as balls, spoons or toy animals		
Modifiers, qualities	*In response to:*	*Used in phrases such as:*
HOT, SOUR, SWEET	WHAT TEMPERATURE THAT?/ (Of cigarette lighter) Ken: TEMPERATURE THAT?/ Moja: HOT/	THAT HOT/ HOT WATER/ SANDWICH HOT/
e.g., HOT—Substances that are hot, such as water or soup or meat; sources of heat, such as stove or furnace, whether lit or not		

Table 3.1 (continued)

Markers and Traits

	In response to:	Used in phrases such as:
AGAIN—Requesting continuation and repetition of grooming, swinging, tossing and other activities	WHAT WANT?/ (After Moja breaks a balloon) Moja: BLOW AGAIN/ Kathy: NO, FINISH PLAY BLOW, YOU BREAK THAT/ Moja: BLOW/	AGAIN TICKLE/ AGAIN UP/AGAIN UP/ AGAIN AGAIN PEEKABOO/
CAN'T—Unable to do a task, as after many attempts to unlock a door, open a jar, break a stick; unable to answer a question; often used in toilet situations; could also be understood as a refusal	CAN YOU POTTY MORE?/ YOU TRY POTTY/CAN YOU BREAK THAT?/ (After putting on outdoor clothes) Dar: CAN'T/ Pat: CAN'T WHAT?/ Dar: OUT/	DIRTY CAN'T/ POTTY CAN'T/ OUT OPEN CAN'T/
COME/GIMME—Requesting someone to approach; requesting an out-of-reach object or an object someone is holding	WHAT WANT?/WHAT NOW?/ WHAT ME DO?/ (Betty working in kitchen) Tatu: COME/ Betty: WANT WHAT?/ Tatu: CHASE/	COME HUG/ GIMME MILK/ GIMME BLANKET/
°DIRTY—Feces; stains on clothes, furniture, shoes, and soiled items; defecating and urinating	WHAT THAT?/NAME THAT/ WHO POTTY THERE?/	THAT DIRTY/THAT THAT SHOE DIRTY/DIRTY DIRTY SORRY/DIRTY GOOD/

Markers and Traits

	In response to:	*Used in phrases such as:*
	(Of toilet in playroom) Chris: THAT WHAT?/ Tatu: POTTY/ Chris: WHAT NAME SMELL?/ Tatu: POTTY…DIRTY/	(potty chair)
ENOUGH—Ending routine activities such as a meal, a bath, a lesson	YOU FINISH?/ (At end of lunch) Washoe: ENOUGH/ Roger: ENOUGH WHAT?/ Washoe: ENOUGH EAT TIME/	ENOUGH FOOD/ ENOUGH SWALLOW ENOUGH/ OUT ENOUGH ENOUGH TOOTHBRUSH/ (end of supper)
FINISH—Ending routine activities, such as a meal, a toilet session, a bath	WHAT NOW?/MORE EAT?/ MORE CLEAN?/ (Brushing teeth after breakfast) Vaughn: MORE TOOTH- BRUSH/ Tatu: FINISH/	SCHOOL FINISH/ FINISH POTTY/ FINISH HURRY/
FUNNY—An epithet, usually for oneself; during tickling, chasing and other playful interactions; occasionally, when being pursued after mischief	WHO FUNNY?/ (During lesson in ASL) Susan: WHO FUNNY?/ Washoe: FUNNY FUNNY YOU/	FUNNY ME/ FUNNY FUNNY WASHOE/ TICKLE FUNNY/ FUNNY SUSAN FUNNY/

Table 3.1 (continued)

Markers and Traits

	In response to:	Used in phrases such as:
GOOD—An epithet, usually for oneself; part of requests, especially for eyeglasses, watch or other breakable belongings of companion; part of apologies and appeasement after mischief; could also be understood as a promise to "be good"	YOU BAD GIRL/YOU GOOD GIRL?/ NO CAN'T GO THERE/ (Before going outdoors) Tatu: GOOD GOOD OUT Naomi: YOU SURE?/ Tatu: GOOD OUT/	GOOD GOOD GOOD ME/ GOOD MOJA/ SORRY GOOD/ TATU GOOD OUT GO/
GOODBYE—At departures, when persons announce they will leave or as they actually depart	WHAT SAY NOW?/TIME ME LEAVE/ HE LEAVE/ (Greg preparing to leave) Greg: ME LEAVE NOW/ Moja: GOODBYE/	GOODBYE DAR/ OUT GOODBYE/
HELP—Requesting assistance with difficult tasks, such as operating locks and keys, cracking nuts, opening bottles, or making difficult signs	WHAT WANT?/ (Of garage door) Washoe: IN HELP KEY/ Roger: WHERE IN?/ Washoe: IN OPEN THERE/ (Of a book) Susan: WHAT THAT?/ Moja: HELP/ Susan: THAT BOOK/ Moja: BOOK/	OPEN HELP/ IN HELP/ HELP UP/

Markers and Traits

	In response to:	Used in phrases such as:
HURRY—Requesting someone to approach, bring an object, unlock a door, or do other things quickly	WHAT WANT?/WHAT NOW?/ YOU WANT OUT?/ (Tony is fixing meal) Dar: HURRY GIMME/ Tony: WANT?/ Dar: CARROT/	HOME HURRY/ HURRY COME/ OPEN HURRY/ EAT TATU HURRY/
MORE—Requesting continuation and repetition of tickling, chasing, brushing and other activities; requesting additional helpings of milk, juice, cookies and other edibles	WHAT WANT?/WHAT DO?/ FINISH?/ (Washoe hands weeding tool to Susan) Washoe: MORE/ Susan: MORE WHAT?/ Washoe: MORE OPEN/ (on ground) (Susan holding grape) Washoe: MORE/ Susan: MORE WHAT?/ Washoe: MORE ME BERRY/	MORE GO/ MORE TICKLK/ MORE MILK/ MORE SODAPOP DAR/

Table 3.1 (continued)

Markers and Traits

	In response to:	*Used in phrases such as:*
NO—Negation; used in reply to commands, questions, and statments; also, in response to actions such as a stranger's offer to pick up subject; threats to throw snowballs or splash water at the subject, and occasionally, offers of food	YOU WANT SHOE THERE?/ WANT GO HOME?/ ME EAT THAT?/COME, TIME SLEEP/FINISH OUT/ (Of Washoe's doll) B.T.G.: THAT MY BABY?/ Washoe: NO NO MINE/ (simultaneous signs) (Of toy cow) Tim: WHAT THAT?/ Moja: HORSE/ Tim: "uh uh" (vocalizes) Moja: NO COW/	BATH NO/ BED NO NO/ HOT NO/ (after unplugging heater)
PLEASE—Requesting a drink, a berry, a hat, going outside, and other objects and activities	ASK POLITE/ASK NICE/ (Pat holding a cookie) Dar: GIMME COOKIE/ Pat: ASK NICE/ Dar: PLEASE GIMME/	PLEASE FLOWER/ PLEASE OUT/ PLEASE TICKLE THERE/
SORRY—An epithet for oneself; part of apology and appeasement after an escape, a toilet accident, breaking something, and other offenses	YOU GOOD NOW?/ASK PARDON/YOU SIGN/ (After a potty accident) Betty: YOU POTTY THERE, BAD/ Tatu: SORRY/	SORRY GOOD/ ME SORRY/ WASHOE SORRY/ COME HUG SORRY SORRY/

Markers and Traits

	In response to:	Used in phrases such as:
TIME—Accouncing or requesting the next event of the daily routine and other imminent events	WHAT NOW?/WHAT TIME NOW?/ (In barn, at lunchtime) Moja:TIME/ Ken:WHAT TIME?/ Moja:HOME/	TIME VACUUM/ TIME EAT?/ TIME TOOTHBRUSH/ TIME DAR OUT/
WANT—Requesting objects and activities	WHAT YOU WANT?/YOU WANT TICKLE?/WANT GROOM?/ (Before going outdoors) Linn:WHAT TIME?/ Washoe:OUT OUT/ Linn:WHO OUT?/ Washoe:WASHOE WANT OUT/	WANT IN/ WANT MORE DRINK/ WASHO WANT CEREAL/ WANT ROGER PEEKABOO/

Table 3.1 (continued)

Markers and Traits

	In response to:	Used in phrases such as:
WHAT—Interesting out-of-view objects, such as contents of backpacks, pockets, clasped hands; pictures or objects for which the sign is unknown to subject; could be understood as question	ASK/, but usually self-initiated (Of picture of gorilla) Moja: THAT WHAT/ Tom: THAT GORILLA/ Moja: THAT ME/ (During tickle play with teddy bear) Susan: WANT TICKLE MORE?/ Moja: TICKLE/ Susan: WHO TICKLE YOU?/ Moja: THAT WHAT/ (of teddy bear) Susan: BABY/ Moja: BABY/	WHAT THAT?/ PLEASE WHAT WHAT SEE EAT/ (closed refrigerator)
WHO—Persons or their pictures, and subject's mirror image; could be understood as question	I KNOW WHO COME SOON/ ASK ME MY NAME/, but usually self-initiated (Of Naomi's photo on driver's license) Tatu: THAT WHO?/ Naomi: THAT ME NAOMI/ Tatu: THAT NAOMI/	WHO THAT?/ THAT WHO ?/ WHO YOU?/

Markers and Traits

	In response to:	Used in phrases such as:
YES—Agreement; used in reply to questions offering objects or activities	YOU WANT THAT?/ YOU WANT TICKLE?/ WANT MORE?/ (Sharing crackers) Tim: WANT MORE?/ Moja: YES/	MILK YES/ WRISTWATCH YES/ OUT YES/

Phrases

Examples of appropriate uses of signs in phrases appear in column 4 of Table 3.2 and throughout this volume. As soon as Washoe had eight or ten signs in her vocabulary, she began to construct phrases of two or more signs. Before long multiple-sign constructions were common. The early development of Washoe's multiple-sign constructions followed closely the development of human children learning their first language (B. Gardner & Gardner, 1971, pp. 161–178). Later, we found the same pattern of development in the signing of Moja, Tatu, and Dar (R. Gardner & Gardner, 1978, pp. 56–58; B. Gardner & Gardner, 1980, pp. 344–359). Students of children's language have described these same developments as the first sentences of human children (e.g., Brown, 1973, pp. 63–201).

The individual terms within these phrases and sentences formed basic meaningful patterns such as agent-action (SUSAN BRUSH, YOU BLOW), action-object (CHASE DAR, OPEN BLANKET), action-location (GO UP, TICKLE THERE), possession (BIB MINE, HAT YOURS), nomination (THAT CAT, THAT SHOE), and recurrence (MORE COOKIE, MORE GO). Longer constructions could specify more than one agent of an action (YOU ME IN, YOU ME GREG GO), or specify agents, actions, and locations (YOU ME DRINK GO, YOU ME OUT SEE), or specify agents, actions, and objects of action (YOU GIVE GUM MOJA, YOU TICKLE ME WASHOE). Meanwhile, systematic tests reported in Chapter 5 show how the the cross-fosterlings could use these same terms as sentence constituents in their answers to questions.

Segmentation. Constructive units of speech are marked off by vocal contours that punctuate utterances and distinguish a hesitant pause in vocalization from a true stop. Sign languages have visual devices that serve the same function. Stokoe et al., (1965) described these devices as follows:

> . . . in about 90% of sign language utterances, the hands of the signer at the end return to the same position of repose from which they began to move linguistically. The position of repose almost always involves contact of the hands with each other, some other part of the body, an article of furniture, or some other solid object. . . . Another kind of juncture . . . occurs when the signer is interrupted, and is marked by cessation of activity with the hands halted in the position and with the configuration they had at the moment of interruption. There are two kinds of subsequent behavior—a continuation of the utterance or a conclusion of the utterance, marked by movement of the hands from the halted stage to the position of repose. (p. 275)

Typically, Washoe, Moja, Pili, Tatu, and Dar terminated an utterance by relaxing their hands to loose fists, while their arms moved down from the signing space and came to rest on a nearby surface or on the lower body. In another common type of termination, their hands abandoned the configuration held while signing and then contacted and handled some object. The specific manipulatory activity was quite varied: turning pages in a book, grasping food or eating utensils, grooming themselves or a companion, and handling playthings. Still another type of termination was observed when the hands assumed support of the body. Again the specific posture was varied, the hands might touch the ground, or grasp a ledge above head level, or take hold of a companion.

As in the case of speech, hesitant pauses can be distinguished from true stops. There are several clear examples of this in the film *Teaching Sign Language to the Chimpanzee Washoe* (R. Gardner & Gardner, 1973; see also the transcript of that film in R. Gardner & Gardner, 1974). When in the film, Susan asks WHAT THAT? (of a doll stuffed into a shoe), Washoe replies BABY IN . . . IN SHOE (R. Gardner & Gardner, 1974, p. 170). By holding her hands poised in space throughout the pause Washoe indicates that she has not yet finished. The thought is only completed when she drops her hands and picks up her doll. The end point of each construction was nearly always plainly visible as can be seen throughout the videotape and film records. The high level of agreement between independent observers who are also accustomed to the rules of segmentation in ASL is illustrated in Chapter 6.

Creativity. Without deliberately teaching the chimpanzees to construct multiple-sign utterances, the human signers normally modelled simple phrases and sentences in their daily conversation. But Washoe, Moja, Pili, Tatu, and Dar could all invent novel combinations for themselves. Thus, Washoe called her refrigerator the OPEN FOOD DRINK and her toilet the DIRTY GOOD even though her human companions referred to these as the COLD BOX and the POTTY CHAIR. When asked WHAT THAT, Moja described a cigarette lighter as a METAL HOT, a thermos flask as a METAL CUP DRINK COFFEE, and a glass of Alkaseltzer, as a LISTEN DRINK.

In Oklahoma, Washoe frequently called the swans in the moat around her island WATER BIRD even though Roger Fouts called the swans DUCKS. Fouts (1975) reported a systematic study conducted in Oklahoma in which the chimpanzee Lucy was asked to name a series of fruits and vegetables for herself. Among the ojects that had never been named for Lucy in ASL were radishes which she called CRY HURT FOOD, and watermelon which she called CANDY DRINK. The number and variety of chimpanzee-invented combinations in the records indicates that the cross-fosterlings used the signs productively to construct new terms to suit new referents.

Inappropriate Usage

We recorded unexpected and inappropriate uses as well as appropriate uses, and the patterns of error often tell a great deal about the structure of the immature vocabularies. One common pattern was to confuse signs within the same conceptual category, as in CAT for DOG or BLACK for RED; another was to confuse signs that are formed in a similar way, as in BUG for FLOWER or TREE for CRACKER (cf. R. Gardner & Gardner, 1984; Chapter 4 this volume). Sometimes the pattern of errors revealed still more about the way a very young primate might divide the referential world, as in the following examples.

When FLOWER started to become a common item in Washoe's vocabulary, it was reported in several inappropriate contexts that all seemed to include prominent odors; for example, Washoe signed FLOWER when opening a tobacco pouch and also when entering the Gardner kitchen at a time when there was a chicken boiling on the stove. Taking our cue from these observations, we modelled and molded the SMELL sign in appropriate contexts. For some time, FLOWER (in the single index, single nostril form) persisted as an error, but gradually, a highly reliable, well-formed SMELL sign emerged.

When Moja was 31 months old, the sign ORANGE, used to refer to the fruit, became a reliable item in her vocabulary and met the fifteen-day criterion described below. One day in her 54th month, Moja commented on the brilliant orange reflection of the sun in the orange taillight of a nearby parked automobile by signing ORANGE to her human companion. Later the same month she signed ORANGE for some orange-colored medicine (other colors in Moja's vocabulary at that time were RED, WHITE, and BLACK). After that, we systematically asked her the color of orange objects, and ORANGE to refer to orange color met the criterion, also.

Errors

When in the judgment of a teacher the chimpanzee sign was an error, the teachers would correct the pupil by making the correct sign, themselves, or by molding the hands of the chimpanzee into the correct sign. As in the case of human children, correction had to be administered sparingly and there were severe limits on how much correction could interfere with more interesting ongoing activities. Early in Project Washoe we learned that all forms of drill were counterproductive (cf. B. Gardner & Gardner, 1971, pp. 140–141; Chapter 1 this volume).

At one time or another, each of the cross-fosterlings would attempt to answer questions with what seemed to the teacher to be a random string of related or unrelated signs, as if the pupil were guessing at the correct answer. When this happened it was always tempting to give some credit, especially if the correct sign was the last in the series of guesses. But it was equally clear why this strategy must be discouraged. Therefore, strings of signs that appeared to be guesses were treated as errors whether or not a correct answer appeared in the series. Occasionally an inexperienced member of the foster family would fail to observe this rule. Fortunately, the result—a rapid increase in the number of random strings—was easy to detect in the daily records and it was equally easy to show the new recruit just why the rule against accepting strings of guesses must be strictly observed. The success of the systematic testing procedures described in Chapter 4 depended on our having discouraged guessing strategies of this sort outside of the formal testing situations.

FIELD RECORDS

Systematically controlled studies of the contexts in which the cross-fostered chimpanzees used the signs of ASL were carried out with samples of the signs and contexts as in Chapters 2, 4, 5, and 6. Within the formal studies of Chapters 2, 4, and 6 independent observers identified the signs and agreement was always very high. This agreement demonstrates that the observers were observing the same signs when they recorded them with the same English gloss. The observers also agreed in the terms that they used to describe the shapes of the signs in the daily field records, and Table 3.2 presents a summary of a sample of the field records of individual signs. But, before presenting Table 3.2, let us consider the technical details of the recording procedures.

Criterial Observations

Each item of vocabulary had to meet detailed criteria of form and usage before it was listed as a reliable sign. In terms of form it had to correspond either to a sign made by human adults, or to an immature variant similar to those seen among human children. Decisions were guided by the judgment of fluent signers who were also familiar with signing in young children. In the case of usage, spontaneity was defined in terms of informative prompting. If the sign was made without informative prompting—such as direct modelling or guidance that could have induced any portion of the target sign—then it was judged to be spontaneous. To be appropriate, however, it had to be prompted by the verbal and situational context, and by the presence of a suitable addressee. Early in Project Washoe, we developed procedures for determining when a sign first entered the vocabulary and when it had become a reliable item (cf. B. Gardner & Gardner, 1971, pp. 140–141).

When three separate and independent observations of a new sign had been reported by three different observers, and all three had been judged to be well-formed, unprompted, and appropriate, then the new sign was placed on a special list of candidates for reliability. While a sign was on this list, each observation was recorded until at least one well-formed, spontaneous, and appropriate observation had been reported for each of fifteen consecutive days. If any day was missed—that is, if none of the observations on that day were judged to be well-formed, spontaneous, and appropriate—then the count was restarted. When the fifteen-day criterion had been met, the sign was added to the list of reliable vocabulary items. By that time, most if not all of the members of the foster family had contributed independent observations to the record.

Since we were both teaching and testing the new signs as they entered the

vocabulary, a great deal of modelling, molding, and informative prompting occurred on the same days as the criterial observations. After any prompted utterance of a sign, the chimpanzee had to make at least one more utterance in
which there was no example of the criterial sign, before the next use of that
sign could be scored as unprompted. A simple way to accomplish this was to
ask some question for which some other sign or signs would be the correct answer, e.g., WHOSE THAT? or WHAT NAME THAT? or WHAT COLOR
THAT? of some irrelevant object.

There was a great deal of variation in the number of days required to meet
the criterion. Some signs became reliable in just fifteen days, most required
several weeks, and some required months. In all cases the date of the third
independent observation, the one that met the criterion for putting the sign on
the list of candidates for reliability, was recorded as the date that the sign entered the vocabulary.

The three initial reports and the fifteen reports in the criterion series were
each judged for acceptable diction by at least three human members of the
foster family of that particular chimpanzee subject. Difficult cases were discussed by the whole staff at regular weekly meetings and decisions were made on
the basis of the likelihood of confusion with other signs and the acceptability
of similar variants in human children. After Project Washoe, we always had at
least one and usually several members of the staff whose experience with young
deaf children guided us in these decisions. Appropriateness, based on context
notes, was judged by at least three familiar human companions and difficult
cases were decided at weekly meetings of the entire staff. At such a meeting
we decided, for example, that the use of the sign SODAPOP for juice was inappropriate, as was the use of CANDY for gum.

Sign of the Day

Once established as an item of vocabulary, the form and usage of each sign
was reassessed regularly to be sure that old signs did not drop out as new signs
entered the vocabulary, and also to chart development (R. Gardner & Gardner,
1978, pp. 48-53). Early in the second project with Moja, Pili, Tatu, and Dar we
developed the following procedure. For six days of every week at least one of
the signs on the reliable list was designated as the sign of the day (SOD). On
that day, we attempted to record every observation of the SOD and each observation was recorded in as much detail as in the original fifteen-day reliability
series. The SOD signs for each chimpanzee subject were posted each day in
several strategic places indoors and outdoors, and all of the human participants
in the project attempted to describe all observations of the SOD. The special
SOD forms also included separate spaces for recording the frequency of inappropriate use of the sign, as well as inappropriate use of other signs where the
SOD would have been appropriate.

When the reliable list was short, it was easy to sample each sign in the vocabulary as SOD at least once each quarter. When there were so many signs on the list that it would take more than three months to sample the whole list at the rate of one sign per day, we designated more than one sign per day as SOD. In this way, each sign was sampled for detailed description at least once per quarter. Thus, we have detailed descriptions of the uses and the shapes of all the reliable signs for each developmental period. From this record, we can trace the development of diction as the cross-fostered chimpanzees became more adept in their signing.

Some signs, such as TICKLE and CHASE, referred to favorite activities that required no special props whatever and we could count on a large sample of adventitious observations of these on any given day. Other signs were particular favorites in common situations. For example, while the other cross-fosterlings were attracted to bright colors, Tatu strongly preferred black. On outings she collected black stones, and at home she had a collection of black belts, gloves, socks, and watchbands that she had cadged from visitors and friends. Tatu was always calling our attention to black objects by signing BLACK, or THAT BLACK. In the case of favorite signs, each quarterly sample yielded a large number of descriptions. If the SOD failed to appear adventitiously, or if it seemed unlikely that it would appear adventitiously, each observer was to attempt to elicit it, at least once, by providing appropriate contexts and appropriate questions.

As in the case of the observations recorded for the fifteen-day reliability series, each description in the SOD records was reviewed by at least two, but usually several more, members of the staff for appropriate and unprompted context as well as for technical completeness of the description. Sometimes the number of descriptions of a particular sign in a particular quarter that met all criteria for inclusion in the present summary was quite small. Usually, this was because very few observations met the stringent criteria rather than because the sign was used rarely.

PCM Description

Each time that we published fresh results of Project Washoe, we also published a detailed description of the uses and shapes of the signs in Washoe's then-current vocabulary (B. Gardner & Gardner, 1971, 1975; R. Gardner & Gardner, 1969). In describing Washoe's early vocabularies we could consult all of the observers at the regular weekly meetings, together with motion picture and still photography, video tapes, and Washoe, herself. The last description, which was published in B. Gardner and Gardner (1975, appendix), was written during the first three months after Washoe had left Reno with Roger Fouts to take up residence at the Institute for Primate Studies, University of Oklahoma. B. T. Gardner and R. A. Gardner wrote these descriptions in consultation with

S. G. Nichols, the third person who had been a member of the foster family throughout Project Washoe, and with G. R. Gaustad, who had been a member for the last three years of Project Washoe.

In writing these descriptions we borrowed heavily from the system devised by Stokoe, Casterline, and Croneberg for their *Dictionary of American Sign Language* (1965), henceforth in this chapter *DASL*. The *DASL* divides each sign into three aspects. The first aspect is the *place* on the body or in space where the sign is made—e.g., cheek, chest, in front of signer, etc. The second aspect is the *configuration* of the hand—e.g., fisted or open hand, which fingers are extended, how the hand is oriented toward the place. The third aspect is the type and direction of the *movement* of the hand—e.g., simple contact or rubbing, upward or downward, straight or circular movement. In these descriptions, we used common English terms where the *DASL* uses a special set of symbols. We used all of the basic *DASL* distinctions as a foundation for our system and included additional English terms to add descriptive detail as required for our special problems and our special purposes. It will be convenient to refer to descriptions in terms of place, configuration, and movement as *PCM descriptions*.

In the second project with the chimpanzees Moja, Pili, Tatu, and Dar we profited in many ways from the pioneering work of Project Washoe. Now, as a standard practice, PCM descriptions were entered into the logs immediately if possible, but nearly always within an hour of their observation. Special data forms were provided for this purpose with spaces for each of the three *DASL* aspects of the sign, as well as a space for the context in which it appeared, that is, events immediately preceding it, other signs that may have been combined with it, and any conversational exchange that may have been part of the context.

At the beginning of the second project, the authors of the present chapter devised a system of standard descriptive terms that all observers could use to record their descriptions of any and all of the signs of the chimpanzees. We based the system on our experience in describing Washoe's vocabulary, on our study of other descriptive systems, particularly the *DASL*, and also on our consultation with members of the deaf community, particularly those who were members of the cross-fostering families.

New recruits learned the descriptive system from more senior participants. We even wrote a special laboratory manual for this purpose. Part of the training of observers consisted of practical exercises in description that were criticized and corrected by more senior observers. The first field records of the beginning observers were also discussed in detail. Meanwhile, at each weekly staff meeting, all new signs that were on the fifteen-day reliability run and all SOD signs for the coming week were demonstrated and discussed. In this way we were able to maintain a reasonably uniform standard of descriptions throughout the

Fig. 3.5 Three signs with the same configuration but different place:
Washoe (58 months) signs PEN (top).
Moja (47 months) signs POTTY (bottom, left).
Tatu (57 months) signs GLASS (bottom, right).

course of the second project, even though we had to keep track of larger vocabularies, more subjects, and more observers.

The observers were, of course, encouraged to add terms where necessary. When such additions proved to be generally useful they were incorporated into the system. In this way the system grew and developed with the vocabularies of the chimpanzees and the experience of the observers.

On any given day, only some of the observations could be described in such detail, of course. With respect to new signs, detailed field notes were made for the first three observations and for all of the observations before the criterion of reliability was satisfied, up to and including the fifteen consecutive observations that finally met the criterion. With respect to reliable signs, the SOD procedure furnished systematic samples of detailed field notes.

A SAMPLE OF SIGN DESCRIPTIONS

Table 3.2 summarizes a sample of the description of the shapes of the signs. All of the signs in the table had met the criteria of reliability before Washoe, Moja, Tatu, and Dar left the Reno laboratory.

Subjects

Chimpanzee Pili died of leukemia during his 24th month, when only 35 of the signs in his vocabulary had met our criterion of reliability. Because he died so young, we have omitted Pili from this sample. The vocabularies of Moja, Tatu, and Dar increased throughout the time that they were cross-fostered in our laboratory, and grew to 168 signs for 80-month-old Moja, 140 signs for 65-month-old Tatu, and 122 signs for 58-month-old Dar. During the last year that they were in our laboratory, four quarterly SOD samples were carried out for each vocabulary. Through a clerical error, however, the four Tatu samples were carried out over a period of one year and 19 days.

Because all three vocabularies grew during the last year, some recently acquired signs appeared in less than four SOD samples. Wherever there were less than ten SOD descriptions of a new sign, the SOD descriptions were supplemented with the descriptions recorded for the fifteen-day reliability run. During her last year in our laboratory, Moja's vocabulary was larger and her foster family was smaller, hence it was appreciably more difficult to obtain qualifying SOD descriptions for her vocabulary during that year. Consequently, there were less than ten qualifying descriptions for 26 of the 168 items in Moja's vocabulary in her last four SOD records. We supplemented these 26 items with the descriptions obtained in the last quarter of the next to the last year. Finally, some of the signs in all three vocabularies were the name signs of members of the foster family who had left before the last year. In these cases we included SOD descriptions of the name sign in question that were obtained during the last year in which the human or chimpanzee named had been a member of the family.

The median number of qualifying descriptions per sign was 18 and all but 12 items (all in Moja's vocabulary) yielded at least 10 qualifying descriptions. The descriptions of the 430 vocabulary items of Moja, Tatu, and Dar that appear in Table 3.2 are based on a total of 8,225 qualifying descriptions. The 133 items in Washoe's vocabulary at the end of her tenure as a cross-fosterling in the Reno laboratory were included by converting, where necessary, the terms of description in B. Gardner and Gardner (1975) to the terms developed for Moja, Tatu, and Dar.

Observers

All of the human members of the foster families contributed the observations in this sample. They consisted of twenty individuals. Fifteen of this number participated as members of more than one of the three foster families. All but three had participated for more than one year and the median amount of participation was two years. Six of the observers had been members of the foster family of Moja, Tatu, or Dar from the day that the chimpanzee arrived newborn in Reno. Five had formerly been long-term members of Washoe's foster family.

Tabulation

In order to produce the summary descriptions in Table 3.2, many of the terms in the field records had to be grouped into slightly coarser categories, the reliability of the tabulation procedure had to be measured, and variations in form had to be indicated.

Standard Terms. We tabulated the records with respect to six aspects of the shape of a sign. To begin with there were the three basic aspects described already, *place* where the sign was made, the *configuration* of the hands, and the *movement* of the hands. The records contained information about three additional aspects. First, there was the *orientation* of the hand, whether the palm or fingers were oriented up or down, toward or away from the signer, and so on. Sometimes the orientation of the arm and wrist were also informative, whether they were bent or straight, horizontal or vertical, and so on. Second, there was the *contactor*, the specific part of the moving hand that contacted the place. Third, there was the *direction* of the movement, whether it was up or down, in a circle, or toward or away from a landmark such as the lips. Each record in the sample summarized here was tabulated according to these six aspects. When a sign was made with one hand contacting the other hand, two configurations and two orientations were listed, one for the moving hand, and one for the contacted hand.

As a first step in tabulation we reduced the number of equivalent or nearly equivalent terms such as "forehead" and "brow," "pinkie" and "little finger," or "clasp" and "grasp." In these cases we chose one of the set of equivalent terms and tabulated all equivalent terms under that label. In many cases, fine detail in the reports had to be grouped more coarsely for practical tabulation. Thus, whether reports used the term "lips," "upper lip," "just above upper lip," "lower lip," "under lower lip," or "just below lower lip," we tabulated them as, simply "lips." And, whether reports used the term, "contact," "touch," "poke," "tap," "strike," "hit," "slap," "pat," "rests on," "laid against," "pushes into," or "placed on," we tabulated them as, simply "contact." This reduced the number of terms that could appear in Table 3.2 to 86 distinct terms for place, 32 terms for configuration, 42 terms for orientation, 28 terms for contactor (but overlapping with the terms for place), 31 terms for movement, and 32 terms for direction of movement.

Reliability. The three authors of this chapter, together with a graduate student who had been a member of Tatu's foster family for Tatu's last eight months in Reno, tabulated all of the qualifying records for the 430 signs in the vocabularies of Moja, Tatu, and Dar. Two independent tabulators transcribed the information in each recorded observation from the field notes into the standard terms for each aspect—place, configuration of one or two hands, orientation of one or two hands, contactor, movement, and direction. They also tabulated whether the place contacted was ipsilateral or contralateral to the moving hand, whether the place was on the body of the signer or the addressee, and whether the sign was accompanied by a sound (as in the kissing sound that Washoe, Moja, and Dar often made when signing GOOD).

The results of the two independent tabulations for each sign were then compared for agreement. There were 57,523 agreements out of 58,718 total judgments, roughly 98% agreement. Virtually all of the disagreements were clerical errors that were settled by retabulating the disputed records. In the few remaining cases of disagreement, the tie was broken by enlisting a third independent tabulator. The tabulation, then, is an accurate representation of the original field records.

Allophonic and Allocheric Variation. A spoken word is formed by continuously varying movements of several speech organs such as the lips, the tongue, and vocal cords. The burst of sound can be analyzed into the units called phonemes that distinguish one word from the other words in a language. A sign of ASL is formed by continuously varying movements of the many parts of the hand and arm. Stokoe applied the concepts and methods of phonological analysis to ASL to identify the fundamental units of gesture that distinguish one sign from the other signs of ASL. In ordinary conversation, the precise auditory shape of a given word varies with the speaker and with the context, particularly the phrase in which it appears. Forms that native speakers treat as equivalent and may only notice when the differences are pointed out to them are called *allophones*. A similar situation exists in ASL, and Stokoe (1960, p. 30) has called these *allochers*.

The *DASL* uses 26 distinct terms for place, 19 for configuration, 15 for movement, and 9 for direction of movement (which serve for orientations as well)—rather fewer terms than we have used here. Stokoe (1978, pp. 34–50) recognizes that observers can discriminate more distinctions than the *DASL* uses, but be argues that these distinctions are allocheric; that they are equivalent because signs of ASL can be distinguished without them. Thus, we distinguished five different places in the mid-face region of the face (nose, nostril, eye, cheek below the eye, and outer corner of the eye) while the *DASL* lumps these into one equivalent mid-face region. Stokoe is probably correct about the allocheric equivalence of these fine distinctions, but it seemed safer to preserve here the additional distictions that we could extract from the chimpanzee records.

For some of the signs an aspect, most often the orientation or the contactor, was left unspecified in the field notes. For example, the thumb and index of the pincer hand form the configuration of many of the signs in the chimpanzee vocabularies. The pincer hand must have some orientation, e.g., palm up, palm down, or fingers point to side. Nevertheless, in the case of BERRY and CAT and many other signs, the field notes for Moja, Tatu, and Dar specify the pincer configuration without specifying the orientation of the hand. We conclude that orientation was an allocheric aspect of BERRY and CAT. Following this reasoning, whenever an aspect of a sign is specified in less than 50% of the records, it was left out of Table 3.2 on the grounds that variants in that aspect were allocheric for that sign—the sign could be recognized without it. Following the same line of reasoning, when the records contained more than four different terms, that aspect is listed as variable in Table 3.2. Finally, a term that appeared in 10% or less of the records was defined as rare and omitted from the table.

TABLE 3.2: THE SHAPES OF THE SIGNS

Legend

The following serves as an extended legend to explain the columns of Table 3.2.

Gloss. The first column in Table 3.2 lists an English gloss for each of the 430 different signs in the table. In most cases this gloss is the English word that is also used to gloss the same sign form in one or more of the following sources: the *DASL*; Bornstein, Kannapell, Saulnier, Hamilton, and Roy, 1973; O'Rourke, 1978; or Watson, 1964. Occasionally, usage in the Reno foster families seemed to require a slightly different English gloss from the one that we found in these sources. In those cases the Reno gloss is listed first, and the gloss that can be found in one or more of the sources for the same sign form is listed in parentheses beside it.

As is often the case in translating from one language to another, there were cases in which the same ASL sign required different English glosses in different contexts. In Table 3.2 these cases are indicated by writing the glosses in pairs, such as FOOD/EAT and PEN/WRITE. When translating ASL utterances into English we have used the most appropriate of the two English glosses, but only credit the chimpanzees with a single item of vocabulary.

We have already described how we adopted the form glossed as PEEKA-BOO from the chimpanzees. In Table 3.2, the form of TICKLE is a variant of the ASL sign for TOUCH, Washoe's CEREAL is a combination of MORNING and SPOON, and her CUCUMBER is a combination of GREEN and SLICES (patterned after TOMATO which in the sources is a combination of RED and SLICES). Five other signs, BIB, BLINDFOLD, GARBAGE, GROOM, and SWAB, were originally obtained from two or more informants in the deaf community, but we have not yet found these forms in published sources.

The signs are listed alphabetically by gloss except that common vocabulary terms are listed first and proper names of the chimpanzee and human members of the foster families are listed together at the end of the table.

Subject (#). The second column in Table 3.2 lists the chimpanzees that had each sign in their reliable vocabulary by the end of the period that we sampled. The chimpanzees are indicated by first initial, *W* for Washoe, *M* for Moja, *T* for Tatu, and *D* for Dar. There were 133 signs in Washoe's vocabulary, 168 in Moja's, 140 in Tatu's, and 122 in Dar's. In parentheses beside each chimpanzee initial is a number that represents the order in which that sign entered that chimpanzee's vocabulary as determined by the date of the third independent observation.

PCM. The remaining three columns of the table contain the descriptions of *place, configuration*, and *movement* for each sign. As already explained, descriptions of orientation, contactor, and direction of movement are included where relevant and available. Each row can be read as a recipe for making a sign. Even those readers without any previous acquaintance with ASL should be able to make a reasonable approximation of each sign for themselves from these descriptions.

The description for each sign, which is listed in the first row beside the English gloss, is the form that the human members of the foster families in Reno modelled for the cross-fosterlings. We can refer to this as the *target* form. For the most part, the target form that we modelled corresponds closely to the form in the published sources. Where the target form differs from the sources, we have included the published source form in brackets together with the target form that we modelled.

Discrepancies were minor. In the case of PIPE, WATER, and the number signs ONE and TWO, an aspect in the source form was altered in the target to make the signs easier for chimpanzee hands to form. In the case of KISS, POTTY, LIPSTICK, and SWING, the target was a simplified, babyish form obtained from fluent signers who had extensive experience with young signing children. In the remaining discrepancies between the targets and the published sources, the records of the target form show that the models omitted repetition for the movement of COMB, HANKY, LAUGH, and RED. In a few cases, we modelled one form (A) for Washoe and Moja and a synonym (B) for the later subjects, Tatu and Dar.

The descriptions of the chimpanzee forms are listed in the rows below each target form. When two terms are listed for an aspect of chimpanzee form we give a rough indication of relative frequency; the term that appeared more frequently in the records is listed first, as in "both upper arms or both elbows." The quantifier "mostly" indicates terms that appeared in 90%–50% of the records, as in "mostly hands move in opposite directions." The quantifier "sometimes" indicates terms that appeared in 49%–10% of the records, as in "contact sometimes repeated."

One or more of the chimpanzee subjects made a characteristic sound or facial expression when signing BLOW, GOOD, KISS and a dozen other signs. These included a kissing sound made with GOOD and KISS, a sniffing sound that Washoe made when she signed FUNNY and Dar made when he signed FLOWER, and audible exhalations that Moja made when she signed YES and Tatu made when she signed WHO. Protrusion of the lips created a distinctive facial expression when Tatu signed WHO and BLOW and when Dar signed TONY M. These sounds and facial expressions are listed for cases in which they appeared in 10% or more of the records.

Notes. The superscript "a" identifies vocabulary items in which 10% or more of the records described the place as "on addressee." Placing a sign on the body of the addressee is an immature form of signing inflection observed in human children and in signing chimpanzees, also. In this way signs such as QUIET placed on the lips of the addressee, SWALLOW placed on the throat of the addressee, and TICKLE placed on the hand of the addressee, become YOU QUIET, YOU SWALLOW, and YOU TICKLE (see Chapter 6 this volume for a detailed analysis).

The superscipt "h" identifies vocabulary items in which 10% or more of the records described a head movement as well as a hand movement. Hand and arm movements are the only movements described in the published sources, except for NO and YES which only have head movements. In the cases of BLANKET, CEREAL, DIRTY, and ICECREAM one or more of the cross-fosterlings moved the head as well as the hands some of the time. Thus, Moja sometimes moved her head, rather than her hand, from side to side when she

Table 3.2
The Shapes of the Signs

Gloss Subject (#)	Place (P)	Configuration (C)	Movement (M)
AGAIN	Palm, of open hand, palm up	Open hand, palm up	Turns palm down then fingertips contact
Moja (133)	Palm, palm up or palm to side	Open hand	Fingertips contact
AIRPLANE	Space in front of Signer	Little finger, together with index or thumb or index and thumb, extended from fist, palm down	Moves away
Washoe (115)	Space in front of Signer	Little finger extended from fist	Moves away
APPLE	Cheek	Fist or hooked index extended from fist	Knuckles contact then twist
Washoe (58)	Cheek	Fist	Rubs down
Moja (18)	Cheek	Hooked index extended from fist or fist	Knuckles contact sometimes repeated
Tatu (26)	Cheek	Contracted hand or fist	Knuckles or index edge rubs, or contacts then twists or bends
Dar (46)	Cheek[c]	Contracted hand or fist, palm down or palm to P	Knuckles contact
BABY	Forearms	Both open hands, forearms crossed	Hands contact, then arms may rock side to side
Washoe (39)	Elbows	Both curved hands, forearms crossed	Grasp

Gloss Subject (#)	Place (P)	Configuration (C)	Movement (M)
Moja (51)	Forearms or upper arms	Forearms crossed	both hands grasp
Tatu (52)	Wrist or forearm, palm to Signer or palm down	Curved hand, palm to Signer or palm down	Grasps then rocks side to side
Dar (105)	Upper arms or elbows	Both open hands, forearms crossed	Hands grasp then arms move up or up and down
BALL	Fingertips and thumbtips	Both curved hands, palms facing	Fingertips and thumbtips of opposite hands contact
Moja (126)	Fingertips and thumbtips or knuckles and thumbtips	Both curved hands or open hands, palms facing	Fingertips and thumbtips or knuckles and thumbtips, of opposite hands contact
Tatu (111)	Fingertips	Both curved hands or open hands, palms facing	Fingertips of opposite hands contact
Dar (37)	Fingertips	Both open hands or curved hands or spread hands, palms to Signer or palms facing	Fingertips of opposite hands contact

Table 3.2 (continued)

Gloss Subject (#)	Place (P)	Configuration (C)	Movement (M)
BANANA			
Washoe (47)	Index, extended from fist, index points up	Index or hooked index extended from fist	Knuckle of index rubs repeatedly along toward base
Moja (64)	Tip of index, extended	Hooked index extended	Index grasps then pulls toward Signer
Tatu (32)	Index mostly edge of index	Index extended	Tip of index rubs along toward base sometimes repeated
Dar (55)	Index, extended from fist or from open hand	Index extended from fist	Index or index and thumb rubs along or to and fro
	Back of index or index, extended from fist or index of open hand	Index extended	Index mostly tip of index rubs along or to and fro
BATH			
Washoe (132)	Chest	Both fists	Knuckles rub up and down, hands may move in opposite directions
Moja (132)	Chest	Both fists	Rub up and down
Tatu (83)	Chest[a]	Fist mostly both fists	Knuckles rub up and down, mostly hands move in opposite directions
Dar (69)	Midriff or chest	Both fists	Knuckles rub up and down, mostly hands move in opposite directions
	Chest	Both fists	Knuckles rub up and down, mostly hands move in opposite directions

Gloss / Subject (#)	Place (P)	Configuration (C)	Movement (M)
BEAR	Chest near shoulders	Both claw hands, palms to P and forearms crossed	Fingertips rub repeatedly down
Moja (153)	Shoulders or upper arms	Both open hands or claw hands, palms to P and forearms crossed	Rub up and down or grasp or contact
BED	Cheek or temple^c	Open hand, fingers point up	Palm contacts
Washoe (45)	Temple	Open hand	Palm contacts
Moja (77)	Cheek and ear or cheek^c	Open hand, fingers point up	Palm contacts
Tatu (99)	Cheek or temple^c	Open hand, fingers point up	Palm contacts
Dar (72)	Cheek or temple^c	Open hand, fingers point up	Palm contacts
BELT	Midriff	Both curved hands or thumb and index extended from fist	Fingertips rub to sides while hands approach or separate
Moja (145)	Midriff or thigh	Both indexes extend from fists or from open hand	Indexes mostly tips of indexes rub to sides
Tatu (137)	Midriff	Both pincer fists or tapered hands, palm to P	Rub or move, side to side or to side

Table 3.2 (continued)

Gloss Subject (#)	Place (P)	Configuration (C)	Movement (M)
BERRY	Tip of thumb, extended from fist	Pincer hand	Index and thumb grasp
Washoe (81)	Thumb	Pincer hand	Index and thumb grasp
Moja (65)	Thumb mostly tip of thumb or tip of index, extended	Pincer hand or pincer fist or fist	Grasps
Tatu (40)	Thumb or tip of thumb, extended from fist or from open hand	Pincer hand or tapered hand or fist	Grasps or grasps and pulls
Dar (31)	Tip of thumb or index, extended from fist or from open hand	Pincer hand or contracted hand	Grasps or grasps and pulls
BIB	Chest	Both indexes extended from fists	Tips of indexes rub to sides and then up
Moja (38)	Chest	Index extended mostly both indexes extended	Indexes mostly tips of indexes rub repeatedly to sides or diagonally up
Tatu (30)	Chest	Both indexes extended from fists or pincer hands or claw hands	Tips of indexes or finger-tips rub up and down or up or diagonally up
Dar (16)	Chest or midriff	Both indexes extended	Indexes mostly tips of indexes rub to sides or diagonally up or up and down

Gloss Subject (#)	Place (P)	Configuration (C)	Movement (M)
BIG	Space in front of Signer	Both open hands, palms facing and fingers point forward	Separate
Moja (106)	Space in front of Signer	Both open hands, palms facing	Separate or fingertips contact then hands separate
BIRD	Lips	Thumb and index extended from fist, palm forward	Index contacts thumb repeatedly
Washoe (49)	Lips	Pincer hand	Index and thumb grasp repeatedly
Moja (25)	Lips	Pincer hand, palm to Signer and thumb up	Index and thumb grasp
Tatu (46)	Lips	Pincer hand or index extended from fist	C grasps P or index contacts thumb, sometimes repeated
Dar (41)	Lips	Index extended from fist or pincer hand, palm to side or forward or down or to Signer	Index contacts thumb or C grasps P, repeatedly
BITE	Index edge, of arm or of open hand, palm down	Curved hand	Grasps
Washoe (96)	Index edge of hand	Curved hand	Grasps
Moja (162)	Index edge of hand or inside of wrist	Curved hand or claw hand	Grasps
Tatu (140)	Palm and back or index edge or back, of open hand, palm down or palm to Signer	Curved hand	Grasps

Table 3.2 (continued)

Gloss Subject (#)	Place (P)	Configuration (C)	Movement (M)
BLACK			
Washoe (78)	Brow	Index extended from fist, index points to side	Tip of index rubs to side
Moja (91)	Brow	Index extended	Index rubs to side
Tatu (101)	Brow or top of head	Index or index and second fingers extended	Tip of index or tips of index and second fingers rub to side
Dar (89)	Brow[a]	Index extended, index points to side	Tip of index rubs to side, sometimes grasps index of Addressee and puts it through the movement
	Brow	Index extended, index point to side	Tip of index rubs to side
BLANKET			
Moja (140)	Midriff then neck	Both open hands, palms to P and fingers point toward each other	Move up while turning to palms down then contact neck
Tatu (75)	Underside of chin	Both curved hands or fists, palms down or palms to Signer	Knuckles or backs of hands contact
Dar (62)	Chin or underside of chin	Both fists or open hands, palms down or palms to Signer	Knuckles or backs of hands contact[h]
	Underside of chin	Both fists or contracted hands, palms to Signer or or palms down	Knuckles or backs of hands contact

Gloss Subject (#)	Place (P)	Configuration (C)	Movement (M)
BLINDFOLD	Both eyes	Both indexes extended from fists, palms to P and indexes point toward each other	Indexes contact, may rub to sides
Moja (144)	Eyes mostly both eyes	Index extended mostly both indexes extended	Indexes mostly tips of indexes contact or rub to sides
BLOW (breeze)	Space in front of lips [space near face]	Open hand [both hands], palm to Signer and fingers point up	Moves repeatedly toward and away
Moja (135)	Lips	Open hand	Palm contacts then moves away mostly repeated
Tatu (131)	Space in front of lips or lips	Open hand, palm to Signer and fingers point to side or point up	Moves or contacts then moves, away or toward and away, sometimes lips blow audibly
Dar (113)	Space in front of lips	Open hand, palm to P and fingers point up or to side	Moves away
BOOK	Palms	Both open hands, palms facing	Palms of opposite hands contact then turn to palms up
Washoe (44)	Palms	Both curved hands, one palm up and other palm down	Palms of opposite hands grasp
Moja (86)	Palms	Both open hands, (one palm up and other palm down), with hands parallel or hands crossing	Palms of opposite hands contact

Table 3.2 (continued)

Gloss Subject (#)	Place (P)	Configuration (C)	Movement (M)
BOY (man)		Curved hand, palm down	Fingers and thumb close to tapered hand
Washoe (109)		Pincer hand	Index and thumb grasp and pull
Moja (80)		Pincer hand, palm down or thumb up	Index and thumb grasp
Tatu (104)		Curved hand or pincer hand, palm down or index edge to P	Thumb and index or thumb and fingers, grasp or open and close
Dar (109)		Pincer hand or pincer fist, palm down	Index and thumb or thumb and fingers, grasp or grasp and pull
BREAD	Back of fingers, of curved hand, palm to Signer and fingers point to side	Curved hand, palm to P	Fingertips rub repeatedly toward little finger edge
Moja (154)	Back or knuckles, of open hand, palm to Signer	Open hand or curved hand, palm to P	Fingertips rub toward little finger edge sometimes repeated
BREAK	Index edges	Both fists, palms down	Index edges of opposite hands contact then separate while turning to palms up or palms facing
Moja (131)	Index edges or index edge of one hand and little finger edge of other hand	Both fists, palms down or one palm up and other palm down	Edges of opposite hands contact, then separate or twist

Note: For BOY (man) rows, Place column:
- BOY (man): Temple
- Washoe (109): Brow
- Moja (80): Brow
- Tatu (104): Temple or brow
- Dar (109): Brow or temple

103

Gloss Subject (#)	Place (P)	Configuration (C)	Movement (M)
BRUSH (rub)	Back of wrist or of forearm	Fist, palm to P	Rubs to and fro
Washoe (26)	Back of hand	Fist, palm down	Rubs repeatedly to and fro
Moja (17)	Various places on arm or on head	Open hand or fist, palm to P	Rubs to and fro or along
Tatu (17)	Forearm or back of forearm	Curved hand or fist, palm to P	Rubs to and fro
Dar (11)	Various places on arm, or on thigh	Curved hand or open hand, palm to P	Rubs to and fro or along
BUG	Nose	Thumb and first two fingers spread, palm to side	Thumb contacts then fingers wiggle
Washoe (73)	Nose	Thumb extended from curved hand	Thumb contacts
Moja (69)	Nose	Thumb extended from open hand	Tip of thumb contacts
Tatu (77)	Nose	Thumb extended from open hand or from spread hand, palm down or palm to Signer	Thumb mostly tip of thumb contacts sometimes repeated
Dar (67)	Nose	Thumb extended from open hand	Thumb mostly tip of thumb contacts
BUTTERFLY	Thumbs	Both spread hands or open hands, palms to Signer and hands crossing	Thumbs of opposite hands interlock then fingers wiggle
Washoe (123)	Thumbs	Both curved hands, palms to Signer and hands crossing	Thumbs of opposite hands interlock

Table 3.2 (continued)

Gloss Subject (#)	Place (P)	Configuration (C)	Movement (M)
CANDY	Chin	Index and second fingers extended from fist, palm to Signer	Tips of index and second fingers rub repeatedly down
Moja (148)	Lips	Index and second fingers extended from open hand, palm to Signer and fingers point up	Index and second fingers mostly tips rub down
Tatu (90)	Chin	Index and second fingers extended	Tips of index and second fingers contact or rub down sometimes repeated
CAN'T	Tip of index, extended from fist, palm down	Index extended from fist, palm down	Tip of index contacts while moving down
Washoe (90)	Tip of index, extended	Index extended	Index contacts then hands separate while C moves down
Moja (41)	Tip of index, extended, index points to side	Index entended, index points to side	Tip of index contacts while moving down sometimes repeated
Tatu (21)	Index, extended from fist, palm down	Index extended from fist, palm down	Index or tip of index contacts repeatedly or contacts while moving down, mostly grasps Addressee's indexes and puts them through the movement

105

Gloss Subject (#)	Place (P)	Configuration (C)	Movement (M)
Dar(25)	Index, extended from fist, palm down	Index extended from fist, palm down	Index mostly tip of index contacts while moving up and down or toward and away, mostly both hands move in opposite directions, sometimes repeated
CAR	Space in front of Signer	Both fists, palms facing	Move up and down, hands move in opposite direction
Washoe (85)	Space in front of Signer	Both fists, forearms extended and hands apart	Move up and down, hands move in opposite direction
Moja (90)	Space in front of Signer	Both fists or open hands, (forearms extended and hands apart) palms facing	Shake up and down (hands move in opposite directions)
Tatu (127)	Space in front of Signer	Both fists, (forearms extended and hands apart) palms facing or palms to Signer	Move or shake, up and down (hands move in opposite directions)
Dar (114)	Space in front of Signer	Both fists, (forearms extended and hands apart) palm facing or palms down	Move or shake up and down (hands move in opposite directions)

Table 3.2 (continued)

Gloss Subject (#)	Place (P)	Configuration (C)	Movement (M)
CARROT	Palm, of open hand	Thumb extended from fist	Tip of thumb rubs repeatedly along or toward little finger edge
Moja (127)	Palm, of open hand, palm up or palm to side	Thumb extended, palm to Signer	Tip of thumb contacts or rubs toward edge of hand
Tatu (66)	Palm, of open hand	Thumb extended from fist	Tip of thumb rubs toward edge of hand or toward wrist
Dar (63)	Palm, of open hand	Thumb extended	Tip of thumb rubs toward edge of hand or along
CAT	Cheek	Pincer hand, palm to side	Index and thumb rub repeatedly to side
Washoe (35)	Cheek	Pincer hand	Index and thumb grasp and pull to side
Moja (52)	Cheek or corner of mouth[c]	Pincer hand	Index and thumb grasp and pull
Tatu (51)	Cheek[c]	Pincer hand	Index and thumb grasp and pull
Dar (60)	Cheek[c]	Pincer hand	Index and thumb grasp and pull sometimes repeated
CATCH	Back, of fist	Curved hand	Grasps or contacts
Washoe (20)	Back of wrist	Curved hand, palm down	Contacts repeatedly

Gloss Subject (#)	Place (P)	Configuration (C)	Movement (M)
Moja (55)	Back, of open hand or fist	Open hand or curved hand	Palm contacts repeatedly or grasps
Tatu (64)	Various places on back of hand or wrist, of fist or curved hand or open hand, palm down	Open hand or curved hand	Palm or fingers, grasp or contact
Dar (39)	Various places on back of hand or wrist, of open hand or curved hand or fist	Curved hand	Palm grasps or contacts
CEREAL (A)	Inside of forearm then lips	Index and second fingers extended from fist, palm up	Tips of index and second fingers contact forearm then lips
Washoe (120)	Inside of forearm	Index extended	Index contacts
CEREAL (B)	Chin	Index extended from fist, palm down and index points to side	Edge of index rubs to side, while index bends and straightens repeatedly
Moja (128)	Lips or chin	Open hand or index extended from open hand or from fist	Edge of index rubs[h] side to side
Tatu (73)	Chin	Index or hooked index extended from fist, points to side	Index rubs to side sometimes repeated
Dar (68)	Chin or underside of chin	Index extended from fist or open hand, palm down or Palm to P, index points to side	Edge of index rubs[h] side to side or to side

107

Table 3.2 (continued)

Gloss Subject (#)	Place (P)	Configuration (C)	Movement (M)
CHAIR	Backs of index and second fingers, extended from fist, palm down	Index and second fingers extended from fist may be bent, palm down and crossing P	Insides of index and second fingers contact
Washoe (72)	Back, of spread hand	Index extended	Index inserts between fingers of P
Moja (117)	Back of index edge, of open hand	Index and second fingers extended	(Insides of) index and second fingers (contact)
CHASE	In space near wrist, of fist, palm to side and forearm extended	Fist	Moves up and down or in circle while approaching wrist
Moja (67)	Inside of forearm, forearm extended	Fist	Knuckles contact mostly repeated
Tatu (43)	Inside of wrist or inside of forearm, (forearm extended)	Fist or contracted hand	Knuckles contact sometimes repeated
Dar (36)	Heel of palm or inside of wrist, (forearm extended or extended vertically)	Contracted hand or fist	Knuckles contact
CHEESE	Heel of palm, of open hand, palm up	Open hand, palm down	Heel of palm contacts while twisting
Washoe (77)	Palm of hand	Open hand, palm down	Palm rubs along toward wrist
Moja (115)	Heel of palm, of open hand, palm up	Open hand, palm down	Heel of palm contacts sometimes repeated

Gloss Subject (#)	Place (P)	Configuration (C)	Movement (M)
Tatu (59)	Palm or heel of palm, of open hand, palm up	Open hand, palm down and crossing P	Palm or heel of palm contacts while twisting, or contacts only
Dar (58)	Heel of palm or palm, of open hand or contracted hand, palm up	Open hand or contracted hand	Heel of palm or palm contacts sometimes repeated
CLEAN	Palm, of open hand, palm up	Open hand, palm down	Palm rubs along or to and fro, may repeat
Washoe (40)	Palm of hand	Open hand, palm down	Rubs along toward tips
Moja (81)	Palm, of curved hand or open hand, palm up	Curved hand, crossing P	Palm rubs to and fro
Tatu (69)	Palm, of open hand, palm up	Open hand	Palm rubs to and fro or along, mostly repeated
Dar (38)	Palm, of open hand, palm up	Open hand	Palm rubs to and fro sometimes repeated
CLIMB	Back of index and second fingers, extended from fist, palm forward and fingers point up	Index and second fingers extended from fist	Tips of index and second fingers contact alternately and repeatedly, while moving up along P
Washoe (84)	Knuckles of index or second finger	Index extended	Index contacts repeatedly
CLOTHES	Chest	Both spread hands, fingers point toward each other	Fingertips rub repeatedly down
Washoe (34)	Chest	Both open hands, palms to Signer	Fingertips rub down

Table 3.2 (continued)

Gloss Subject (#)	Place (P)	Configuration (C)	Movement (M)
COAT	Chest	Both fists, thumbs may be extended, palms to P	Thumbs or knuckles [thumbs only] rub down
Moja (59)	Chest	Both fists	Knuckles rub up and down or down
Dar (79)	Chest	Both fists	Knuckles rub down or up and down
COFFEE	Index edge, of fist, palm to side or index edge up	Fist, palm to side or index edge up	Little finger edge rubs in circle
Moja (118)	Index edge, of fist	Fist	Little finger edge rubs side to side
Tatu (63)	Index edge, of fist, index edge up	Fist, palm to side or palm up	Little finger edge or back of fist rubs side to side or in half-circle
Dar (73)	Index edge, of fist or of wrist, index edge up	Fist, index edge up or palm down	Little finger edge or knuckles rub side to side
COMB	Top of head	Claw hand	Rubs [repeatedly] to side
Washoe (59)	Top of head then temple	Curved hand, palm to P	Rubs to side
Moja (49)	Top of head	Claw hand or open hand	Rubs to side or diagonally forward
Tatu (55)	Head mostly top of head	Claw hand	Rubs to side
Dar (22)	Top of head	Open hand or claw hand, palm down	Rubs to side

Gloss Subject (#)	Place (P)	Configuration (C)	Movement (M)
COME/GIMME	Space in front of Signer	Open hand or index extended from fist, may use both hands, palm up or palm to Signer, forearm extended	Fingers or wrist or elbow beckons
Washoe (1)	Space in front of Signer	Open hand, palm up	Wrist or fingers beckon
Moja (1)	Space in front of Signer	Curved hand or spread hand	Arm extends toward Addressee or away from Signer, then sometimes beckons
Tatu (5)	Space in front of Signer	Open hand, palm to side or palm up	Arm extends away from Signer or toward Addressee, then fingers beckon or wiggle
Dar (3)	Space in front of Signer	Open hand, palm up or palm to side	Arm extends away from Signer or toward Addressee or object, then sometimes beckons or shakes
COOKIE	Palm of open hand, palm up	Curved hand, palm to P	Fingertips and thumbtip contact then twist in circle
Moja (116)	Palm, of open hand	Contracted hand	Knuckles contact
Tatu (47)	Palm, of open hand, palm up	Contracted hand or curved hand	Knuckles contact
Dar (35)	Palm, of open hand, palm up or palm to side	Contracted hand	Knuckles contact sometimes repeated

Table 3.2 (continued)

Gloss Subject (#)	Place (P)	Configuration (C)	Movement (M)
CORN	Teeth	Index extended from fist, palm down and index points to side	Approaches, may rotate at wrist, teeth may pantomime biting
Moja (167)	Teeth or mouth	Index extended from fist or open hand, palm down and index points to side	Index inserts then teeth bite sometimes repeatedly
Tatu (110)	Teeth	Index extended from open hand, palm down and index points to side	Index inserts then teeth bite
Dar (95)	Teeth	Index extended from open hand or from fist, palm down and index points to side	Index inserts then teeth bite
COVER/BLANKET	Back, of open hand, palm down	Open hand, palm down	Rubs to side or along toward wrist
Washoe (21)	Back of hand	Open hand, palm down	Rubs toward Signer
COW	Temple	Thumb and little finger extended from fist	Tip of thumb contacts, then hand may nod up and down or forward
Washoe (79)	Brow	Thumb extended	Thumb contacts
Moja (95)	Temple	Thumb extended from curved hand or from fist	Tip of thumb contacts

Gloss Subject (#)	Place (P)	Configuration (C)	Movement (M)
Tatu (65)	Temple or top of head or brow	Thumb extended from open hand or from curved hand or from fist, palm down or palm forward	Thumb mostly tip of thumb contacts or contacts then rotates forward
Dar (47)	Top of head or cheek	Thumb extended from curved hand or open hand	Thumb mostly tip of thumb contacts
CRACKER	Elbow, forearm vertical	Fist, palm to P or palm down	Contacts repeatedly
Moja (143)	Elbow	Fist	Knuckles contact repeatedly
Tatu (112)	Elbow, forearm vertical	Fist, palm to P or palm down	Contacts mostly repeated
Dar (93)	Elbow, forearm vertical or forearm extended	Fist or contracted hand, palm to P or palm down	Contacts mostly repeated

Table 3.2 (continued)

Gloss Subject (#)	Place (P)	Configuration (C)	Movement (M)
CRY	Cheek below eye	Hooked index or index extended from fist, may use both hands, palm to Signer and index points up	Tip of index rubs down
Washoe (98)	Cheek below eye	Index extended	Index rubs down
Moja (110)	Eye[c] mostly cheek below eye	One or both indexes extended	Index mostly tip of index rubs down sometimes repeated
Tatu (120)	Eyes mostly cheeks below eyes	Both indexes or hooked indexes extended from fists; or other finger extended from spread hands, palms to Signer	Tips of extended fingers rub down or diagonally down
Dar (101)	Eye[c] mostly cheek below eye or outer corner of eye	Index extended mostly both indexes extended from fists, palms to Signer	Tip of index rubs down
CUCUMBER (green slices)	Space in front of Signer; then index edge, of fist, palm down	Index extended from fist	M1: Shakes; then M2: Edge of index rubs down
Washoe (93)	Edge of index, extended; then space to side of Signer	Index extended	M1: Index rubs along toward tip; then M2: Arm extends and hand shakes
CUP	Palm, of open hand, palm up	Curved hand	Little finger edge contacts, then hand may move up

Gloss Subject (#)	Place (P)	Configuration (C)	Movement (M)
Moja (112)	Palm, of open hand, palm up	Curved hand or fist	Little finger edge contacts then moves up and away from P, or contacts only, sometimes repeated
Tatu (98)	Palm, of open hand, palm up	Curved hand or fist, index edge up or palm up	Little finger edge contacts
Dar (103)	Palm, of open hand, palm up	Curved hand or fist, palm to side	Little finger edge contacts
DIAPER	Thighs	Both indexes extended from fists, palms down or palms to Signer	Index contacts thumb repeatedly
Moja (76)	Thighs	Pincer hand mostly both hands	Indexes and thumbs grasp
Tatu (16)	Thighs	Both pincer hands or open hands, palms to P	Indexes contact thumbs repeatedly, or hands grasp or rub P
Dar (17)	Thighs	Both indexes extended from fists	Indexes mostly tips of indexes rub up
DIFFERENT	Tips of indexes	Both indexes extended from fists, palms down and indexes crossing	Tips of indexes of opposite hands contact then separate
Washoe (106)	Tip of index, extended	Hooked index extended	Index grasps then hands separate

Table 3.2 (continued)

Gloss Subject (#)	Place (P)	Configuration (C)	Movement (M)
DIRTY			
	Underside of chin	Spread hand, palm down	Back of hand contacts then fingers wiggle
Washoe (61)	Underside of chin	Open hand, palm down	Back of wrist contacts repeatedly, often forcefully so that teeth click together audibly
Moja (50)	Underside of chin	Open hand or fist, palm down	Back of wrist or of hand contacts sometimes repeated
Tatu (42)	Underside of chin	Various hand shapes from spread hand to fist, palm down	Back of wrist or of hand or of forearm contacts[h]
Dar (91)	Underside of chin	Fist, palm down	Back of hand or of wrist contacts sometimes repeated
DOG	Thigh [then space in front of signer]	Open hand [then snapping hand]	Palm contacts repeatedly [then snap fingers]
Washoe (22)	Thigh	Open hand	Palm contacts repeatedly
Moja (47)	Leg[a] or thigh or both legs	One or both open hands	Palm contacts repeatedly
Tatu (33)	Thigh or leg	Open hand	Palm contacts repeatedly
Dar (43)	Thigh[c]	Open hand	Palm contacts repeatedly
DOWN	Space below Signer	Index extended from fist, index points down	Moves down

Gloss / Subject (#)	Place (P)	Configuration (C)	Movement (M)
Washoe (37)	Space below Signer	Open hand or index extended from open hand, fingers point down	Points down or contacts ground
Moja (13)	Space below Signer	Open hand or index extended from open hand, fingers point down	Arm extends down or fingertips contact ground
Tatu (7)	Space below Signer	Open hand, fingers point down	Arm extends down
Dar (7)	Space below Signer	Open hand or contracted hand or index extended, fingers point down	Arm extends down
DRINK Washoe (13)	Lips	Thumb extended from curved hand or from fist	Thumb approaches or contacts, then hand rotates up
Moja (4)	Lips	Thumb extended from fist	Thumb contacts
Tatu (2)	Mouth or teeth or lips	Thumb extended	Thumb mostly tip of thumb inserts or contacts
Dar (5)	Mouth or lips	Thumb extended from curved hand or from fist or from open hand	Thumb or tip of thumb, inserts or contacts, then hand rotates up, or inserts only
	Lips	Thumb extended from curved hand or from fist, or hand of Addressee held by Signer	Thumb or tip of thumb contacts, sometimes with kissing or sucking sound

Table 3.2 (continued)

Gloss Subject (#)	Place (P)	Configuration (C)	Movement (M)
EARRING	Ear	Pincer hand	Index and thumb grasp or grasp and shake
Tatu (96)	Ear or both ears	One or both pincer hands	Index and thumb grasp and pull down
Dar (98)	Ear[c]	Pincer hand	Index and thumb grasp mostly grasp and pull
ENOUGH	Index edge, of fist	Open hand	Palm rubs repeatedly away from Signer
Washoe (70)	Index edge, of fist	Curved hand	Palm rubs to side
FINISH	Space in front of Signer	Open hand or spread hand, may use both hands	Turns to palm down
Moja (58)	Palms of Addressee	Both open hands	Contact then mostly rotate or shake while in contact
Tatu (39)	Hand mostly both hands of Addressee	Various hand shapes from fist to open hand	Grasps hands of Addressee then rotates them to palm down or palm up
FLOOR	Index edges	Both open hands, palms down	Index edges of opposite hands contact, may repeat
Washoe (127)	Index edges	Both open hands, palms down	Index edges of opposite hands contact
FLOWER	Nose	Tapered hand, palm to Signer	Fingertips contact one nostril after the other

119

Gloss Subject (#)	Place (P)	Configuration (C)	Movement (M)
Washoe (19)	Nose	Curved hand, palm to Signer	Fingertips contact, sometimes one nostril after the other
Moja (36)	Nose	Open hand, palm to Signer and fingers point up or to side	Fingertips contact sometimes repeated
Tatu (31)	Nose	Pincer hand	Tips of index and thumb contact or approach, sometimes contact one nostril after the other
Dar (53)	Nose	Tapered hand or pincer hand, palm to Signer or palm down	Thumb and fingertips or thumb and index contact mostly repeated, sometimes with sniffing sound
FOOD/EAT	Lips	Tapered hand, palm to Signer	Fingertips contact or approach
Washoe (18)	Lips	Curved hand, palm to Signer	Fingertips contact
Moja (10)	Lips	Open hand	Fingertips contact sometimes repeated
Tatu (12)	Lips	Tapered hand or curved hand or open hand, palm to Signer or palm down	Fingertips contact sometimes repeated or approach
Dar (8)	Lips	Tapered hand or pincer fist or pincer hand or contracted hand, palm to Signer	Fingertips or knuckles contact, sometimes lips smack audibly

Table 3.2 (continued)

Gloss Subject (#)	Place (P)	Configuration (C)	Movement (M)
FORK Washoe (118)	Palm, of open hand Palm of hand	Index and second fingers extended and spread Spread hand	Tips of index and second fingers contact repeatedly Tips of index and second fingers contact
FRIEND Tatu (80) Dar (92)	Indexes Indexes Indexes[a]	Both hooked indexes extended from fists, one palm up and other palm down Both hooked indexes extended from fists, one palm up and other palm down Both hooked indexes extended from fists, one palm up or to Signer and other palm down; or one hooked index extended from fist and one index of Addressee	Indexes interlock then turn (to reverse palm orientation) and repeat Indexes of opposite hands interlock Indexes interlock or one hooked index grasps index of Addressee
FUNNY Washoe (15)	Nose Nose	Index and second fingers extended from fist, palm to Signer Index extended	Tips of index and second fingers rub down Index contacts, with snorting sound
GARBAGE (cabbage)	Temple	Claw hand, palm to P and fingers point up	Heel of palm contacts

Gloss Subject (#)	Place (P)	Configuration (C)	Movement (M)
Tatu (119)	Temple	Claw hand or contracted hand, palm to P and fingers point up	Heel of palm contacts sometimes repeated
GIRL Washoe (105)	Cheek	Thumb extended from fist	Tip of thumb rubs down
Moja (75)	Cheek	Thumb extended	Thumb rubs down
Tatu (105)	Cheek	Thumb extended from fist	Thumb rubs down
Dar (121)	Cheek	Thumb extended from fist or from open hand	Tip of thumb rubs down
	Cheek[c]	Thumb extended from curved hand or from open hand or from fist	Thumb or tip of thumb rubs down
GLASS	Teeth	Index or hooked index extended from fist	Tip of index contacts
Moja (92)	Teeth	Index extended	Tip of index contacts
Tatu (113)	Teeth	Index extended from fist, palm down	Tip of index contacts
Dar (90)	Teeth	Index mostly hooked index extended	Tip of index contacts

Table 3.2 (continued)

Gloss Subject (#)	Place (P)	Configuration (C)	Movement (M)
GLASSES			
	Eye/s	Thumb and index extended from fist, may use both hands, palm to side and fingers point to side	Rubs to side while closing index and thumb
Moja (109)	Brow	Index extended mostly both indexes extended from fists, palms to P	Indexes mostly insides of indexes rub to sides
Tatu (134)	Both eyes	Both indexes extended from fists or pincer fists, palms to P or palms down	Indexes or edges of indexes and thumbs rub to sides
GLOVE	Back, of open hand, palm down and fingers point forward	Open hand, palm down and fingers point forward	Fingers rub along toward wrist
Moja (138)	Back of hand	Open hand or claw hand	Rubs along toward wrist
Tatu (139)	Back, of fist[a], palm down	Open hand or pincer fist	Fingertips or tips of indexes or claw hand, palm down and thumbs or fingers rub along toward wrist sometimes repeated
Dar (106)	Back, of open hand or of fist, palm down and fingers point forward	Open hand, palm down and fingers point forward	Fingers or fingertips rub along toward wrist sometimes repeated
GO	Space in front of Signer	Index extended from fist or from open hand	Rotates away from Signer by bending wrist or elbow
Washoe (8)	Space in front of Signer	Open hand	Arm extends away from Signer

Gloss Subject (#)	Place (P)	Configuration (C)	Movement (M)
Moja (2)	Space in front of Signer	Open hand	Arm extends away from Signer or toward location
Tatu (1)	Space in front of Signer	Open hand or index extended from open hand or from fist, palm down or palm to side	Points or arm extends, toward location or away from Signer
Dar (6)	Space in front of Signer	Index extended from fist or from open hand or open hand	Arm extends or hand moves, toward location or away from Signer
GOOD	Lips	Open hand, palm to Signer	Fingertips contact then move away
Washoe (60)	Lips	Open hand	Palm contacts then moves away, often with kissing sound
Moja (26)	Lips	Open hand	Palm contacts, mostly with kissing sound
Tatu (18)	Lips	Open hand	Palm or fingertips contact then mostly move away, sometimes repeated
Dar (33)	Lips	Open hand, fingers point to side	Palm contacts, sometimes with kissing sound

Table 3.2 (continued)

Gloss Subject (#)	Place (P)	Configuration (C)	Movement (M)
GOODBYE			
Washoe (128)	Lips then space in front of Signer	Open hand, palm to Signer	Fingertips contact then turn palm forward and wave up and down
Moja (22)	Lips then space in front of Signer	Open hand	Palm contacts then arm extends away
	Lips or lips then space in front of Signer	Open hand	Palm contacts lips, then mostly moves away or forward sometimes while shaking, mostly with kissing sound
Tatu (44)	Lips or lips then space in front of Signer	Open hand	Palm contacts then arm extends
GRAPES			
Moja (99)	Back, of open hand, palm down	Claw hand, palm to P	Fingertips contact repeatedly while moving along toward tips
	Back, of open hand	Open hand or curved hand, palm to P	Fingertips rub along toward tips or toward edge of hand sometimes repeated, or contact repeatedly
Tatu (79)	Back, of open hand, palm down	Open hand or claw hand, palm to P	Fingertips or palm rubs toward index edge of hand or along toward tips or contacts, repeatedly
GRASS (A)	Space in front of Signer	Both indexes extended from fists [one hand only]	Move to sides while twisting, index may contact thumb repeatedly [no contact]

Gloss Subject (#)	Place (P)	Configuration (C)	Movement (M)
Washoe (83)	Space to sides of Signer	Both indexes extended	Arms extend and hands shake
GRASS (B)	Underside of chin	Spread hand, palm up and fingers point forward	Palm moves up toward P or contacts P, may repeat
Moja (73)	Underside of chin	Open hand, palm up and fingers point to side	Palm contacts
Dar (112)	Underside of chin	Open hand or curved hand, palm up and fingers point to side	Palm contacts
GREEN Washoe (76)	Space in front of Signer Space to side of Signer	Index extended from fist Index extended	Twists or shakes Arm extends and hand shakes
GROOM	Back of forearm	Pincer hand	Index and thumb grasp repeatedly
Moja (60)	Back of hand[a] or back of forearm or other place to be groomed	Pincer hand or curved hand	Index and thumb grasp and pull
Tatu (117)	Back of forearm or other place to be groomed	Pincer hand	Index and thumb grasp or grasp and pull, repeatedly
Dar (27)	Forearm[a]	Pincer hand	Index and thumb grasp or grasp and pull, sometimes repeated

Table 3.2 (continued)

Gloss Subject (#)	Place (P)	Configuration (C)	Movement (M)
GUM	Cheek	Index and second fingers extended and separated	Fingertips contact then fingers bend and straighten repeatedly
Moja (27)	Cheek[c]	Index extended from fist	Tip of index contacts sometimes repeated
Tatu (34)	Cheek	Index and second fingers extended from open hand hand or extended and spread	Fingertips contact then bend or contact then bend and straighten repeatedly
Dar (28)	Cheek[a,c]	Index extended or open hand	Tip of index or fingertips contact or index rubs down
HAMMER	Space in front of Signer	Both fists, forearms extended	One fist moves repeatedly up and down
Washoe (69)	Space in front of Signer	Both fists, forearms extended	One fist rotates down
HANDS	Wrist, of open hand	Open hand, crossing P	Little finger edge rubs to side then reverse role of P and C hands and repeat
Washoe (91)	Wrist	Spread hand, palm to Signer and crossing P	Rubs to side then reverse role of P and C hands and repeat
HANKY	Nose	Pincer hand	Index and thumb grasp and pull down [repeatedly]
Moja (68)	Nose	Pincer hand	Index and thumb grasp

127

Gloss Subject (#)	Place (P)	Configuration (C)	Movement (M)
Tatu (97)	Nose	Pincer hand	Index and thumb grasp or grasp and pull down
Dar (44)	Nose	Pincer hand or pincer fist	Grasps mostly grasps and pulls
HAT	Top of head	Open hand, palm down	Palm contacts repeatedly
Washoe (27)	Top of head	Open hand	Palm contacts
Moja (29)	Top of head	Open hand	Palm contacts repeatedly
Tatu (24)	Top of head	Open hand	Palm contacts repeatedly
Dar (23)	Top of head	Open hand	Palm contacts mostly repeated
HEAR/LISTEN	Ear	Index extended from fist in HEAR; curved hand in LISTEN	Tip of index contacts or points toward P in HEAR; index edge contacts in LISTEN
Washoe (5)	Ear	Index extended	Index contacts
Moja (23)	Ear[c]	Index extended in HEAR; open hand, palm to P in LISTEN	Index mostly tip of index inserts or points in HEAR; palm or fingers or finger-tips contact in LISTEN
Tatu (19)	Ear[c]	Index extended in HEAR; open hand or curved hand in LISTEN	Index mostly tip of index contacts in HEAR; edge of hand or fingers contact in LISTEN
Dar (26)	Ear[c]	Index extended from open hand, palm down in HEAR; open hand or curved hand, fingers point up in LISTEN	Tip of index contacts or inserts in HEAR; palm or index edge contacts in LISTEN

Table 3.2 (continued)

Gloss Subject (#)	Place (P)	Configuration (C)	Movement (M)
HELP	Little finger edge, of fist, palm to side or index edge up	Open hand	Palm contacts or contacts then hands move up
Washoe (54)	Palm of hand	Fist	Contacts repeatedly
Moja (102)	Palm, of open hand, palm up	Fist or contracted hand or curved hand	Knuckles or little finger edge contacts
HOLE	Space in front of Signer or space near referent	Pincer hand	Index contacts thumb repeatedly or hand moves in circle
Washoe (122)	Space in front of Signer	Pincer hand	Index rubs thumb repeatedly
Moja (134)	Space in front of Signer	Index and thumb or pincer hand	Index contacts thumb or hand moves away
HOME	Cheek or lips then cheek	Tapered hand	Fingertips repeatedly contact cheek, or contact lips then cheek
Moja (141)	Cheek[c] or side of chin, or lips then cheek	Open hand or curved hand, palm to Signer and fingers point up	Fingertips contact one P repeatedly, or contact lips then cheek
Tatu (94)	Cheek	Tapered hand or open hand or curved hand	Fingertips contact mostly repeated
Dar (70)	Cheek[a]	Open hand or tapered hand	Fingertips contact mostly repeated
HORSE	Temple	Index and second fingers extended from fist, palm forward and fingers point up	Back of hand contacts while fingers nod repeatedly forward

129

Gloss Subject (#)	Place (P)	Configuration (C)	Movement (M)
Moja (124)	Head or temple	Index and second fingers extended or index extended from open hand or from fist	Extended finger/s, or tip/s, of extended finger/s contact
Tatu (53)	Temple or top of head	Thumb and index extended or index and second fingers extended from fist	Thumb and index or thumb contacts
HOSE (pistol)	Space in front of Signer	Thumb and index extended from fist	Thumb and/or index bend and straighten
Washoe (113)	Space in front of Signer	Index extended	Index bends and straightens repeatedly
HOT	Space in front of lips then space in front of Signer	Claw hand, palm to Signer	Approaches then moves away while turning to palm down
Washoe (117)	Space in front of lips	Spread hand, palm to Signer	Approaches and lips blow
Moja (44)	Space in front of lips or lips then space in front of Signer	Open hand or curved hand	Approaches, or contacts then shakes down, mostly with audible exhalation
Tatu (28)	Lips then space in front of Signer, or space near face	Open hand or claw hand or tapered hand, palm down or palm to Signer	Fingertips contact then hand turns and arm extends away, or approach face then shake
Dar (49)	Space in front of lips or space near hot object	Claw hand or open hand, palm to Signer or palm down	Approaches then mostly moves away while turning, or waves up and down

130

Table 3.2 (continued)

Gloss Subject (#)	Place (P)	Configuration (C)	Movement (M)
HOUSE			
	Fingertips	Both open hands, palms facing and fingers point up	Fingertips of opposite hands contact then separate while moving hands down
Washoe (110)	Fingertips	Both open hands, palms facing and fingers point up	Fingertips of opposite hands contact
HUG	Chest	Both fists, palms to Signer and forearms crossed	Hands contact
Washoe (48)	Chest and upper arm	Both curved hands, forearms crossed	Hands grasp
Moja (9)	Midriff and upper arm	Forearms crossed	Both hands grasp
Tatu (8)	Chest or upper arms	Palms to P and forearms crossed	Both hands squeeze or contact
Dar (15)	Upper arms	Both open hands, palms to P and forearms crossed	Hands grasp or contact
HURRY	Space in front of Signer	Index and second fingers extended from fist, palm to side and fingers point forward [both hands]	Shakes up and down
Washoe (9)	Space in front of Signer	Spread hand, bent at wrist	Shakes
Moja (45)	Space in front of Signer	Open hand, bent at wrist	Shakes up and down or side to side
Tatu (71)	Space in front of Signer	Open hand or curved hand, palm to side	Shakes up and down
Dar (78)	Space in front of Signer or space to side of Signer	Open hand sometimes with extended arm	Shakes

Gloss Subject (#)	Place (P)	Configuration (C)	Movement (M)
HURT	Space in front of Signer or near site of injury	Both indexes extended from fists, indexes point toward each other	Tips of indexes of opposite hands approach each other, may repeat
Washoe (14)	Near site of injury	Both indexes extended	Tips of indexes of opposite hands approach each other
Moja (89)	Near site of injury	Both indexes extended from fists	Tips of indexes of opposite hands contact each other
Tatu (50)	Space in front of Signer or near site of injury	Both indexes extended from fists, indexes point toward each other	Indexes mostly tips of indexes contact sometimes repeated or approach each other
Dar (40)	Space in front of Signer or near site of injury	Both indexes extended from fists, indexes point toward each other	Tips of indexes of opposite hands contact or approach each other
ICE (cold)	Chest	Both fists, palms facing	Elbows contact P, while hands approach opposite hands or hands shake repeatedly
Washoe (126)	Midriff	Both fists	Contact repeatedly

Table 3.2 (continued)

Gloss Subject (#)	Place (P)	Configuration (C)	Movement (M)
ICECREAM	Lips	Fist, palm down	Index edge rubs repeatedly down, tongue may pantomime licking
Washoe (103)	Tongue	Fist	Knuckles rub down
Moja (113)	Lips[a]	Fist	Index edge rubs[h] side to side or down
Tatu (49)	Lips	Fist, palm down	Index edge rubs[h] repeatedly to side
Dar (54)	Lips	Fist, palm down	Index edge rubs down sometimes repeated
IN/ENTER (A)	Palm, of tapered hand or curved hand, palm to side	Tapered hand, palm down	Fingertips insert
Washoe (24)	Palm, of curved hand	Curved hand, palm to Signer and fingers point down	Inserts
Tatu (123)	Fingers, of open hand or or curved hand or tapered hand, palm down or to Signer or to side	Open hand or curved hand, palm to Signer or palm down	C hand grasps fingers of P hand; or fingers of P hand insert in C hand
Dar (81)	Palm, of curved hand or tapered hand, palm to side or palm to Signer	Open hand, palm to Signer or palm down, fingers point down	Fingertips of C hand insert in P hand; or P hand repeatedly grasps fingertips of C hand

Gloss Subject (#)	Place (P)	Configuration (C)	Movement (M)
IN/ENTER (B)	Palm, of open hand or curved hand, palm down or palm to Signer	Open hand or curved hand, palm down	Back of hand rubs away from Signer
Moja (54)	Palm, of curved hand, palm down	Open hand, palm down and crossing P	Back of C rubs repeatedly to and fro
KEY	Palm, of open hand	Hooked index extended from fist	Knuckles of index contact then twist
Washoe (38)	Palm of hand	Hooked index extended from fist	Index contacts then twists
Moja (57)	Palm, of open hand	Hooked index extended from fist	Knuckles of index contact
Tatu (57)	Palm, of open hand	Hooked index or hooked second finger extended from fist	Knuckles of extended finger or index contacts then twists
Dar (119)	Palm, of open hand, palm up	Index or hooked index extended from fist	Tip of index or knuckles of index contact sometimes repeated or contact and bend

134

Table 3.2 (continued)

Gloss Subject (#)	Place (P)	Configuration (C)	Movement (M)
KISS	Lips then cheek	Open hand or tapered hand or index extended from fist, palm to Signer [open hand only]	Fingertips or tip or index contact lips then cheek
Washoe (88)	Lips	Curved hand	Fingertips contact then hand rotates then knuckles contact
Moja (20)	Lips or lips then cheek[a]	Index extended	Tip of index contacts sometimes repeated
Tatu (135)	Lips or lips then cheek[a]	Index extended	Index repeatedly contacts lips or contacts lips then cheek, sometimes lips kiss index audibly
Dar (118)	Lips	Pincer first or index extended from fist	Index and thumb or tips of index and thumb or index contacts repeatedly, sometimes lips kiss index audibly
KNIFE	Edge of index, of index or index and second fingers extended from fist	Index and second fingers extended from fist, crossing P	Fingers rub repeatedly along toward tips
Washoe (102)	Edge of index, extended	Index extended	Index rubs along toward tip
Moja (146)	Edge of index or back of extended index and second fingers	Index and second fingers extended or index extended from fist	Extended finger/s rub along or to and fro or side to side, sometimes repeated

Gloss / Subject (#)	Place (P)	Configuration (C)	Movement (M)
LAUGH	Both corners of mouth	Both indexes extended from fists	Tips of indexes rub [repeatedly] to sides and up
Washoe (112)	Both corners of mouth	Both hooked indexes extended	Indexes grasp and pull to sides
Moja (111)	Both corners of mouth	Both indexes mostly hooked indexes extended	Indexes grasp and pull to sides
Tatu (60)	Both corners of mouth	Both indexes or hooked indexes extended	Indexes grasp and pull to sides
Dar (71)	Both corners of mouth[a]	Both indexes extended	Indexes or tips of indexes grasp and pull to sides
LEAF	Index, extended from fist, index points to side	Spread hand	Wrist contacts then hand twists
Washoe (71)	Inside of wrist, of open hand	Index extended	Index contacts
Moja (149)	Inside of wrist	Hooked index extended from fist or index extended from open hand	Knuckle or tip of index contacts sometimes repeated
LIGHT	Space in front of Signer or space above Signer	Tapered hand	Opens to spread hand
Washoe (74)	Space in front of Signer	Fist	Opens hand
Moja (14)	Space above Signer	One or both fists	Fingertips rub palm or fist opens to open hand
Tatu (62)	Space in front of Signer	Tapered hand	Opens to spread hand or opens and closes, repeatedly
Dar (42)	Space above or to side or in front of Signer	Tapered hand or fist or pincer hand	Hand opens sometimes repeated

Table 3.2 (continued)

Gloss Subject (#)	Place (P)	Configuration (C)	Movement (M)
LIPSTICK	Lips	Pincer hand or index extended from fist or tapered hand, palm to P [hooked index extended from fist]	Tip of index rubs to side or side to side or in circle [not in circle]
Moja (33)	Lips	Index extended	Tip of index rubs to side or along
Tatu (81)	Lips	Tapered hand or pincer fist or pincer hand or index extended from fist, palm to P	Fingertips rub in cicle or to side or side to side
LOCK	Inside of wrist, of fist	Fist, palm down	Turns to palm up then back of wrist contacts
Washoe (124)	Inside of wrist, of fist	Fist, palm down and crossing P	Wrist contacts
ME	Chest	Index extended from fist	Tip of index contacts
Washoe (28)	Chest	Index extended	Index contacts
Moja (12)	Chest	Open hand or index extended	Fingertips or tip of index contacts
Tatu (10)	Chest	Index extended or open hand	Tip of index or fingertips contact sometimes repeated
Dar (9)	Chest	Index extended	Tip of index contacts
MEAT	Index edge, of open hand	Pincer hand	Index and thumb grasp, then may move up and away from P

137

Gloss Subject (#)	Place (P)	Configuration (C)	Movement (M)
Washoe (67)	Index edge of hand	Pincer hand	Index and thumb grasp
Moja (56)	Index edge of hand	Pincer hand or fist	Index and thumb grasp
Tatu (89)	Index edge, of open hand, palm to Signer or palm to side	Pincer hand	Index and thumb grasp
Dar (66)	Index edge of hand	Pincer hand	Index and thumb grasp
MEDICINE	Palm, of open hand, palm up	Second finger extended from spread hand	Tip of second finger rubs in circle
Moja (136)	Palm of hand	Second finger extended from open hand or open hand or index extended from fist	Tip of extended finger or tips of index and second fingers contact
Tatu (88)	Palm, of open hand, palm up	Second finger extended from open hand	Second finger or tip of second finger contacts or rubs along or toward edge of hand
Dar (74)	Palm, of open hand	Second finger extended from open hand or from spread hand	Second finger mostly tip of second finger contacts or rubs

Table 3.2 (continued)

Gloss Subject (#)	Place (P)	Configuration (C)	Movement (M)
METAL	Chin	Hooked index extended from fist, plam to side and index points up	Knuckle of index contacts [rubs forward]
Moja (93)	Chin	Index mostly hooked index extended	Index mostly knuckle of index contacts sometimes repeated
Tatu (129)	Chin	Hooked index extended from fist or fist, palm to side and index points up	Knuckle of index contacts
Dar (116)	Chin or underside of chin	Hooked index extended from fist or contracted hand or fist, palm to Signer or palm to side	Knuckle of index or knuckles contact
MILK	Space in front of Signer	Curved hand, palm to side	Closes to fist repeatedly
Moja (37)	Space in front of Signer	One or both fists, palm to side	Squeeze and mostly finger-tips rub palm (repeatedly)
Tatu (13)	Space in front of Signer	Curved hand or fist, palm to side	Closes to fist repeatedly or fist squeezes
Dar (18)	(Fingertips) of Addresee hand	Curved hand or open hand, palm to side or palm down (fingers parallel to Addressee's fingers)	(Fingertips) grasp P then squeeze, or grasp P then hand repeatedly closes to fist
MINE	Chest	Open hand	Palm contacts
Washoe (33)	Chest	Open hand	Palm contacts
Moja (46)	Chest	Open hand	Palm contacts mostly repeated

Gloss / Subject (#)	Place (P)	Configuration (C)	Movement (M)
Tatu (41)	Chest or midriff	Open hand	Palm contacts sometimes repeated
Dar (14)	Chest	Open hand	Palm contacts mostly repeated
MIRROR	Space near face	Open hand, palm to Signer and fingers point up	Twists
Washoe (119)	Space near face	Open hand, palm to Signer	Approaches
Moja (147)	Wrist mostly back of wrist, of open hand, palm to Signer, fingers point up or forearm vertical	Open hand or curved hand	Grasps
MORE	Fingertips	Both tapered hands, palms facing	Fingertips of opposite hands contact, may repeat
Washoe (2)	Fingertips	Both open hands, palms to Signer	Fingertips of opposite hands contact
Moja (3)	Fingertips	Both open hands	Fingertips of opposite hands contact
Tatu (3)	Fingertips or knuckles	Both open hands or tapered hands, palms to Signer or palms facing	Fingertips or knuckles of opposite hands contact repeatedly
Dar (1)	Knuckles or fingertips	Both contracted hands or open hands	Knuckles or fingertips of opposite hands contact sometimes repeated

Table 3.2 (continued)

Gloss Subject (#)	Place (P)	Configuration (C)	Movement (M)
NO	Head	N/A	Shakes side to side
Washoe (75)	Head	N/A	Shakes side to side
Moja (8)	Head	N/A	Shakes side to side
Tatu (9)	Head	N/A	Shakes side to side
Dar (12)	Head	N/A	Shakes side to side
NUT	Teeth	Thumb extended from fist	Thumb rubs away
Washoe (129)	Teeth	Thumb extended from fist	Thumb rubs
Moja (71)	Teeth	Thumb extended	Thumb mostly tip of thumb rubs away
Tatu (25)	Teeth	Thumb extended, palm down	Thumb rubs away or down
Dar (32)	Teeth	Thumb extended, palm down	Thumb mostly tip of thumb rubs away
OIL (grease)	Little finger edge, of open hand, index edge up	Pincer hand	Index and thumb grasp and move down and away from P
Washoe (42)	Little finger edge of hand	Pincer hand	Index and thumb grasp and move down
Moja (30)	Little finger edge, of open hand, index edge up or palm up	Pincer hand	Index and thumb grasp
Tatu (35)	Little finger edge of hand	Pincer hand	Index and thumb grasp mostly grasp and move away from P

Gloss Subject (#)	Place (P)	Configuration (C)	Movement (M)
Dar (45)	Little finger edge, of open hand, index edge up	Pincer hand	Index and thumb grasp mostly grasp and move down
ONE	On flat surface or palm, of open hand [space in front of Signer]	Index extended from fist, [index points up]	Tip of index contacts [hand moves away from Signer]
Moja (151)	On flat surface or space in front of Signer	Index extended mostly both indexes extended from open hands or from fists	Tips of indexes contact P sometimes repeated or hand moves away from Signer
Tatu (138)	Palm[a] of hand, palm up	Index extended from fist or from open hand, palm down	Index mostly tip of index contacts sometimes repeated
ONION	Outer corner of eye	Hooked index extended from fist	Knuckle of index contacts then twists repeatedly
Moja (130)	Outer corner of eye	Hooked index extended from fist	Knuckle contacts sometimes repeated
Tatu (132)	Outer corner of eye or cheek below eye or temple	Fist or contracted hand or hooked index extended from fist	Knuckle/s contact mostly contact and twist sometimes repeated
Dar (111)	Outer corner of eye[c]	Hooked index extended from fist or contracted hand or fist, palm to Signer or palm down	Knuckle/s or index edge contacts sometimes repeated

Table 3.2 (continued)

Gloss Subject (#)	Place (P)	Configuration (C)	Movement (M)
OPEN	Index edges	Both open hands, palms forward or palms down	Index edges of opposite hands contact then hands separate, may rotate to palms facing or palms up
Washoe (6)	Index edges	Both open hands, palms down	Index edges of opposite hands contact then hands separate while rotating
Moja (35)	Object or surface to be opened	Both open hands	Palms contact then mostly move away from P
Tatu (23)	Object or surface to be opened	Open hand mostly both hands	Palms contact then mostly move away from P or to sides
Dar (20)	Object or surface to be opened	Open hand or claw hand mostly both hands	Palms contact then move up or away from P
ORANGE	Lips	Curved hand, palm to side	Index edge contacts then hand closes to fist repeatedly
Moja (63)	Lips	Fist	Index edge contacts or contacts and squeezes, mostly with kissing sound
Tatu (68)	Lips	Curved hand, palm to side or fist	Index edge contacts P then C repeatedly closes to fist or fist squeezes
Dar (99)	Lips	Open hand or curved hand or fist, palm down	Index edge contacts P then C closes to fist sometimes closes repeatedly or fist squeezes

143

Gloss Subject (#)	Place (P)	Configuration (C)	Movement (M)
OUT			
Washoe (11)	Palm, of curved hand	Tapered hand	Inserts then moves up out of grasp
Moja (34)	Palm, of curved hand	Open hand, palm to Signer and fingers point down	Moves up out of grasp
Tatu (27)	Palm, of curved hand	Open hand	Moves up out of grasp
Dar (29)	Palm, of curved hand	Open hand or tapered hand	Moves up out of grasp
	Palm, of curved hand	Open hand or tapered hand	Inserts then moves out of grasp or moves out of grasp
PANTS			
Washoe (36)	Thighs	Both open hands, fingers point down	Fingertips rub repeatedly up
Moja (97)	Midriff	Both open hands, palms to P	Fingertips rub up
	Legs	Both open hands	Palms rub up and down or contact only

Table 3.2 (continued)

Gloss Subject (#)	Place (P)	Configuration (C)	Movement (M)
PEA/BEAN	Back or edge, of index extended from fist	Pincer hand	Index and thumb contact or grasp, repeatedly while moving along toward tip
Moja (168)	Index or knuckle of index, extended from open hand or from fist or open hand	Pincer hand or index extended from fist	Index and thumb grasp repeatedly
Tatu (103)	Edge of index or back of index, extended	Pincer hand	Index and thumb grasp successive places while moving along P or grasp repeatedly
Dar (88)	Index mostly edge of index, of open hand	Pincer hand or index extended from fist	Index and thumb grasp mostly repeated
PEACH	Cheek	Spread hand, palm to P	Fingertips rub down while closing to tapered hand
Moja (166)	Cheek[c]	Open hand or curved hand, palm to P and fingers point up	Fingertips rub down
Tatu (82)	Cheek	Open hand or spread hand, palm to P	Fingertips rub down or close while rubbing down or grasp and pull repeatedly
Dar (84)	Cheek[c]	Open hand or spread hand, palm to P	Fingertips rub down
PEEKABOO	Both eyes	Open hand, palm to P and fingers point to side	Palm contacts

145

Gloss Subject (#)	Place (P)	Configuration (C)	Movement (M)
Washoe (46)	Both eyes	Open hand, fingers point to side	Palm contacts
Moja (53)	Both eyes	Open hand mostly both hands, palms to P	Palms contact
Tatu (87)	Both eyes or eyes and nose	Open hand, palm to P and fingers point to side	Contacts or approaches
Dar (57)	Both eyes or eyes and nose	Open hand, fingers point to side	Palm contacts
PEN/WRITE	Palm, of open hand, palm up	Pincer hand or tapered hand or hooked index extended from fist	Fingertip/s rub to side, may repeat
Washoe (50)	Palm of hand	Index extended	Index rubs along toward wrist
Moja (48)	Palm, of open hand, palm up	Index extended from fist	Tip of index rubs along mostly toward tips
Tatu (108)	Palm, of open hand, palm up	Pincer hand or pincer fist or tapered hand or index extended from fist	Fingertips rub to side or or side to side or along
PIN	Chest	Pincer hand	Index and thumb contact
Washoe (100)	Chest near shoulder	Pincer hand	Index and thumb grasp
PIPE	Lips	Thumb and little finger extended from fist, palm to side	Little finger [tip of thumb] contacts
Washoe (97)	Lips	Thumb and little finger extended from fist	Little finger contacts

Table 3.2 (continued)

Gloss Subject (#)	Place (P)	Configuration (C)	Movement (M)
PLEASE	Chest	Open hand, palm to P and fingers point to side	Rubs in circle
Washoe (17)	Chest	Open hand, palm to P	Rubs to side
Moja (24)	Chest	Open hand or curved hand, palm to P	Rubs to side
Tatu (38)	Chest	Open hand, palm to P	Rubs to side or side to side, or rubs to side while closing to fist
Dar (24)	Chest	Open hand, palm to P	Rubs to side or rubs to side while closing to fist sometimes repeated
POTTY (urinate)	Nose	Index extended from fist	Tip of index contacts, may repeat
Moja (16)	Nose[a]	Index extended	Tip of index contacts
Tatu (15)	Nose	Index extended	Tip of index contacts
Dar (13)	Nose[a]	Index extended, palm to Signer	Tip of index contacts
PURSE	Between chest and upper arm	Open hand, palm to Signer	Inserts
Washoe (101)	Between chest and upper arm	Open hand	Inserts
QUIET	Lips	Index extended from fist, index points up	Edge of index contacts

Gloss Subject (#)	Place (P)	Configuration (C)	Movement (M)
Washoe (53)	Lips	Index extended from fist, index points up	Index contacts, often with "sssh" sound
Moja (31)	Lips[a]	Index of Addressee held by Signer or index of glove held by Signer or index extended from fist	Edge of index contacts, sometimes with "sssh" sound
Tatu (20)	Lips[a]	Index extended, index points up	Index or edge of index contacts
Dar (107)	Lips[a]	Index extended from fist or from open hand	Edge or back of index, contacts or approaches
RED	Lips	Index extended from fist, index points up	Tip of index rubs [repeatedly] down
Washoe (63)	Lips	Index extended	Index rubs to side
Moja (72)	Lips	Index extended from fist, index points up	Index mostly tip or edge of index rubs down
Tatu (91)	Lips	Index extended	Index mostly tip or edge of index rubs down
Dar (64)	Lips or chin	Index extended from fist	Tip of index rubs down sometimes repeated

Table 3.2 (continued)

Gloss Subject (#)	Place (P)	Configuration (C)	Movement (M)
RIDE	Center hole, made by tapered hand	Hooked index and second fingers extended from fist, palm down	Index and second fingers interlock and both hands move away
Washoe (80)	Index and second fingers, of spread hand, palm down	Curved hand, palm down	Grasps
Moja (78)	Thumb, extended from fist	Fist	Grasps and mostly both hands shake
Tatu (72)	Thumb, extended from open hand or from fist or from curved hand	Fist or curved hand	Grasps then mostly both hands move forward or rock side to side
RING	Tip or knuckle of third finger, of spread hand	Pincer hand	Index and thumb grasp, then may rub along toward base
Moja (101)	Knuckle, of extended index	Pincer hand	Index and thumb grasp
ROCK	Back, of fist, palm down	Fist, palm down	Knuckles contact repeatedly
Moja (74)	Back of hand or back of wrist	Fist, palm to P	Knuckles contact repeatedly
Tatu (122)	Back, of fist or of open hand, palm down	Fist, palm down or palm up	Knuckles contact repeatedly
Dar (104)	Back, of fist, palm down	Fist	Knuckles contact sometimes repeated
RUN	Palm, of open hand, palm to side and fingers point forward	Open hand, palm to P	Rubs repeatedly up and away

Gloss Subject (#)	Place (P)	Configuration (C)	Movement (M)
Washoe (111)	Palms	Both open hands, palms facing and index edges up	Fingertips rub toward Signer, hands move alternately and repeatedly
SAME	Edges of indexes	Both indexes extended from fists, palms down	Index edges of opposite hands contact
Washoe (107)	Edges of indexes	Both indexes extended	Edges of indexes of opposite hands contact
SANDWICH (A)	Palm of curved hand, palm up	Open hand	Little finger edge inserts then P grasps C
Moja (157)	Back of open hand, palm up or palm to Signer	Open hand or curved hand, palm to P and crossing P	Palm contacts and hand grasps
SANDWICH (B)	Lips	One hand curved and other hand open [both open hands], palms to Signer [palms down and fingers point to P]	Curved hand grasps open hand [hands contact], and hands approach P or fingertips of open hand contact P
Tatu (85)	Lips	One hand curved, palm to side; other hand open, palm to Signer and fingers point to P	Curved hand grasps open hand, and hands approach P or fingertips of open hand contact P
Dar (94)	Mouth or lips	One hand curved, crossing other hand or palm to side; other hand open, palm to Signer or palm down, fingers point to P	Curved hand grasps open hand, and fingertips of open hand insert in P or contact P

Table 3.2 (continued)

Gloss Subject (#)	Place (P)	Configuration (C)	Movement (M)
SCHOOL	Palm, of open hand, palm up	Open hand, palm to P and crossing P	Fingers contact repeatedly
Moja (83)	Palm, of open hand, (palm up)	Open hand, palm down and crossing P	Palm contacts (repeatedly)
SEE	Both eyes or eye	Index and second fingers extended and spread, fingers point up	Contacts or approaches, then moves away
Washoe (41)	Outer corner of eye	Index extended	Index contacts
Moja (32)	Eye or corner of eye[c]	Index extended	Tip of index contacts
Tatu (37)	Corner of eye or eye	Index extended from open hand or from fist or open hand, palm to Signer	Index or tip of index contacts
Dar (80)	Eye or corner of eye[c]	Index extended from fist or from open hand or open hand, palm to Signer or palm down	Tip of index or index or second finger contacts
SHIRT	Chest	Pincer hand	Index and thumb grasp and pull
Moja (70)	Chest	Pincer hand or pincer fist	Index and thumb grasp and pull
Tatu (48)	Chest or midriff	Pincer hand	Index and thumb grasp and pull or grasp
Dar (51)	Chest[a]	Pincer hand	Index and thumb grasp and pull

Gloss Subject (#)	Place (P)	Configuration (C)	Movement (M)
SHOE			
Washoe (29)	Index edges	Both fists, palms down and side by side	Index edges of opposite hands contact repeatedly
Moja (39)	Index edges or edges	Both fists, palms down	Index edges of opposite hands contact
		Both fists, palms down or one palm up and other palm down	Edges of opposite hands contact sometimes repeated
Tatu (45)	Index edges	Both fists, palms down or palms to Signer, side by side	Index edges of opposite hands contact repeatedly
Dar (30)	Index edges	Both fists, palms down and side by side	Index edges of opposite hands contact mostly repeated
SLEEP			
Tatu (115)	Space near face	Spread hand, palm to Signer	Moves down while closing to tapered hand
	Face	Open hand, palm to Signer and fingers point up	Rubs down
SMALL			
Moja (105)	Space in front of Signer	Both open hands, palms facing and fingers point forward	Opposite hands approach each other without contacting
	Fingertips or palms	Both open hands, palms facing and fingers point forward	Fingertips or palms of opposite hands contact

Table 3.2 (continued)

Gloss Subject (#)	Place (P)	Configuration (C)	Movement (M)
SMELL	Nose	Open hand, palm to Signer	Moves or rubs up, may repeat
Washoe (32)	Nose	Open hand, palm to Signer and fingers point to side	Rubs up or to side
Moja (40)	Nose	Open hand, palm to Signer and fingers point up or to side	Contacts or rubs or moves, up or up and down, repeatedly
Tatu (70)	Nose	Open hand, palm to Signer and fingers point to side	Rubs up or contacts, sometimes repeated
Dar (56)	Nose	Open hand, palm to Signer and fingers point to side	Contacts or moves up, or moves toward and away then contacts
SMOKE	Lips	Index and second fingers extended and spread, palm to Signer	Index and second fingers contact then move repeatedly away
Washoe (68)	Lips	Index and second fingers extended from spread hand, palm to Signer	Index and second fingers contact
Moja (161)	Lips	Index and second fingers extended or extended and spread, from open hand or from fist, palm to Signer	Tips of index and second fingers contact
SODAPOP	Index edge, of fist, palm to side	C1: Second finger or index extended from spread hand, palm down; then C2: Open hand, palm to P	M1: Tip of extended finger inserts into or contacts center hole made by P; then M2: Palm contacts

153

Gloss Subject (#)	Place (P)	Configuration (C)	Movement (M)
Moja (108)	Index edge, of fist	C1: Index extended; then C2; Open hand	M1: Tip of index inserts; then M2: Palm contacts sometimes repeated; mostly C2 and M2 only, i.e., POP
Tatu (54)	Index edge, of fist, palm to side	C1: Index or second finger extended from spread hand, palm down and finger points to P; then C2: Open hand	M1: Tip of extended finger inserts; then M2: Palm contacts; sometimes C2 and M2 only, i.e., POP
Dar (59)	Index edge, of fist, palm to side	C1: Index extended from open hand or from fist; then C2: Open hand	M1: Index or tip of index inserts; then M2: Palm contacts; sometimes C2 and M2 only, i.e., POP
SORRY Washoe (16)	Chest	Fist	Knuckles rub in circle
Moja (61)	Chest	Fist	Knuckles rub to side
	Chest	Fist	Knuckles rub up and down
Tatu (74)	Chest	Fist	Knuckles rub up and down
Dar (52)	Chest	Fist	Knuckles rub diagonally down or up and down or repeatedly contact
SOUR	Chin or corner of mouth	Index extended from fist	Tip of index contacts then twists
Tatu (86)	Chin	Index extended, palm to Signer	Tip of index contacts

Table 3.2 (continued)

Gloss Subject (#)	Place (P)	Configuration (C)	Movement (M)
SPIN	Space in front of Signer	Index extended from fist, index points down	Rotates repeatedly
Washoe (86)	Space in front of Signer	Index extended from open hand, index points down	Rotates at wrist
SPOON	Palm, of open hand, palm up	Index and second fingers extended from fist, palm up	Backs of fingers contact then move repeatedly up toward face
Washoe (82)	Palm of hand then lips	Curved hand	Fingertips contact palm then lips
Moja (114)	Palm, of open hand	Index and second fingers extended from open hand, palm up	Knuckles or tips of index and second fingers rub along toward wrist or contact only
STAMP (letter)	Lips then palm, of open hand	Thumb extended from fist	Tip of thumb contacts lips then palm
Washoe (114)	Palm of hand then lips	Thumb extended	Thumb contacts palm then lips
Moja (94)	Lips or tongue then palm of hand	Thumb or index extended	Thumb or tip of extended finger contacts lips or tongue then palm, or contacts lips or tongue only
Tatu (136)	Lips or tongue then palm of hand	Thumb extended from open hand or from fist	Thumb or tip of thumb contacts lips or tongue then palm

155

Gloss Subject (#)	Place (P)	Configuration (C)	Movement (M)
Dar (120)	Lips then palm, of open hand, palm up or palm to Signer	Thumb extended from fist or from open hand or from curved hand	Thumb or tip of thumb contacts lips then palm, or rubs down lips then contacts palm
STRING (thread)			
Washoe (62)	Little finger, extended from fist	Pincer hand	Index and thumb grasp and pull
Moja (137)	Little finger	Pincer hand	Index and thumb grasp and pull to side
Tatu (106)	Little finger, extended	Pincer hand or pincer fist	Index and thumb grasp and pull or grasp
Dar (83)	Little finger, extended from fist or little finger of open hand	Curved hand or index extended from fist or pincer hand	Grasps mostly grasps and pulls
	Little finger, extended from open hand or little finger of open hand	Curved hand or pincer hand or index extended from fist or fist	Grasps and pulls
SWAB	Ear	Index extended from fist	Tip of index inserts then twists or contacts then twists
Moja (142)	Ear[c]	Index extended	Index or tip of index inserts, then twists or rubs
Tatu (126)	Ear[c]	Index extended, palm down	Index mostly tip of index inserts then twists
Dar (76)	Ear[c]	Index extended from fist or from open hand or from claw hand, palm down or palm to Signer	Tip of index inserts then twists or rubs, or contacts only

Table 3.2 (continued)

Gloss Subject (#)	Place (P)	Configuration (C)	Movement (M)
SWALLOW			
Washoe (121)	Throat	Index extended from fist	Tip of index rubs down
	Throat	Index extended	Index contacts
Moja (85)	Neck or throat[a]	Index or hooked index extended	Index or tip of index or knuckle of index rubs down or contacts sometimes repeated
Tatu (118)	Throat[a]	Index extended from fist	Tip of index rubs down sometimes repeated
Dar (87)	Throat[a]	Index extended	Tip of index rubs down or contacts
SWEET	Lips	Open hand or index and second fingers extended from fist, palm to Signer and fingers point up	Fingertips rub down, may repeat
Washoe (3)	Tongue	Index and second fingers extended from spread hand	Tips of index and second fingers contact
Moja (87)	Lips	Open hand, palm to Signer and fingers point up	Fingertips rub down sometimes repeated
Tatu (61)	Lips	Open hand, palm to Signer and fingers point up	Fingertips rub down sometimes repeated
Dar(48)	Lips	Open hand, palm to Signer and fingers point up	Fingertips rub down
SWING	Wrist [back of index and second fingers, extended], forearm extended	Curved hand [index and second fingers extended]	Grasps [contacts] then hands rock repeatedly side to side or toward and away

Gloss Subject (#)	Place (P)	Configuration (C)	Movement (M)
Tatu (93)	Wrist	Curved hand or open hand, palm to P	Grasps then rocks side to side or toward and away
TABLE	Back of forearm and open hand, palm down and forearm horizontal	Open hand, palm down and forearm horizontal	Palm and forearm contact
Moja (129)	Back of forearm, forearm horizontal	Open hand	Contacts sometimes repeated
Dar (82)	Elbow or forearm, forearm horizontal	Open hand or fist	Palm or knuckles contact
TELEPHONE	Ear and lips	Thumb and little finger extended from fist	Tips of thumb and little finger contact
Washoe (116)	Ear then corner of mouth	Thumb and little finger extended from fist	Thumb contacts ear then little finger contacts mouth
THAT/THERE	Space in front of Signer or on object	Index extended from fist	Index points toward location or object or contacts
Washoe (10)	Space in front of Signer or on object	Index extended from open hand or open hand	Index points toward location or contacts
Moja (19)	Space in front of Signer or on object	Index extended from open hand or open hand	Points or arm extends, toward location or object, or contacts
Tatu (11)	On object or in space in front of Signer	Index extended	Index or tip of index, contacts or points toward location or object
Dar (10)	On object or in space in front of Signer	Index extended	Index or tip of index, contacts sometimes repeated or points

Table 3.2 (continued)

Gloss Subject (#)	Place (P)	Configuration (C)	Movement (M)
TICKLE			
Washoe (7)	Back of hand	Index extended from fist	Index rubs to side
	Back of hand	Hooked index extended from fist	Index rubs to side
Moja (6)	Back of hand[a]	Index extended	Tip of index rubs
Tatu (6)	Back of hand[a]	Index extended from fist	Index rubs to side
Dar (2)	Back of hand[a]	Index extended	Index rubs to side
TIME			
	Back of wrist	Index or hooked index extended from fist	Tip of index contacts
Washoe (99)	Back of wrist	Hooked index extended	Index contacts
Moja (100)	Wrist[a] mostly back of wrist	Index extended	Tip of index contacts repeatedly
Tatu (58)	Wrist[a] or back of wrist	Index extended, palm down	Tip of index contacts sometimes repeated
Dar (108)	Back of wrist[a]	Index extended from fist, palm down	Index mostly tip of index contacts
TOMATO			
	Lips; then index edge, of fist, palm down	Index extended from fist, palm to Signer; then palm down	M1: Tip of index rubs down lips; then M2: Edge of index rubs down edge of fist
Washoe (92)	Lips; then edge of index	Hooked index extended	M1: Index rubs to side on lips; then M2: Rubs along index toward tip
Moja (119)	Lips; then extended index or index edge of fist	Index extended	M1: Index mostly tip of index rubs down or contacts lips; then M2: Rubs along or contacts index

159

Gloss Subject (#)	*Place* (P)	*Configuration* (C)	*Movement* (M)
TOOTHBRUSH	Teeth	Index extended from fist, index points to side	Rubs side to side or up and down
Washoe (12)	Teeth	Index extended side	Edge of index rubs side to
Moja (21)	Teeth	Index extended from fist or from open hand or open hand	Edge or inside of index rubs to side or side to side
Tatu (14)	Teeth	Index extended, palm to Signer or palm down	Edge of index rubs side to side
Dar (21)	Teeth	Index extended from fist or from open hand or open hand, fingers point to side and palm down	Index mostly edge of index rubs side to side

Table 3.2 (continued)

Gloss Subject (#)	Place (P)	Configuration (C)	Movement (M)
TOOTHPASTE	Teeth; then index, extended tended from fist	C1: Index extended from fist; then C2: Thumb extended from fist	M1: Index contacts or rubs to side on teeth; then M2: Thumb rubs along toward tip on index
Moja (121)	Teeth; then index, extended	Index extended	M1: Edge of index rubs or contacts teeth; then M2: Index mostly tip of index rubs on index
Tatu (95)	Teeth; then extended in-dex or index of open hand, palm down	C1: Index extended or open hand; then C2: Thumb extended or index extended or open hand	M1: Index mostly edge of index rubs to side or side to side on teeth; then M2: Index or thumb or tip of extended finger rubs along index
Dar (86)	Teeth; then knuckles of index or back of index, extended	Index extended	M1: Index or edge of index rubs side to side or to side on teeth; then M2: Index or tip of index rubs along or along toward tip on index; mostly M2 before M1
TREE	Palm or back, of open hand, forearm hori-zontal	Spread hand or open hand, forearm vertical	Elbow contacts then hand twists and fingers wiggle
Washoe (64)	Elbow, forearm vertical	Curved hand	Palm contacts
Moja (66)	Elbow, forearm vertical or diagonal	Open hand	Contacts mostly repeated

Gloss Subject (#)	Place (P)	Configuration (C)	Movement (M)
Tatu (78)	Elbow, forearm vertical or diagonal	Open hand	Palm contacts
Dar (117)	Elbow, forearm vertical or arm bent	Open hand	Palm contacts sometimes repeated
TWO	On flat surface or palm, of open hand [space in front of Signer]	Index and second fingers extended and spread, [fingers point up]	Tips of index and second fingers contact [hand moves away from Signer]
Moja (152)	On a flat surface	Both indexes and second fingers extended from open hands or extended and spread	Index and second fingers mostly tips of index and second fingers contact sometimes repeated
UP	Space above Signer	Index extended from fist, index points up	Moves up or arm extends up, may repeat
Washoe (4)	Space above Signer	Open hand, fingers point up	Points up
Moja (5)	Space above Signer	Open hand mostly both hands, fingers point up	Arms extend up
Tatu (4)	Space above Signer	One or both open hands or indexes extended from open hands	Arm extends up
Dar (4)	Space above Signer	Open hand mostly both hands	Arms extend up

Table 3.2 (continued)

Gloss Subject (#)	Place (P)	Configuration (C)	Movement (M)
VACUUM	Palm, of open hand, palm up	Spread hand	Fingertips rub repeatedly along toward wrist
Moja (156)	Palm, of open hand, palm up	Open hand	Fingertips rub repeatedly along toward wrist
Tatu (130)	Palm, of open hand, palm up	Open hand or curved hand or claw hand, palm down	Fingertips, rub along toward wrist or toward edge of hand, sometimes repeated, or rub while closing
Dar (97)	Palm, of open hand, palm up	Open hand or spread hand, palm down	Fingertips rub repeatedly along toward wrist
WANT (hungry)	Chest	Curved hand, palm to Signer	Fingertips rub down
Washoe (130)	Chest	Curved hand, palm to Signer	Rubs down
WATER	Lips	Thumb contacts little finger with others extended and spread, palm to side and fingers point up	Little finger edge or edge of index [edge of index only] contacts, may repeat
Washoe (104)	Lips	Curved hand, palm to side	Index edge contacts
Moja (104)	Lips	Open hand or curved hand, palm to side	Little finger edge contacts
Tatu (121)	Lips or lips and chin	Spread hand, fingers point up and palm to P; or open hand, fingers point up and little finger edge or index edge to P	Contacts sometimes repeated

163

Gloss Subject (#)	Place (P)	Configuration (C)	Movement (M)
WE	Chest	Index extended from fist moves to side then contacts again	Tip of index contacts then
Washoe (65)	Chest, often chest of Addressee	Index extended	Index contacts then moves to side then contacts again
WHAT	Palm, of spread hand or open hand	Index extended from fist	Tip of index rubs toward little finger edge
Moja (98)	Palm	Index extended	Index rubs toward edge of hand
WHITE	Chest	Spread hand, palm to Signer and fingers point to side	Fingers and thumb contact then close to tapered hand while moving away
Washoe (66)	Chest	Pincer hand	Index and thumb grasp and pull away
Moja (88)	Chest	Open hand or pincer hand, palm to P	Open hand closes to fist while grasping, or pincer hand grasps mostly grasps and pulls
Tatu (125)	Chest	Open hand or spread hand, palm to P	Grasps and/or squeezes
Dar (122)	Midriff or chest	Open hand, palm to P	Grasps and pulls or grasps or closes to fist while grasping and pulling

Table 3.2 (continued)

Gloss Subject (#)	Place (P)	Configuration (C)	Movement (M)
WHO	Space in front of lips	Index or hooked index extended from fist, index points to lips	Wiggles or moves in circle
Washoe (133)	Space in front of lips	Hooked index extended, index points to lips	Approaches, and lips blow
Tatu (133)	Space in front of lips, or lips then space in front of lips, lips protruded	Index or index extended from fist, (index points to lips)	Wiggles, or contacts then wiggles, or contacts then moves away, sometimes lips blow audibly
WINDOW	Index edge, of open hand, palm to Signer and fingers point to side	Open hand, palm to Signer and fingers point to side	Little finger edge contacts repeatedly
Washoe (87)	Index edge of hand	Open hand, palm to Signer and fingers point to side	Little finger edge contacts
WIPER (napkin)	Lips and chin	Open hand, palm to Signer	Fingers rub repeatedly down or in circle
Washoe (25)	Lips and chin	Open hand	Palm rubs up or to side
Moja (42)	Chin or lips and chin	Open hand	Palm or fingertips rub to side or side to side or to side and down
Tatu (29)	Lips or chin	Open hand	Palm or fingers rub down and to side
Dar (34)	Lips and chin or lips	Open hand, fingers point to side	Palm rubs down
WOOD	Back, of open hand, palm down	Open hand	Little finger edge rubs side to side

165

Gloss / Subject (#)	Place (P)	Configuration (C)	Movement (M)
Moja (165)	Back of wrist or wrist	Open hand or fist	Little finger edge or wrist rubs to and fro or along
Tatu (124)	Back of forearm or fist	Fist, index edge up or palm up	Little finger edge or forearm rubs to side or side to side
Dar (115)	Radial edge or back, of forearm or of wrist, forearm horizontal	Fist, palm to side	Rubs to and fro or along
WRESTLE	Fingers	Both spread hands	Fingers of opposite hands interlock then both hands move repeatedly to and fro
Moja (122)	One or two fingers or all fingers	Both open hands	Fingers of opposite hands interlock then shake or interlock only
WRISTWATCH Moja (96)	Back of wrist	Pincer hand, palm to P	Index and thumb contact
Tatu (109)	Back of wrist	Open hand or curved hand	Grasps
Dar (96)	Back of wrist[a]	Curved hand or open hand	Grasps or contacts
	Back or wrist	Open hand or curved hand	Palm grasps
YES Moja (125)	Head	N/A	Nods up and down
	Head	N/A	Nods up and down or down, mostly with audible exhalation

Table 3.2 (continued)

Gloss Subject (#)	Place (P)	Configuration (C)	Movement (M)
YOU			
Washoe (23)	Addressee	Index extended from fist	Index points or contacts
Moja (11)	Chest of Addressee	Index extended	Index contacts
Tatu (22)	Chest of Addressee	Open hand or index extended	Fingertips or tip of index contacts
Dar (19)	Chest of Addressee	Index extended	Index or tip of index contacts
	Chest of Addressee	Index extended or open hand or both indexes extended, palm down or palm to side	Index mostly tip of index or fingertips, contact or point
YOURS			
Washoe (89)	Addressee	Open hand, palm to P and fingers point up	Approaches P
Moja (103)	Chest of Addressee	Open hand	Contacts
Tatu (107)	Chest of Addressee	Open hand	Back of hand or palm contacts
Dar (100)	Chest of Addressee	Open hand, fingers point to side or point up	Palm contacts or approaches P
	Chest of Addressee	Open hand	Palm or little finger edge contacts or approaches P

Proper Name Subject (#)	Place (P)	Configuration (C)	Movement (M)
ARLENE K.	Hip	Fist, palm to P and knuckles down	Knuckles contact
Tatu (100)	Hip	Fist	Knuckles contact
B.T.G. Washoe (51)	Cheek	Index extended from fist	Edge of index rubs down
Moja (7)	Cheek^c	Index extended from fist or hooked index	Index rubs down
			Index mostly tip or edge of index contacts sometimes repeated or rubs down
Tatu (36)	Cheek	Index extended from fist	Edge or tip of index rubs down or to side or contacts
BART H.	Palm, of open hand, palm forward and fingers pointed up	Index and second fingers extended from fist	Tips of index and second fingers contact
Tatu (84)	Palm or index edge, of open hand, palm down and fingers point forward	Open hand or index and second fingers extended from open hand, palm up and crossing P	Index and second fingers mostly tips of index and second fingers contact
BETTY S.	Upper arm^c	Open hand, palm up and fingers point to side	Little finger edge contacts
Dar (65)	Upper arm^c	Open hand	Palm contacts mostly repeated
CLAYTON V.	Lips	Index and second fingers extended and spread	Index and second fingers contact, may repeat
Moja (107)	Lips	Index and second fingers extended and spread	Index and second fingers mostly tips of index and second fingers contact

168

Table 3.2 (continued)

Proper Name Subject (#)	Place (P)	Configuration (C)	Movement (M)
DAR	Ear	Index extended from fist, palm forward and index points up	Index rubs forward
Tatu (76)	Ear	Index extended from fist	Index mostly tip of index rubs
Dar (50)	Ear	Index extended from fist, palm forward or palm to rear, index points up	Index contacts while moving forward
DENNIS S.	Teeth	Hooked index extended from fist	Tip of index contacts
Washoe (94)	Teeth	Hooked index extended from fist	Index contacts
DON M.	Chin	Fist, index edge to P	Grasps repeatedly
Washoe (131)	Chin	Fist	Grasps repeatedly
GREG G.	Chest near shoulder[c]	Index extended from fist, index points to side	Index edge contacts
Washoe (52)	Chest near shoulder[c]	Index extended	Index contacts
Moja (155)	Shoulder[c]	Index and second fingers or index extended from fist	Fingertip/s contact
HAROLD P.	Ear	Fist or thumb extended from fist	Thumb and fingers grasp and pull
Moja (84)	Ear	Curved hand or thumb extended from fist	Grasps and pulls down or grasps and shakes or grasps only

169

Proper Name Subject (#)	Place (P)	Configuration (C)	Movement (M)
JEFF B.	Ear	Fist	Thumb and fingers grasp
Moja (150)	Ear^c	Pincer fist or curved hand or pincer hand	Grasps and pulls to side or grasps only
JIM R.	Chest near shoulder	Little finger extended from fist	Little finger rubs down then to side
Moja (160)	Chest near shoulder	Open hand	Fingertips rub down sometimes repeated
KEN B.	Both hips	Both open hands, palms to rear and fingers point down	Index edges contact
Moja (158)	Leg mostly both legs	Both open hands contact	Index edges or palms
LARRY S.	Chin	Thumb and index extended from fist	Tip of index contacts
Washoe (108)	Chin	Index extended	Index contacts
LINN A.	Midriff	Thumb and index extended from fist	Index rubs to side
Washoe (125)	Midriff	Index extended	Index rubs to side
MARK L.	Center of brow	Open hand, palm down and fingers point to Signer	Fingertips contact
Tatu (114)	Center of brow	Open hand	Contacts

Table 3.2 (continued)

Proper Name Subject (#)	Place (P)	Configuration (C)	Movement (M)
MARTI G.	Chin	Thumb contacts little finger with others extended, palm to P and fingers point up	Fingertips contact repeatedly
Tatu (92)	Chin	Open hand, palm to P and fingers point up	Contacts
MOJA	Palm, of open hand	Thumb contacts little finger with others extended, may be bent	Fingertips or knuckles rub along toward tips or to and fro
Moja (43)	Palm, of open hand	Open hand	Fingertips rub (along toward wrist)
Tatu (67)	Palm, of open hand, palm up	Contracted hand	Knuckles rub along or side to side or to and fro
NAOMI R.	Side of chin or chin	Thumb extended from spread or from open hand, palm to side	Tip of thumb contacts
Washoe (57)	Cheek	Thumb extended	Thumb contacts
Moja (28)	Chin or side of chin	Thumb or thumb and index, extended from open hand or from claw hand	Thumb or tip of thumb contacts sometimes repeated
Tatu (128)	Chin or side of chin or cheek	Thumb extended from open hand or from spread hand	Thumb or tip of thumb contacts
PAT D.	Chin	Pincer hand	Index and thumb grasp repeatedly

Proper Name Subject (#)	Place (P)	Configuration (C)	Movement (M)
Moja (163)	Chin	Pincer fist, palm down	Index and thumb grasp and pull
Dar (110)	Chin	Pincer hand	Index and thumb grasp and pull
R.A.G.			
	Center of brow	Index extended from fist, index points down or to side	Edge of index contacts or rubs down
Washoe (55)	Center of brow	Index extended from fist, palm down	Edge of index contacts
Moja (82)	Brow[a] mostly center of brow	Index extended	Tip of index rubs down or contacts
Tatu (102)	Brow mostly center of brow	Pincer hand or index extended from fist, palm down	Fingertips or index rubs to side or down
Dar (61)	Brow[a] mostly center of brow	Index extended from fist or from open hand, index points down or to P	Tip of index contacts or rubs down
RICHARD R.	Elbow, forearm vertical	Index and second fingers extended and crossed	Index and second fingers contact repeatedly
Moja (159)	Elbow	Index and second fingers extended from fist or from open hand	Tips of index and second fingers contact
ROGER F.	Ear	Pincer hand	Index and thumb grasp and pull down
Washoe (30)	Ear	Pincer hand	Index and thumb grasp and pull

Table 3.2 (continued)

Proper Name Subject (#)	Place (P)	Configuration (C)	Movement (M)
RON B.	Temple	Open hand, palm down or palm to side	Index edge contacts
Moja (79)	Brow or top of head	Open hand or contracted hand, palm to side or palm forward	Index edge or wrist contacts
RON R.	Midriff	Index and second fingers extended and crossed	Tips of index and second fingers contact repeatedly
Washoe (95)	Midriff	Index extended	Index contacts repeatedly
SUSAN N.	Top of head	Fist, palm down	Rubs to rear while turning to palm up
Washoe (43)	Top of head	Open hand	Palm rubs to rear
Moja (15)	Top of head	Fist or open hand, palm down	Contacts sometimes repeated or rubs to side
Tatu (116)	Top of head or brow	Pincer fist, palm down	Tips of index and thumb rub to side or side to side
Dar (75)	Top of head	Fist, palm down	Rubs to side or contacts, sometimes repeated
SUSAN W.	Back of wrist or radial edge of wrist	Fist	Little finger edge rubs to side or to and fro or along
Moja (120)	Wrist or arm	Fist or open hand	Little finger edge or back of fist rubs to side or along or to and fro
TATU	Upper arm[c]	Fist, palm to P	Knuckles contact
Moja (123)	Upper arm[c]	Fist	Knuckles contact

Proper Name Subject (#)	Place (P)	Configuration (C)	Movement (M)
Tatu (56)	Upper arm[c]	Fist	Knuckles contact
Dar (77)	Shoulder[c]	One or both fists	Knuckles contact repeatedly
TIM D.	Tops of shoulders	Both curved hands, palms down	Fingertips contact
Moja (164)	Both shoulders or tops of shoulders	Both open hands, palms to P or palms down	Fingertips contact
TOM T.	Chest near shoulder	Fist	Knuckles contact repeatedly
Moja (62)	Chest	Fist or contracted hand	Knuckles contact repeatedly
TOM V.	Outer corner of eye	Index and second fingers extended and spread, fingers point up	Edge of index contacts
Dar (85)	Outer corner of eye	Open hand or index and second fingers of open hand separated, palm down or to Signer or to side and fingers point up or to side	Index and second fingers contact sometimes repeated
TONY M.	Lips	Both indexes extended from fists, indexes point toward each other	Tips of indexes rub to sides
Dar (102)	Lips, protruded	Both indexes extended	Indexes or tips of indexes rub to sides or down

Table 3.2 (continued)

Proper Name Subject (#)	Place (P)	Configuration (C)	Movement (M)
VAUGHN H.	Elbow	Index and second fingers extended and spread	Index and second fingers contact
Moja (139)	Elbow	Index and second fingers extended and spread	Index and second fingers contact
WASHOE	Ear	Thumb contacts little finger with others extended and spread	Index rubs forward
Washoe (31)	Ear	Open hand, fingers point up	Rubs forward
WENDE S.	Neck	Thumb contacts little finger with others extended and spread	Fingertips rub repeatedly down
Washoe (56)	Neck	Open hand, palm to P	Fingertips rub

signed CEREAL and up and down when she signed ICECREAM. The human members of the foster families did not model these head movements, but historical records of ASL as used in the deaf community show that some ASL signs such as BORING and THINK were once formed by moving both head and hand, although only the hand moves in the modern form (Klima & Bellugi, 1979, pp. 70–71).

The superscript "c" identifies vocabulary items in which 10% or more of the records describe the active hand as contacting a place on the contralateral side of the body even though the target place modelled for the cross-fosterlings was on the ipsilateral side. For example, Moja signed PEACH by rubbing the fingertips of her right hand downwards on her left cheek. We found no relation in our records between this form variant and the context notes. However, in nearly all cases the contralateral place was the cheek or the ear. With a long chimpanzee arm it may be easier to reach over and touch the contralateral side of the head than to stay on the ipsilateral side.

The three authors of this chapter reviewed all of the summary descriptions and compared them with photographic and video-taped records of all four chimpanzees. In eight cases of the many hundreds that are possible we found a value of an aspect of a sign of a particular chimpanzee that was not mentioned in the summary description. In each case the sign was adequately described without this additional detail, but we have added the detail in parentheses for completeness.

Comments

Table 3.2 together with Table 3.1 can serve as a dictionary of the signs in the vocabularies of Washoe, Moja, Tatu, and Dar, a resource to be consulted when the shape and use of a sign must be specified. In addition, Table 3.2 is arranged for easy comparisons between the chimpanzees with respect to the contents of their vocabularies and the sequence of acquisition (cf. B. Gardner & Gardner, 1980, pp. 341–344) as well as the shapes of the signs. Where the shapes of the chimpanzee signs differ from the target forms, they usually all differ in the same way, as in BLANKET and TREE. In comparing the chimpanzee forms with the target forms that were modelled for them, readers should remember that the articulation of very young human signers, like the articulation of very young human speakers, is often an immature version of the adult model (Orlansky & Bonvillian, 1988, pp. 284–287). In Table 3.2, most of the deviations from adult models are very similar to immature patterns that have been reported for the early signing of human children.

Very young human children, for example, tend to use an enlarged signing area, sometimes reaching above their heads for signs such as MORE (Schlesinger & Meadow, 1972, pp. 65–66). In the same way, the earliest version of MORE that we saw in the cross-fostered chimpanzees was made overhead

Fig. 3.6 Signing on the addressee: Pili (21 months) signs TICKLE on his own hand, but Moja (33 months) places the sign on the hand of the addressee.

Fig. 3.7 Immature variants of MORE: The infants Washoe (16 months) and Pili (3 months) sign MORE overhead, while Washoe at 57 months signs MORE at chest level.

rather than at chest level (see R. Gardner & Gardner, 1973, for filmed examples). Although Washoe, Moja, Tatu, and Dar had all outgrown this version of MORE when their signs were sampled for this table, an enlarged signing area can still be seen in COME, DOWN, GO, and UP.

As we might expect, the youngest human signers offer crude approximations of difficult configurations. The most frequently mentioned example is the substitution of a pointing index for more complex hand configurations (McIntire, 1977; Schlesinger & Meadow, 1972, pp. 65–66). Table 3.2 shows similar reduction to the pointing index in the signs of Washoe, Moja, Tatu, and Dar. The cross-fostered chimpanzees usually matched relatively simple configurations, such as fist, open hand, pincer, thumb extended, index extended, and hooked index, but failed at more complex configurations requiring the "M", "R", "T", "W" or "3" of the American hand alphabet and number system.

The pattern of difficulty is much the same as Boyes-Braem (1973) and McIntire (1977) describe in the development of human children. Precise control of the middle, ring, and little fingers is required for the more complex configurations but is acquired later than precision of thumb and index fingers in human children (Kinsbourne & Warrington, 1963). The more complex configurations that children and chimpanzees find difficult are underused in the signs of ASL. Along similar lines, some configurations require a signer to extend the thumb, index, or index and second fingers from a fist. In many signs of this sort, the chimpanzees extended the correct finger or fingers, but left the remaining fingers in a relaxed position.

Like human children, Washoe, Moja, Tatu, and Dar often produced simpler movement patterns than their adult models. They might only reproduce the first of two movements, as in PEACH. The basic direction, whether up and down, side to side, or toward and away from the center of the body, was matched well, but changing directions seemed to be more difficult. The circular rub in COFFEE and SORRY, or the to side and then up in BIB and LAUGH was reduced to one component of the complex directional movement. Again, like human children they contacted the place, sometimes quite sharply, where the adult form only requires pointing to or moving toward the place.

References

Aiken, E.G., & Lau, A.W. (1967). Response prompting and response confirmation: A review of recent literature. *Psychological Bulletin, 68*, 330–341.

Battison, R., & Jordan, I.K. (1976). Cross-cultural communication with foreign signers: Fact and fancy. *Sign Language Studies, 10*, 53–68.

Berko-Gleason, J. (1958). The child's learning of English morphology. *Word,* *14,* 150–177.

Bornstein, H., Hamilton, L.B., & Kannapell, B.M. (1969). *Signs for instructional purposes.* Washington, DC: Gallaudet College Press.

Bornstein, H., Kannapell, B.M., Saulnier, K.L., Hamilton, L.B., & Roy, H.L. (Eds.) (1973). *Basic pre-school Signed English dictionary.* Washington, DC: Gallaudet College Press.

Boyes-Braem, P. (1973). The acquisition of handshape in American Sign Language. Unpublished manuscript. La Jolla, CA: Salk Institute.

Brown, R. (1973). *A first language.* Cambridge, MA: Harvard University Press.

Fouts, R.S. (1975). Communication with chimpanzees. In G. Kurth & I. Eibl-Eibesfeldt (Eds.), *Hominisation und verhalten,* (pp. 137–158). Stuttgart: Gustav Fischer Verlag.

Frishberg, N. (1975). Arbitrariness and iconicity: Historical change in American Sign Language. *Language, 51,* 696–719.

Gardner, B.T., & Gardner, R.A. (1971). Two-way communication with an infant chimpanzee. In A. Schrier & F. Stollnitz (Eds.), *Behavior of nonhuman primates,* (Vol. 4, pp. 117–184). New York: Academic Press.

Gardner, B.T., & Gardner, R.A. (1975). Evidence for sentence constituents in the early utterances of child and chimpanzee. *Journal of Experimental Psychology: General, 104,* 244–267.

Gardner, B. T., & Gardner, R. A. (1980). Two comparative psychologists look at language acquisition. In K. Nelson (Ed.), *Child language,* (Vol. 2, pp. 331–369). New York: Gardner Press.

Gardner, R. A., & Gardner, B. T. (1969). Teaching sign language to a chimpanzee. *Science, 165,* 664–672.

Gardner, R. A., & Gardner, B. T. (1973). Teaching sign language to the chimpanzee, Washoe. (16-mm sound film). State College, PA: Psychological Cinema Register.

Gardner, R. A., & Gardner, B. T. (1974). Teaching sign language to the chimpanzee, Washoe. *Bulletin D'Audio Phonologie, 4*(5), 145–173.

Gardner, R. A., & Gardner, B.T. (1978). Comparative psychology and language acquisition. *Annals of the New York Academy of Sciences, 309,* 37–76.

Gardner, R. A., & Gardner, B. T. (1984). A vocabulary test for chimpanzees. *Journal of Comparative Psychology, 98,* 381–404.

Jordan, I. K., & Battison, R. (1976). A referential communication experiment with foreign sign languages. *Sign Language Studies, 10,* 69–80.

Kinsbourne, M., & Warrington, E. K. (1963). The development of finger differentiation. *Quarterly Journal of Experimental Psychology, 15,* 132–137.

Klima, E. S., & Bellugi, U. (1979). *The signs of language.* Cambridge, MA: Harvard University Press.

McIntire, M. L. (1977). The acquisition of American Sign Language hand configuration. *Sign Language Studies, 16,* 247–266.

Nelson, K. (1973). Structure and strategy in learning to talk. *Monograph of the Society for Research in Child Development, 38,* (1–2, Serial No. 149), 1–137.

Orlansky, M.D., & Bonvillian, J.D. (1988). Early sign language acquisition. In M.D. Smith & J.L. Locke (Eds.), *The emergent lexicon,* (pp. 263–292). New York: Academic Press.

O'Rourke, T. J. (1978). *A basic vocabulary: American Sign Language for parents and children.* Silver Spring, MD: T. J. Publishers.

Schlesinger, H. S., & Meadow, K. P. (1972). *Deafness and mental health: A developmental approach.* Berkeley: University of California Press.

Stokoe, W. C. (1960). Sign language structure: An outline of the visual communications systems of the American deaf. *Studies in Linguistics,* Occasional Papers 8. NY: University of Buffalo.

Stokoe, W. C. (1978). *Sign language structure,* revised edition. Silver Spring, MD: Linstok Press.

Stokoe, W. C., Casterline, D., & Croneberg, C. G. (1965). *A dictionary of American Sign Language on linguistic principles.* Washington, D.C.: Gallaudet College Press.

Watson, D. O. (1964). *Talk with your hands.* Menasha, WI: George Banta Co.

Woodward, J. C. (1976). Signs of change: Historical variation in American Sign Language. *Sign Language Studies, 10,* 81–94.

°The sign DIRTY should have been listed with Noun/Verbs and not with Markers and Traits in Table 3.1; the remainder of the description of the usage of DIRTY on page 72 is correct.

4. A Test of Communication

Beatrix T. Gardner and *R. Allen Gardner*

When Washoe was 27 months old she made a hole in the then-flimsy inner wall of her house trailer. The hole was located high up in the wall at the foot of her bed. Before we repaired the hole she managed to lose a toy in the hollow space between the inner and outer walls. When R. A. Gardner arrived that evening she attracted his attention to an area of the wall down below the hole at the level of her bed, signing OPEN OPEN many times over that area. It was not hard for him to understand what the trouble was and eventually to fish out the toy. When the toy was found, it was exciting to realize that a chimpanzee had used a human language to communicate truly new information. It was not long before such situations became commonplace. For example, Washoe's playground was in the garden behind a single-storey house. High in her favorite tree, Washoe was often the first to know who arrived at the front of the house and her companions on the ground learned to rely on her to tell them who was arriving and departing.

Washoe could tell her human companions things that they did not already know. This is what Clever Hans could not do. Clever Hans, it will be remembered, was a German horse that seemed to do arithmetic by tapping out numbers with his hoof. Not the circus trainers or the calvary officers, not the veterinarians or the zoo directors, not even the philosophers and the linguists who studied the case could explain how Clever Hans did it. Nevertheless an experimental psychologist, Oskar Pfungst (1911), unravelled the problem with the following test. Pfungst whispered one number into Clever Hans left ear and Herr von Ost, the trainer, whispered a second number into the horse's right ear. When Clever Hans was the only one who knew the answer, he could not tap out the correct sums. He could not tell his human companions anything that they did not already know.

Since then, controls for "Clever Hans Errors" have been standard procedure in comparative psychology. To date most, if not all, research on human children has been carried out without any such controls. It is as if students of child development believed that, whereas horses and chimpanzees may be sensitive to subtle nonverbal communication, it is safe to assume that human children are totally unaffected.

Early in Project Washoe we devised vocabulary tests to demonstrate that

181

chimpanzees could use the signs of ASL to communicate information (B. Gardner & Gardner, 1971, pp. 158–161; 1974, pp. 11–15; R. Gardner & Gardner, 1974, pp. 160–161). For Washoe's first test we mounted color photographs (mostly cut from magazine illustrations) on 8.5-in. x 5.5-in. cards. An experimenter selected a random sample of six to ten cards and placed them face down in a cupboard of Washoe's trailer the night before a test session. Early in the morning an observer held up the cards one by one and asked Washoe to name them. For each card, the observer wrote down the first sign that Washoe made and then looked at the card and scored the response as correct or incorrect.

In order to extend the test to three-dimensional exemplars, we used plywood boxes, 12-in. high x 13-in. wide x 9.5-in. deep. One side of each box was clear plexiglass, the other sides were opaque. An experimenter selected exemplars randomly from a pool of photographs and objects and placed them one by one in a box. Again, the observer exposed the window side of the box to Washoe without looking inside and wrote down the first sign that Washoe made. We soon abandoned the box test because it was so cumbersome and expensive, but it gave us a valuable piece of information about the difference between photographs and three-dimensional exemplars.

Three-dimensional exemplars of objects like bibs and brushes were easy to get into a small box but exemplars of CAT, DOG, COW, BIRD, and CAR were another matter. In order to present both photographs and three-dimensional exemplars for all categories, we used high-quality figurines and models as well as photographs for the larger objects. We soon noticed that the expensive replicas produced significantly more errors than the photographs. Washoe's favorite error for replicas of cats, dogs, cows, birds, and cars was BABY, but she rarely called any of the photographs of these items BABY. In a sense, she treated the three-dimensional replicas as less realistic than the photographic replicas (B. Gardner & Gardner, 1971, pp. 160–161).

On the basis of these results we developed a procedure that used photographs only. For a more detailed description of the testing procedures and results see B. Gardner & Gardner (1971, pp. 158–161; 1974, pp. 11–15), R. Gardner & Gardner (1973, 1984), and Campbell-Jones (1974).

OBJECTIVES

The first objective of these tests was to demonstrate that the chimpanzee subjects could communicate information under conditions in which the only source of information available to a human observer was the signing of the chimpanzees. To accomplish this, nameable objects were photographed on 35-mm slides. During testing, the slides were back-projected on a screen that could be seen by the chimpanzee subject, but could not be seen by the observer. The slides were projected in a random order that was changed from test to test so that the order could not be memorized either by the observer or by the subject.

The second objective of these tests was to demonstrate that independent observers agreed with each other. To accomplish this, there were two observers. The first observer (O_1) served as interlocutor in the testing room with the chimpanzee subject. The second observer (O_2) was stationed in a second room and observed the subject from behind one-way glass, but could not see the projection screen. The two observers gave independent readings; they could not see each other and they could not compare observations until after a test was completed.

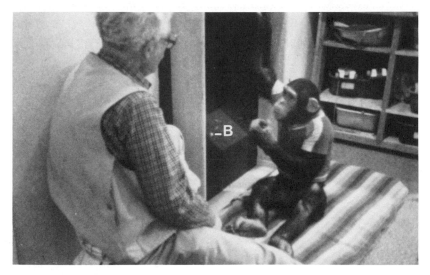

Fig. 4.1   Room 1: The vocabulary testing apparatus used with Moja, Tatu, and Dar. Chimpanzee Dar sits in front of the projection screen, which is recessed within the cabinet. O_1, seated beside the cabinet, can see Dar's signs but cannot see the projection screen. By pressing the white push-button (B), Dar makes a picture appear on the screen. (The vocabulary testing apparatus used with Washoe was slightly different; see B. Gardner & Gardner, 1974, pp. 11–16).

The third objective of these tests was to demonstrate that the chimpanzees used the signs to refer to natural language categories—that the sign DOG could refer to any dog, FLOWER to any flower, SHOE to any shoe, and so on. This was accomplished by preparing a large library of slides to serve as exemplars. Some of the slides were used in pretests that served to adapt subjects, observers, and experimenters to the testing procedure. The slides that were reserved for the tests were never shown during pretests so that the first time that a particular chimpanzee subject saw any one of the test slides was on a test trial and no test slide was shown on more than one test trial. Consequently, there was no way that a subject could get a correct score by memorizing particular pairs of exemplars and signs. That is to say, scores on these tests depended upon the ability to name new exemplars of natural language categories.

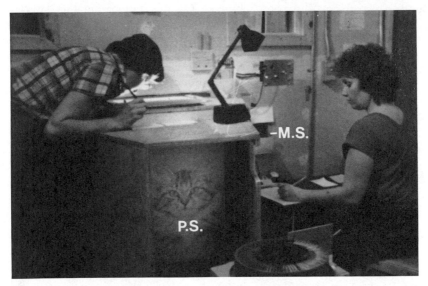

Fig. 4.2 Room 2: A carousel projector shows the test slides. Standing to one side of the cabinet, O_2 can see the subject through the one-way glass window but cannot see the projection screen (P.S.). O_2 writes down what the subject signs and passes the message slip to the experimenter, who also receives written messages from O_1, via the message slot (M.S.). After receiving a message slip from O_1 and O_2, the experimenter steps the carousel to the slide for the next trial.

METHODS

Items and Exemplars

We can use the term *vocabulary item* to refer to a category of objects, such as shoes, flowers, dogs, that could be named by a particular sign; and the term *exemplar* to refer to a unique member of such a category. All of the exemplars in the tests and pretests were 16-in. x 11-in. back-projected images of 35-mm color slides.

Outside of the testing situation, we could use the pictures in ordinary books and magazines—even when the pictures contained objects of many different kinds—because we could point to particular objects or ask questions such as, WHAT BIRD EAT? Under the blind conditions of the tests, however, the objects had to dominate the field of view. The backgrounds had to be very plain since even brightly colored backgrounds were sometimes distracting and would be named instead of the objects. Note in the examples of Figures 4.3a and 4.3b that the objects usually filled the screen regardless of their normal relative size, whether they were bugs, shoes, or cars.

Some of the things the chimpanzees could name, such as grass or water, seemed impossible to present in test slides because they lack any characteristic shape and appear as meaningless forms against a blank background. Some otherwise shapeless objects, such as coffee or facial tissues, could be presented in test slides because they appear in distinctive containers. Still other objects, such as houses and windows, seemed impossible to photograph without backgrounds or foregrounds that contain distracting extraneous detail. An important function of the pretests was to try out different photographic techniques. It was in this way that we learned to avoid vividly colored backgrounds that might be named instead of the featured object.

We had to learn to look at the slides with the eyes of our subjects. For example, dramatic slides of leafy trees yielded mixed results, but shortly after Christmas one year, Tatu suggested something better. As she played with her discarded Christmas tree she named it to herself many times. It turned out that Christmas trees, photographed close-up against the sky, made highly acceptable exemplars both for Tatu and for Dar. The tops of the live evergreens taken with a telephoto lens were also highly acceptable. Even though evergreens come in some variety, we wanted to demonstrate that chimpanzees can also name deciduous trees under test conditions. Once more, Tatu showed us the way. That same winter, on outings in the woods, Tatu frequently called our attention to trees by signing THAT TREE at their bare trunks. After this hint, we discovered that photographs of bare trees in winter made excellent exemplars.

Teaching and Testing

In most laboratory studies of nonhuman beings, the same procedures serve both for teaching and for testing. A monkey or a rat, for example, learns to associate one stimulus with the reward and the other with an empty food dish on the very same trials that are scored for correct and incorrect choices and plotted to show learning curves. Washoe, Moja, Tatu, and Dar were accompanied by a human member of their foster family during virtually all of their waking hours. During that time, the exposure to objects and the ASL names for objects was very large compared with the brief periods spent in vocabulary tests. Moreover, these tests were as different from the routines of the rest of their daily lives as similar testing would be for young children. For caged subjects, a session of testing is probably the most interesting thing that happens in the course of a laboratory day. For Washoe, Moja, Tatu, and Dar, most of the

Fig. 4.3a Exemplars used in tests of vocabulary. Black and white reproductions of APPLE (A), BERRY (B), FLOWER (C) and SHOE (D) used in Tatu's Test 2 and Dar's Test 2.

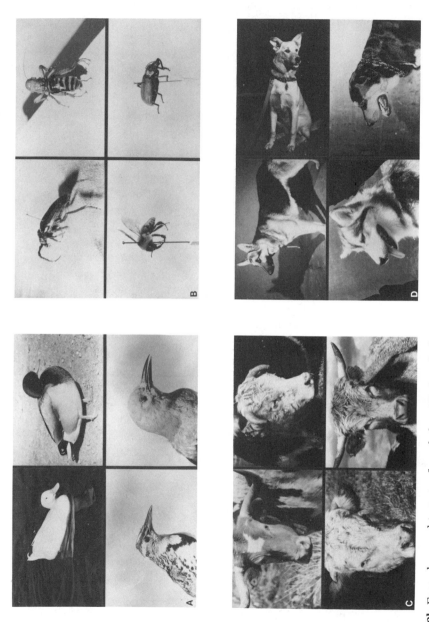

Fig. 4.3b Exemplars used in tests of vocabulary. Black and white reproductions of BIRD (A), BUG (B), COW (C) and DOG (D), used in Tatu's Test 2 and Dar's Test 2.

activities of daily life were more attractive than their formal tests. The cross-fostering regime precluded any attempt to starve them like rats or pigeons to make them earn their daily rations by taking tests.

Getting free-living, cross-fostered, chimpanzees to do their best under the stringent conditions of these tests required a great deal of ingenuity and patience. A basic strategy was to establish the testing routine by a regular program of pretests that were kept short, usually less than thirty minutes, and infrequent, rarely more than two sessions per week. We used the pretests to pilot variations in procedure and to ensure that experimenters, observers, and subjects were all highly practiced at the procedure before the tests.

Rewards

Early in Project Washoe, we learned that when she was too anxious to earn her reward—when she was too hungry or the reward too desirable—then we could expect no more from Washoe than the absolute minimum amount or quality of response necessary to get the reward. Whenever used, food rewards had to be very small—half of a raisin or a quarter of a peanut—more symbolic than nourishing. Attempting to reward Washoe for correct replies in the testing situation created procedural difficulties that we avoided with Moja, Tatu, and Dar by rewarding them for prompt, clear replies, regardless of correctness. Unlike Washoe, the other subjects were distracted by the treats and would often ask for the rewards by name at critical points in the procedure, so that O_1 and O_2 could not tell whether the chimpanzees were asking for a treat or naming a picture. Consequently, we abandoned this procedure entirely for Moja, Tatu and Dar, and they rarely received any rewards after the initial stages of pretesting.

Both the procedure in the observation room and the procedure in the testing room were frequently observed by additional personnel. Whether those serving as O_1 were aware of it or not, they often revealed their approval or disapproval of a cross-fosterling's performance by smiling or frowning and by nodding or shaking their heads as well as by signing such things and GOOD GIRL or SMART BOY.

Target Signs

The correct sign for each vocabulary item was designated in advance of the tests. That sign and that sign only was scored as correct for that item. Although there were aspects of the pictures for which superordinate terms, such as FOOD, or descriptive terms, such as BLACK, might be scored, neither the presence or absence nor the correct or incorrect use of such terms was considered in the scoring of these tests.

Most of the replies consisted of a single sign which was the name of an object. Sometimes, the single noun in the reply was contained in a descriptive phrase, as when Tatu signed RED BERRY for a picture of cherries, or when

Dar signed THAT BIRD for a picture of a duck. These replies contained only one object name and that was the sign that was scored as correct or incorrect. Occasionally, a test reply contained more than one object name, as when Washoe signed FLOWER TREE LEAF FLOWER for a picture of a bunch of daisies. In such cases, the observers designated a single sign for scoring (usually the first) without looking at the picture themselves. For each trial and each observer, then, one sign and one sign only in each report was used to score agreement between O_1 and O_2 and agreement between the reports of the observers and the name of the exemplar.

The vocabulary items that appeared in the tests of Washoe, Moja, Tatu, and Dar are listed in Table 4.1. Differences among the subjects in Table 4.1 reflect differences in their vocabularies as well as a strategy of overlapping tests that would sample the range of picturable objects in the vocabularies without making the tests excessively long. For each test we chose four exemplars of each vocabulary item to illustrate the range of objects that a subject could name with the same sign. Different breeds represented CAT and DOG, different species represented BIRD and BUG, different makes and models represented CAR, and so on (see Figures 4.3a and 4.3b). The number of vocabulary items and the resulting number of trials (items times exemplars) appear in Table 4.2

RESULTS

Table 4.2 shows how the major objectives of the tests were accomplished. The agreement between O_1 and O_2 was high for all seven tests; except for Moja, the agreement ranged between 86% and 95% and all agreement was far beyond chance expectancy. Note that this is the agreement for both correct and incorrect signs. Clearly, the signs made by the chimpanzees were distinct and intelligible. The agreement between the signs reported by O_1 and O_2 and the correct names of the categories is also high; except for Moja, correct scores ranged between 71% and 88% and all scores were far beyond chance expectancy.

The line labelled "expected" in Table 4.2 needs some explanation. When we first described this testing procedure (B. Gardner & Gardner, 1971) we estimated the expected chance performance as 1/N where N is the number of vocabulary items on a test and all items are represented by the same number of exemplars. This estimate was based on the assumption that only the chimpanzees were guessing and that their guessing strategies could only be randomly related to the random sequence of presentation. But this estimate may be too low because it does not take into account the possibility that the observers were guessing. In random sampling without replacement, the probabilities of later events in a sequence depend on earlier events. The observers could have used their knowledge of the items that had appeared earlier to predict

Table 4.1
Vocabulary Items in the Tests of Four Chimpanzees

Items	Chimpanzees				Items	Chimpanzees			
	W	M	T	D		W	M	T	D
Animates					*Foods*				
BABY	+		+	+	APPLE		+	+	+
BIRD	+	+	+	+	BANANA		+	+	+
BUG	+	+	+	+	BERRY		+	+	+
CAT	+	+	+	+	CARROT			+	+
COW	+	+	+	+	CEREAL		+		
DOG	+	+	+	+	CHEESE	+		+	+
HORSE		+			CORN		+	+	+
					FRUIT	+			
Plants					GRAPES		+		
FLOWER	+	+	+	+	GUM		+		
LEAF	+	+			ICECREAM		+	+	+
TREE	+	+	+	+	MEAT	+		+	+
					NUT	+	+	+	+
Clothing					ONION		+		
CLOTHES	+				ORANGE		+		
HAT	+	+	+	+	PEA/BEAN		+		
PANTS	+				PEACH		+	+	+
SHOE	+	+	+	+	SANDWICH			+	+
					TOMATO	+			
Grooming									
BRUSH	+	+	+						
COMB		+	+		*Drinks*				
HANKY			+		COFFEE			+	+
LIPSTICK			+		DRINK	+			
OIL	+		+	+	MILK		+		
TOOTHBRUSH	+	+	+	+	SODAPOP		+	+	+
WIPER	+				*Other*				
					BALL			+	+
Sensory					BOOK	+	+		
LISTENS	+	+			CAR	+		+	+
LOOKS	+	+	+		HAMMER	+			
SMELLS	+				KEY	+	+	+	
					KNIFE		+		
					PEEKABOO			+	
					PIPE	+			
					SMOKE	+	+		

the items that would appear later. Thus, players who can remember the cards that have already been played can win significant amounts at games such as blackjack. Diaconis (1978) and Read (1962) deal with a similar problem in demonstrations of extrasensory perception. When highly motivated subjects in ESP experiments can see each target card after each prediction, their later predictions tend to improve.

Table 4.2
Scores on the Vocabulary Tests of Four Chimpanzees

Chimpanzee Subject		Washoe		Moja	Tatu		Dar	
Test		1	2	1	1	2	1	2
Vocabulary Items (#)		16	32	35	25	34	21	27
Trials (#)		64	128	140	100	136	84	108
Interobserver Agreement (%)		95	86	70[a]	89	91	90	94
Scored Correct by	Observer 1 (%)	86	72	54[b]	84	80	79	83
	Observer 2 (%)	88	71	54[b]	85	79	80	81
Expected* (%)		15	4	4	6	4	7	5

* Assuming that the observer was guessing on the basis of perfect memory for all previous trials that that observer had seen (see text).
[a] Based on 135 trials; O_2 missed 5 trials. [b] Based on 132 trials; 8 unscorable trials.

A general mathematical expression to calculate the effect of random selection without replacement but with trial-by-trial feedback on chance expectancy was developed by Patterson, Gardner, and Gardner (1986). As applied to the vocabulary tests, this expression assumes that both observers: (1) saw each slide after each trial; (2) had perfect memory for the number of exemplars of each vocabulary item that had appeared before the beginning of each trial; and (3) guessed the correct sign on the basis of the number of exemplars of each vocabulary item that remained to be presented. The expected scores for each test are shown in Table 4.2. In all cases, this estimate is a small fraction of the obtained scores. Since O_1 and O_2 reported extra-list intrusions (signs that were not on the target lists) they were using a less efficient strategy than that assumed by Patterson et al. Hence, small as they are, the values in the "expected" line of Table 4.2 overestimate chance expectancy.

The expected score for Washoe's first test is appreciably higher than the expected scores for the other six tests for two reasons. First, this test was shorter than the other tests and predictability depends on the number of vocabulary items—the fewer the items the greater the predictability. Second, and more significant for this discussion, predictability increases as we approach the end of the test. The last trial is completely predictable, since there is only one vocabulary item that could have any remaining exemplars. The next to the last trial may be completely predictable, but there are at most two vocabulary items that could still appear, and so on. In all cases, except for Washoe's first test, both O_1 and O_2 were assigned to test sessions in such a way that no individual served as an observer for more than half of the trials of any single test. The device is similar to the way gambling casinos can defeat card-counting customers by re-shuffling the deck. The smaller number of items and the assignment of the same two observers to both sessions of Washoe's first test account for the higher, but still quite small, expected score on that test.

DISCUSSION

Signs of ASL

The field records summarized in Table 3.2 show how closely the signs in the vocabularies of Washoe, Moja, Tatu, and Dar approximated the target signs of ASL that we modelled for them, allowing of course for childish diction. These daily observations were frequently confirmed under naturalistic conditions by fluent signers who visited the cross-fostering laboratory (e.g., Stokoe, 1983). The double-blind testing procedures described here lent themselves to more rigorous confirmation as follows. Two fluent deaf signers, both then recent graduates of Gallaudet College, each served as O_2 in Washoe's pretests in the summer of 1970. Each of these young men participated in two pretests at a time when each had observed Washoe for less than one hour. Their agreement with O_1 (who had in each case years of experience with Washoe) rose from 67% and 71% on their first session to 89% for both on their second session.

The task that these fluent signers faced should be compared with that of fluent speakers of English identifying the words of equally immature human children after equally brief pre-exposure to the immature speakers and under equally stringent conditions. These two outside observers who were expert at ASL, but unfamiliar with Washoe, read her signs fairly well at first and then improved markedly in their second test session. The improvement did not depend upon learning about specific vocabulary items because the items were changed from the first session to the second session. The initially good agreement with O_1 together with the improvement indicates that Washoe's signs were intelligible to fluent signers with, perhaps, a childish or chimpanzee accent that could be learned fairly quickly.

Concepts

To make sure that the signs referred to conceptual categories, all of the test trials were first trials; that is, each slide was shown to the subject for the first time on the one and only test trial in which it was presented to that subject.

All of the specific stimulus values varied, as they do in natural language categories; that is to say, most human beings would agree that the exemplars in each set belong together. Apparently, Washoe, Moja, Tatu, and Dar agreed with this assignment of exemplars to conceptual categories.

When teaching a new sign, we usually began with a particular exemplar—a particular toy for BALL, a particular shoe for SHOE. At first, especially with very young subjects, there would be very few balls and very few shoes. The same situation is common in human nursery life. Early in Project Washoe we worried that the signs might become too closely associated with their initial referents. It turned out that this was no more a problem for Washoe or any of our other subjects than it is for children. The chimpanzees easily transferred the signs they had learned for a few balls, shoes, flowers, or cats to the full range of the categories wherever they found them and however represented, as if they divided the world into the same conceptual categories that human beings use.

In a significant sense, no animal, human or nonhuman, steps twice into the same perceptual stream. A young monkey that picks a ripe mango in a tree must learn something general about ripe mangoes, because it will certainly never see that particular mango again. A young lion that stalks and kills an impala must learn something general about hunting impalas, because it will certainly never meet that particular impala again. Whatever may be learned about a particular object or event, the most valuable things that are learned have to do with variable aspects of general stimulus classes. What the psychologist must explain is how past experience transfers to new situations; because this is what happens most of the time.

So much experimentation has been limited to precisely repeated stimulus objects or to objects that vary only in simple dimensions, such as color and size, that it would be easy to form the impression that the conceptual abilities of nonhuman beings are severely limited. But, there are notable exceptions. Hayes and Hayes (1953) with chimpanzee Viki, Hicks (1956) and Sands, Lincoln, and Wright (1982) with monkeys, and Herrnstein, Loveland and Cable (1976) with pigeons, for example, have all demonstrated that nonhuman beings can use natural language categories when they are tested with suitably varied stimulus material.

Significant variation among exemplars and testing with true first trials are essential to the definition of natural language categories. More concerned with theoretical definitions of language than with conceptual behavior, the Rumbaughs (Essock, Gill, & Rumbaugh, 1977; Gill & Rumbaugh, 1974; Savage-Rumbaugh, Pate, Lawson, Smith, & Rosenbaum, 1983) have administered hundreds of trials of training and testing with identical exemplars or with minimally varied exemplars. To be sure, in their tests of chimpanzees the Rumbaughs concentrated on the artibrariness of what they call "lexigrams" as used in arbitrarily fixed sequences. It seems likely that the Rumbaugh chimpanzees could have used natural language categories, given the opportunity to do so.

In four years of work with the chimpanzee Nim, Terrace and his associates (Terrace, 1979; Terrace, Petitto, Sanders, & Bever, 1980) never attempted any experimental analysis of reference. Their work is unique in this field in that they never administered any systematic tests at all. Since the time of Kellogg and Kellogg (1933), it is the first study in this field that was entirely restricted to adventitious naturalistic observation without any controls for Clever Hans errors, whatsoever.

Communication and Language

Although concern with grammar has occupied so much of the efforts of developmental psycholinguists, in our view it would be a mistake for psychobiologists to neglect the study of reference. If the development of human verbal behavior requires any significant expenditure of biological resources, then it must return some biological advantages to its possessors. Before it can return any profit, however, a biological trait must operate on the world in some way; it must be instrumental in obtaining benefit or avoiding harm. If clarifying one's ideas is biologically profitable, it must be because in some way clarified ideas provide superior means for operating in the biological world. As for establishing social relations, a system of displays and cries is sufficient to maintain group cohesiveness in most animals. The advantage of a wider variety of signals would seem to be the communication of more information. But, unless verbal behavior refers to objects and events in the external world, it cannot communicate information and it cannot have any such advantage. From this point of view, reference is the biological function of verbal behavior, and the function of grammar or structure in verbal behavior must be to enlarge the scope and to increase the precision of reference.

In the naturally occurring languages of the world, the pairing of words and signs with conceptual categories is arbitrary. This is amply demonstrated by the mutual unintelligibility of languages and the well-documented history of shifts in forms and usage. Washoe, Moja, Tatu, and Dar, if they had been human children—if they had been angels for that matter—could succeed in these vocabulary tests only by associating the signs of ASL with their referents. Angels may have other ways of associating responses with stimuli, but children and chimpanzees must learn arbitrary associations. Thus, to the extent that the communication of information depends upon the arbitrary connection of terms to conceptual categories, then that biological function of a natural language depends upon the rote learning of paired associates.

Duality of Patterning

Chimpanzees who have learned to sign with their hands can respond at any time with any sign in their vocabulary. The conversations are open-ended.

Free of the restricted choices imposed by the artificial, apparatus-bound systems such as those of Premack, Rumbaugh, and their associates, they can make their own errors. In the cross-fostering laboratory, part of the daily record form (see Chapter 3 this volume) was reserved for two kinds of errors: errors in which the signs were used inappropriately and errors in which an inappropriate sign was used when the SOD would have been appropriate. Under those conditions, the bulk of the errors were either conceptual confusions, e.g., CAT for DOG, or formal confusions, e.g., BUG for FLOWER (see Table 3.2).

Those who are unfamiliar with sign languages often suppose that the forms of the signs are highly correlated with their referents. Indeed, in artificial sign languages this is often the case. In the system developed by Paget and Gorman (Crystal & Craig, 1978), for example, all of the signs for animals have similar shapes. In natural languages, however, the terms for items in the same conceptual group tend to be distributed widely over the possible gestural or phonetic forms.

Statistical analysis of the errors made by the chimpanzees under rigorous testing conditions confirmed the observations reported in the daily records (R. Gardner & Gardner, 1984, pp. 393–398). Thus DOG was a common error for pictures of cows, NUT for pictures of berries and so on, showing that conceptual groups such as animates and foods were a source of confusion for the chimpanzees. Incidentally, in this analysis the pattern of errors for the sign CAR and for pictures of cars was more like the pattern for animates than the pattern for inanimates. Formal confusions based on shapes of the signs in Table 3.2 were the second source of errors. Signs made on the cheek such as CAT and APPLE were confused with each other, as were signs made on the nose such as BUG and FLOWER, and signs made on the hand such as SHOE and SODAPOP. The cheremic structure of ASL was a source of errors in the signing of cross-fostered chimpanzees the way the phonetic structure of English is a source of errors in the speech of human beings.

Hockett (1978, pp. 275–276) points out that when errors are based on phonology as well as semantics we have evidence for duality of patterning. Perhaps an example will make this point more clear. Warden and Warner (1928) demonstrated that the German shepherd dog Fellow, a star of movies and vaudeville, could understand instructions in spoken English. In the most critical tests, Fellow's master spoke from behind a screen and instructed him to fetch objects from the next room. Fellow was significantly correct in his responses but he also made errors, such as fetching a collar instead of a dollar, that depend on the sounds of English. Similarly, we would argue that only a chimpanzee that had learned the shapes of the ASL signs would confuse CAT with APPLE or BUG with FLOWER.

As a part of the laboratory procedure, Washoe, Moja, Tatu, and Dar were discouraged from answering questions with a string of guesses. Nevertheless, some test replies contained two or more names for objects. Pairs of signs within such indecisive replies also formed patterns. Conceptual pairs, such as CAT and DOG, or SODAPOP and ICECREAM, and form pairs, such as CAT and APPLE or BUG and FLOWER, were the most common. Sometimes, pairs were repeated, as in CAT DOG CAT DOG, or BUG FLOWER BUG FLOWER. Sometimes, replies contained a string of related signs, as when Washoe signed, CAT BIRD DOG MAN for a picture of a kitten or FLOWER TREE LEAF FLOWER for a picture of daisies. There are several signs that are made by grasping points along the edge of one hand with the thumb and index finger of the active hand; the end of the thumb is grasped in BERRY,, the upper edge of the palm in MEAT, the lower edge of the palm in OIL (see B. Gardner & Gardner, 1975, Appendix; Table 3.2 in this volume). In a typical case, Washoe signed, OIL BERRY MEAT for a picture of frankfurters, as if the correct sign was on the tip of her fingers. Thus, not only the correct replies, but the errors and the very dithering between alternatives, were governed by conceptual relations among the referents and cherological relatons among the signs of ASL.

References

Campbell-Jones, S. (Producer & Director) (1974). The first signs of Washoe. (Film). Boston, MA: WGBH Nova series.

Crystal, D., & Craig, E. (1978). Contrived sign language. In I. M. Schlesinger & L. Namir (Eds.), *Sign language of the deaf*, (pp. 141–168). New York: Academic Press.

Diaconis, P. (1978). Statistical problems in ESP research. *Science, 201*, 131–136.

Essock, S. M., Gill, T. V., & Rumbaugh, D. M. (1977). Language relevant object- and color-naming tasks. In D. M. Rumbaugh (Ed.), *Language learning by a chimpanzee*, (pp. 193–206). New York: Academic Press.

Gardner, B. T., & Gardner, R. A. (1971). Two-way communication with an infant chimpanzee. In A. Schrier & F. Stollnitz (Eds.), *Behavior of nonhuman primates*, (Vol. 4, pp. 117–184). New York: Academic Press.

Gardner, B. T., & Gardner, R. A. (1974). Comparing the early utterances of child and chimpanzee. In A. Pick (Ed.), *Minnesota symposium on child psychology*, (Vol. 8, pp. 3–23). Minneapolis: University of Minnesota Press.

Gardner, B. T., & Gardner, R. A. (1975). Evidence for sentence constituents in the early utterances of child and chimpanzee. *Journal of Experimental Psychology: General, 104*, 244–267.

Gardner, R. A., & Gardner, B. T. (1973). Teaching sign language to the chimpanzee, Washoe. (16-mm sound film). State College, PA: Psychological Cinema Register.

Gardner, R. A., & Gardner, B. T. (1974). Teaching sign language to the chimpanzee, Washoe. *Bulletin D'Audio Phonologie, 4*(5), 145–173.

Gardner, R. A., & Gardner, B. T. (1984). A vocabulary test for chimpanzees. *Journal of Comparative Psychology, 98*, 381–404.

Gill, T. V., & Rumbaugh, D. M. (1974). Mastery of naming skills by a chimpanzee. *Journal of Human Evolution, 3*, 483–492.

Hayes, K. J., & Hayes, C. (1953). Picture perception in a home-raised chimpanzee. *Journal of Comparative and Physiological Psychology, 46*, 470–474.

Herrnstein, R. J., Loveland, D. H., & Cable, C. (1976). Natural concepts in pigeons. *Journal of Experimental Psychology: Animal Behavior Processes, 2*, 285–302.

Hicks, L. H. (1956). An analysis of number-concept formation in the rhesus monkey. *Journal of Comparative and Physiological Psychology, 49*, 212–218.

Hockett, C. F. (1978). In search of Jove's brow. *American Speech, 53*(4), 243–314.

Kellogg, W. N., & Kellogg, L. A. (1933). *The ape and the child.* New York: Hafner Publishing Co.

Patterson, J. C., Gardner, B. T., & Gardner, R. A. (1986). Chance expectancy with trial-by-trial feedback and random sampling without replacement. *American Mathematical Monthly, 93*, 520–530.

Pfungst, O. (1911). *Clever Hans* (C. L. Rahn, Trans.). New York: Henry Holt.

Read, R. C. (1962). Card-guessing with information—a problem in a probability. *American Mathematical Monthly, 69*, 506–511.

Sands, S. F., Lincoln, C. E., & Wright, A. A. (1982). Pictorial similarity judgements and the organization of visual memory in the rhesus monkey. *Journal of Experimental Psychology: General, 111*, 369–389.

Savage-Rumbaugh, E. S., Pate, J. L., Lawson, J., Smith, S. T., & Rosenbaum, S. (1983). Can a chimpanzee make a statement? *Journal of Experimental Psychology: General, 112*, 457–492.

Stokoe, W. C. (1983). Apes who sign and critics who don't. In H. T. Wilder & J. de Luce (Eds.), *Language in primates,* (pp. 147–158). Bloomington: Indiana University Press.

Terrace, H. S. (1979). *Nim.* New York: Knopf.

Terrace, H.S., Petitto, L., Sanders, R. J., & Bever, T. G. (1980). On the grammatical capacity of apes. In K. E. Nelson (Ed.), *Children's language,* (Vol. 2, pp. 371–495). New York: Gardner Press.

Warden, C. J., & Warner, L. H. (1928). The sensory capacities and intelligence of dogs with a report on the ability of the noted dog "Fellow" to respond to verbal stimuli. *Quarterly Review of Biology, 3*, 1–28.

5. Developmental Trends in Replies to Wh-questions by Children and Chimpanzees*

Thomas E. Van Cantfort, Beatrix T. Gardner and R. Allen Gardner

Most of the work in child psycholinguistics has been concerned with the evidence for grammatical competence that can be found in the speech that children use in conversations with a parent or some other familiar adult in the home (Bloom et al., 1980; Brown, 1973; de Villiers et al., 1979; Goodluck & Tavakolian, 1982; Tager-Flusberg, 2982). One source of evidence consists of the relation between question and reply when the question is of the type referred to as a "Wh question" (Brown, 1968; Ervin-Tripp, 1970).

In fact, each interrogative word is a kind of dummy element, an algebraic 'X', standing in the place of a particular constituent of the sentence . . . The dummy word asks for specification of that constituent. It marks the spot where information is to be poured into the sentence, and the form of the dummy—whether *who, what, where, when,* or *why*—indicates the sort of information required. . . . In general, each kind of Wh question calls for an answer which is an instance of a particular major sentence constituent. (Brown, 1968, pp. 280–281)

Even before children are able to produce well formed Wh-questions themselves they reply to the Wh-questions of adults. According to Brown, the first evidence that children have the relevant grammatical competence is found in their ability to produce grammatically correct replies to Wh-questions.

In a sense, the ability to restrict replies to the correct sentence constituent is more significant than the ability to give semantically correct answers. For example, when someone asked Washoe, WHO THAT? while indicating Roger S. Fouts, all semantically correct replies had to include the name sign, ROGER, either alone or in a phrase such as THAT ROGER. Nevertheless, incorrect name signs, such as SUSAN or GREG, were still correct in a way that replies

---

*Based on a dissertation submitted by Thomas E. Van Cantfort to the University of Nevada-Reno in partial fulfillment of the requirements for the PhD degree.

such as HAT or BLACK or TICKLE ME were not. The fact that Washoe usually answered Who demonstrative questions with name signs is in some respects more significant than her ability to associate particular name signs with particular individuals in her acquaintance. The restriction of replies to a correct category is also a more general characteristic of replies to Wh-questions, because there is an important group of questions such as WHO GOOD? and WHAT YOU WANT? that refer to matters of opinion and preference rather than to matters of fact. Strictly speaking, the only objective judgment that an observer can make about the correctness of a reply to such a question is a judgment about the correctness of its sentence constituent.

In their pioneering studies, Brown (1968) and Ervin-Tripp (1970) combed through transcripts of adult-child conversations that had been collected earlier, searching for instances in which the adult interlocutor had asked one of the major question types. For each case, the investigator made an ad hoc judgment as to whether the child's answer contained an appropriate sentence constituent. In Project Washoe, a sample of 50 replies to each of 10 different Wh-questions was obtained and the pitfalls of a retrospective analysis were avoided by applying a set of rules that uniquely assigned Washoe's replies to one and only one of the prespecified categories (B. Gardner & Gardner, 1975). Similarly, in more recent Wh-question studies with children, experimenters gather systematic samples of children's replies to Wh-questions and use a priori rules to analyze the replies (Cairns & Hsu, 1978; Parnell, Patterson, & Harding, 1984; Toler & Bankson, 1976; Tyack & Ingram, 1977).

Replies to Wh-questions

Context notes in the field records showed that Washoe often answered ASL equivalents of Wh-questions with appropriate sentence constituents—she answered Who questions with proper nouns and pronouns, What questions with nouns, Where questions with locatives. (For detailed description of the field records see Chapter 3 this volume; B. Gardner & Gardner, 1971, 1975, 1985; R. Gardner & Gardner, 1978.) In the 50th and 51st month of the project, when Washoe was approximately five years old, a systematic sample of replies to Wh-questions was obtained. The analysis showed that Washoe's replies to the question frames Who, What, Where and Whose contained the appropriate sentence constituents 84% of the time (B. Gardner & Gardner, 1975).

Systematic samples of replies to Wh-questions for Moja, Pili, Tatu, and Dar were gathered from an earlier age. In this chapter, we will examine samples taken year by year throughout the second project to: (1) determine the distribution of sentence constituents in the replies of Moja, Pili, Tatu, and Dar to Wh-questions and look for developmental patterns: (2) compare the samples taken for Moja and Tatu at five years of age with the sample taken for five-year-old Washoe; and (3) compare the developmental pattern of replies to Wh-questions for children and cross-fostered chimpanzees.

METHOD

Subjects

The subjects in this longitudinal study were Moja, Pili, Tatu, and Dar. Replies to Wh-questions were collected for Moja at 32, 38, 43, 62, and 74 months of age; for Pili at 20 months of age; for Tatu at 18, 28, 34, 49, and 61 months of age; and for Dar at 21, 26, 37, and 49 months of age. Only one sample of replies to Wh-questions was collected from Pili, who died of leukemia at two years of age (Muchmore & Socha, 1976). During the period that these samples were taken, subjects were under cross-fostering conditions at the Reno laboratory, and ASL was the only language used in their presence (see Chapter 9 this volume, Table 9.1).

Experimenters

Members of the foster families of Moja, Pili, Tatu, and Dar served as the experimenters who gathered samples of replies to Wh-questions. The majority of the experimenters (58%) participated in more than one Wh-question sample.

The preparation of the experimenters for the Wh-question study included discussion of the purpose of each step of the procedure, and a pretest period in which the experimenters practiced the procedures. In the course of the pretest, the wording of the experimenters' Wh-questions and their recording of the subject's replies was examined, and feedback was provided on the gathering of questions and replies. Examples of well-formed Wh-questions were provided throughout the study.

Question Frames

A question frame in this investigation was constructed by combining one interrogative sign with one or more additional signs in such a way that a category of replies was specified. The category that was specified, for each question frame, is listed in Table 5.1 as the *target category*. Also included in Table 5.1 are typical examples of questions and replies that were recorded during this investigation. This procedure for constructing question frames and specifying target categories closely parallels those of Brown (1968) and Ervin-Tripp (1970) in their studies of this aspect of the spontaneous speech of young children.

Adults ask young children many simple Wh-questions, such as What demonstrative, What object of action, Where and What-do. As children grow older, adults gradually add more advanced Wh-questions, such as Who object, Why, When, Which, and How (cf. Ervin-Tripp & Miller, 1977, pp. 18–21).

The wide range of Wh-questions that is typically asked of human children also appears in the everyday discourse between Moja, Pili, Tatu, and Dar and the experimenters (e.g., WHO CHASE DAR? WHERE YOUR BALL? WHAT NAME THAT? WHOSE SHOE?). The question frames that appeared in the early field records showed developmental trends similar to those of comparable samples of human speech and signing. More advanced types of questions

Table 5.1
Question Frames and Target Categories

Question frame	Target category	Examples of questions and replies	
Who demonstrative	Proper nouns (N)	FIRST WHO ME?/ WHAT YOUR NAME?/	TIM D./ ME TATU/
Who subject object trait	Proper nouns (N) or Pronouns (P)	WHO TICKLE?/ WHO ME CHASE?/ WHO GOOD GIRL?/	YOU TICKLE/ CHASE CHASE MOJA/ B. GARDNER/
Who possessive	Possessives (ps)	WHOSE BABY THAT?/ WHOSE WRIST- WATCH THAT?/	MY BABY/ YOURS/
What quality	Attributes (A)	WHAT MAKE THAT?/ WHAT COLOR SHOE?/	METAL/ SHOE BLACK/
What demonstrative	Common nouns (n)	WHAT THIS?/ WHAT NAME THAT?/	LIGHT/ NUT/
What object of action	Common nouns (n)	TATU DRINK WHAT?/ WHAT ME SWALLOW?/	MILK/ NUT SWALLOW/
What want	Common nouns (n) Verbs (V)	WHAT YOU WANT?/ WHAT YOU WANT?/	EAT GUM/ CHASE/
What predicate	Verbs (V)	WHAT ME DO?/ WHAT WE PLAY?/	LAUGH/ TICKLE THERE/
Where action	Locatives (L)	WHERE YOU WANT GO?/ WHERE GROOM?/ TICKLE WHERE?/	 HOME/ GROOM THERE/ THERE/
Where nominal	Locatives (L)	WHERE YOUR BLANKET?/ WHERE TOOTH- BRUSH?/	 BLANKET THERE/ OUT/
How many	Quantitative (Q)	HOW MANY COWS?/ HOW MANY?/	TWO/ ONE/

appeared for the first time in the later records, and gradually became more frequent among the questions asked and answered. Thus, questions such as WHAT THAT? WHAT WANT? WHERE BIB? were predominant in the early field records, while questions such as WHO CHASE PILI? WHAT DO NOW? HOW MANY? appeared later.

Because this was a developmental study, the question frames for each chimpanzee subject varied from sample to sample and more question frames were used in the later samples. The field records for the immediately preceding three months were consulted in selecting question frames for each new sample. During the pretest, there was some further screening of the question frames that had appeared in the current field records. Only those question frames that usually elicited a signed reply from the subject, whether appropriate or inappropriate, were included in the sample. Table 5.2 lists the thirteen different Wh-question frames that were used in the samples, by subject and by age.

English Glosses

Many problems occur in the word-for-word translation from one language to another, such as from German to French. We face many of the same problems of translation in rendering signs of ASL verbatim into English (Stokoe, Casterline, & Croneberg, 1976, see appendix A). ASL, like Chinese and Hungarian languages, but unlike English, omits articles and the copula *to be* and makes very little use of obligatory auxiliary verbs. At the same time, many of the inflections of ASL have no word-for-sign English equivalent. Because of these inflections, certain morphemes that are obligatory in Standard English are optional in ASL as in the face to face conversation of many spoken languages. Thus, exchanges such as WHERE GROOM? GROOM THERE and WHAT COLOR SHOE? SHOE BLACK read quite well in the original ASL, even though they seem highly telegraphic in the word-for-sign English of this volume.

Procedures

The question frames were listed on special data forms that also provided space for recording the text and context of each question and reply. For the early samples, there were two forms each with four or five different Wh-question frames. Alternate forms were used on alternate days. As the subjects grew older, the number of different Wh-question frames increased. In the later samples, three days and three data forms were required to complete one cycle of the set to be sampled. In this case the three different forms were assigned to days so as to sample evenly over questioners and days of the week.

The data form was given to the experimenters at the beginning of a scheduled four to eight hour interation with the subject. The experimenters were instructed to obtain and record a reply for each question frame on the form. The instructions read as follows:

Record the exact signs of the question asked and, if the subject replies, record the exact signed reply and stop further recording for that question frame. If the subject does not reply, record, "No Reply" and try again later, in a different context or with a different question. It is only necessary to try three times for a reply. If the subject has not replied by the third time stop recording for the question type.

The experimenters were allowed three attempts to elicit a reply from the subject for each question frame. If they were not successful on the first attempt, they changed the question and/or the context. When, for example, Susan Nichols asked Moja, WHERE TICKLE NOW? and failed to obtain a reply, she did not repeat the quesiton. After indoor activities were finished, Susan got a coat

Table 5.2
Number of Questions and Replies by Subject, Age and Wh-question Frame

Subject		T	P	D	D	T	M	T	D	M	M	T	D	T	M	M
Age in months		18	20	21	26	28	32	34	37	38	43	49	49	61	62	74
Who demonstrative	Q		9				11	13	16	13	13	10	13	11	10	11
	R		8				8	10	10	12	12	10	10	10	10	10
Who subject/object/trait	Q	12	11	19	18	12	8	25	29	28	38	38	24	30	37	32
	R	10	8	10	10	10	8	20	20	24	36	30	20	30	30	30
Who possessive	Q					13		13	16	12	13	10	11	12	10	10
	R					10		10	10	12	12	10	10	10	10	10
What quality	Q								15	13	14	11	11	10	11	16
	R								10	12	12	10	10	10	10	10
What demonstrative	Q	18	16	16	12	10	8	11	13	15	13	11	11	10	10	10
	R	10	8	10	10	10	8	10	10	12	12	10	10	10	10	10
What object of action	Q							12				12		10		15
	R							10				10		10		10
What want	Q	12	8	18	12	14	9	12	13	12	14	10	10	10	10	10
	R	10	8	10	10	10	6*	10	10	12	12	10	10	10	10	10
What predicate	Q				15			9	10	16	16	12	10	10	13	12
	R				10			9*	9*	12	12	10	10	10	10	10
Where action/nominal	Q	19	10	22	26	12	11	24	33	40	31	29	23	21	25	28
	R	10	8	10	20	10	8	20	20	24	24	20	20	20	20	19*
How many	Q														10	
	R														10	
Total	Q	61	54	75	83	61	47	119	145	149	152	131	125	124	136	144
	R	40	40	40	60	50	38	99	99	120	132	110	110	120	120	119

M = Moja, T = Tatu, P = Pili, and D = Dar; Q = questions, R = replies
*The quota of replies was not obtained due to experimenter error.

for herself and one for Moja, and then asked, WHERE GO? and Moja replied, OUT. The records included the signed reply as well as notes on other behaviors. For example, when Betty Puryear asked Tatu, WHERE COW FOR TICKLE? the data sheet shows that Tatu responded by handing the toy cow to Betty.

The replies to Wh-questions were collected when the experimenter and subjects were alone together; that is, when they were not being visited by other human companions and/or chimpanzees. The experimenters asked several of the different Wh-question frames as they became appropriate during the daily routine. For example, during grooming the experimenter asked, WHAT THAT? for baby oil and then asked, WHERE OIL TATU?; later in the day during a meal the experimenter asked, WHAT WANT EAT? The instructions permitted different Wh-question frames in the same context and different contexts for the same Wh-question frame, but prevented immediate repetition of the same question in the same context. When, for example, Patrick Drumm asked Dar, WHAT NAME THAT? (for a key) and Dar replied, KEY, then Patrick asked, WHAT THAT MAKE FROM? and Dar replied, KEY METAL.

These procedures were continued until the sample contained the required quota of replies for each question frame. In the earliest samples, as few as eight replies fulfilled the quota; for all the later samples, ten replies were required. The advantage of this technique is that the sampling is blended with the daily activities of the chimpanzees. At the same time, this technique ensures a systematic collection of replies for each of the Wh-question frames.

The Samples of Replies Obtained

This longitudinal study was initiated in June 1975, when the first samples for Moja and for Pili were collected. Tatu and Dar joined the study in following years, and the samples of replies were collected until 1981. (See Van Cantfort [1986] for the beginning and ending dates of samples, and the number of days required to gather the replies for each subject for each sample.) Altogether, the subjects were asked 1,606 questions and gave 1,297 signed replies (see Table 5.2). Responses to Wh-questions were signed replies, action responses, such as retrieving toys in response to Where nominal questions, or no response. Only the signed replies to Wh-questions were analyzed in this study.

RESULTS

Classifying Replies

The rules for classifying the replies of Moja, Pili, Tatu, and Dar followed very closely the rules used to analyze Washoe's replies (B. Gardner & Gardner, 1975, pp. 251–252) for classifying both individual signs and combinations of signs. A few minor adjustments were required for the present study which involved four new chimpanzee subjects, with different vocabularies, and several new Wh-question frames.

Classifying Individual Signs

Following the procedure used to analyze Washoe's replies (B. Gardner & Gardner, 1975), each sign in the replies of Moja, Pili, Tatu, and Dar was sorted into one of a set of target categories of sentence constituents (see Tables 5.3–5.6). In ASL, as in English, signs can be assigned to several sentence constituents. For example, the sign COMB can be used as a noun or as a verb. Stokoe, Casterline, and Croneberg (1976) in their *Dictionary of American Sign Language* (*DASL*) indicate whether each entry has nominal or verbal uses, and this was the basis for sorting Moja, Pili, Tatu, and Dar's signs as nouns and verbs.

1.   The category common nouns (n) included all signs that are considered to be nominals in the *DASL* as well as signs, such as COMB and DRINK, that could be used either as nouns or as verbs. Two other types of nouns were assigned to their own target categories: proper nouns and pronouns.

2.   The category proper nouns (N) included all name signs (e.g., MOJA, NAOMI, etc.). The signs FRIEND, BOY/MALE, and GIRL were also included in proper nouns because the chimpanzees often used these signs to label individuals who lacked a name sign, such as new foster family members, visitors, the handyman, etc. (see Table 3.1 this volume).

3.   The category pronouns (P) included such signs as YOU and ME.

4.   The category verbs (V) included signs that are typically used as verbs in ASL (e.g., CHASE).

5.   The category locatives (L) included signs for places and directions (e.g., HOME and UP).

6.   The category modifiers included possessive pronouns (PS), traits (Tr) (e.g., GOOD), attributes (A) (e.g., RED, WHITE), and quantitatives (Q) (e.g., ONE, TWO).

7.   The category markers included such signs as TIME, CAN'T, GIMME, PLEASE, and MORE.

Tables 5.3–5.6 classify the signs in the replies into the above categories for Moja, Pili, Tatu, and Dar.

Classifying Combinations of Signs

The above classification procedure worked well with single sign replies. However, in Washoe's Wh-question test, 46% of the replies contained more than one sign, and often the different signs belonged to different categories (B. Gardner & Gardner, 1975, p. 252). Similarly, many of Moja, Pili, Tatu, and Dar's replies contained more than one sign, and often the different signs

Table 5.3
Signs in All Samples of Replies for Moja, Classified into General Categories

Proper nouns	Pronouns	Common nouns		Modifiers	Markers	Verbs	Locatives
BOY/MALE	ME	APPLE	HORSE	Possessives	CAN'T	BLOW	HOME
B.T.G.	YOU	BALL	HURT	MY/MINE	COME/GIMME	BREAK	IN
CLAYTON V.		BANANA	ICECREAM	YOURS	DON'T KNOW	CHASE	OUT
DAR		BEAR	KEY		HURRY	CRY	THAT/THERE
GREG G.		BED	MEAT	Traits	MORE	GO	UP
HAROLD P.		BERRY	MILK	GOOD	NO	GROOM	
JAMES R.		BIB	MIRROR	SORRY	PLEASE	LAUGH	
JEFFERY B.		BIRD	NUT		WHAT	OPEN	
MOJA		BLINDFOLD	OIL	Colors		SWALLOW	
PATRICK D.		BRUSH	PEN/WRITE	BLACK	Temporal	TICKLE	
PILI		BUG	POTTY	ORANGE	TIME		
R.A.G.		CAT	RIDE	RED			
RONALD B.		CEREAL	SANDWICH	WHITE			
SUSAN N.		CHAIR	SEE				
TIM D.		COAT	SHIRT	Quantitive			
TOM T.		COMB	SHOE	ONE			
		COW	SMELL	TWO			
		CRACKER	SMOKE				
		DIAPER	SODAPOP				
		DOG	SWAB				
		DRINK	SWEET				
		FLOWER	TOOTHBRUSH				
		FOOD/EAT	TOOTHPASTE				
		GLASSES	TREE				
		GUM	VACUUM				
		HANKY	WIPER				
		HEAR/LISTEN	WRISTWATCH				

Table 5.4

Signs in the 20-Month Sample of Replies for Pili, Classified into General Categories

Proper nouns	Common nouns		Markers	Verbs	Locatives
PILI SUSAN N.	BIB CHEESE DOG DRINK FOOD/EAT GUM	HAT LIGHT MILK SHOE TOOTHBRUSH	CAN'T DON'T KNOW MORE	CHASE PEEKABOO TICKLE	THAT/THERE

Table 5.5
Signs in All Samples of Replies for Tatu, Classified into General Categories

Proper nouns	Pronouns	Common nouns		Modifiers	Markers	Verbs	Locatives
BART H.	ME	APPLE	GRAPES	*Possessives* MY/MINE	CAN'T	BITE	HOME
B.T.G.	YOU	BABY	GUM		COME/GIMME	BLOW	OUT
DAR		BED	HEAR/LISTEN		HURRY	CHASE	THAT/THERE
FRIEND		BELT	LIGHT	*Traits* GOOD	MORE	CRY	
GIRL		BERRY	LIPSTICK		NO	GO	
MARK L.		BIB	MASK		PLEASE	HUG	
MARTHA G.		BRUSH	MEAT	*Colors*	*Temporal*	LAUGH	
MOJA		BUG	MILK	BLACK	FINISH	OPEN	
NAOMI R.		CANDY	NUT	ORANGE		PEEKABOO	
R.A.G.		CARROT	OIL	RED		SLEEP	
TATU		CAT	PEACH	*Materials*		TICKLE	
		CHEESE	POTTY	GLASS			
		CLOWN	RIDE				
		COFFEE	SEE				
		COOKIE	SHOE				
		COW	SMELL				
		CRACKER	SODAPOP				
		DIAPER	SOUR				
		DIRTY	SWEET				
		DRINK	TOOTHBRUSH				
		FLOWER	TREE				
		FOOD/EAT	WIPER				

Table 5.6
Signs in All Samples of Replies for Dar, Classified into General Categories

Proper nouns	Pronouns	Common nouns		Modifiers	Markers	Verbs	Locatives
DAR	ME	BALL	HURT	Possessives	CAN'T	BLOW	HOME
ELIZABETH S.	YOU	BERRY	ICECREAM	MY/MINE	COME/GIMME	CHASE	IN
MOJA		BIB	MEAT	YOURS	MORE	GO	OUT
PATRICK D.		BIRD	MILK		PLEASE	GROOM	THAT/THERE
R.A.G.		BRUSH	NUT	Traits		LAUGH	UP
SUSAN N.		CAT	OIL	GOOD		PEEKABOO	
TATU		CEREAL	PEACH			TICKLE	
TOM V.		CHEESE	POTTY	Colors			
TONY M.		COAT	SHIRT	BLACK			
		COFFEE	SHOE	RED			
		COOKIE	SODAPOP				
		COW	SOUR	Materials			
		DRINK	STRING	GLASS			
		FLOWER	SWEET	METAL			
		FOOD/EAT	TABLE	WOOD			
		GRASS	TOOTHBRUSH				
		GUM	WIPER				
		HAT					

belonged to different categories. The a priori rules for classifying their combinations of signs also followed procedures used in B. Gardner and Gardner (1975) as described below.

In ASL, the locatives IN, OUT, and UP can be used either to designate location, as in MILK OUT, or to designate locative action, as in OUT ME. For this investigation, IN, OUT, and UP were classified as locative verbs (VL) when they appeared in replies that included a pronoun or a name sign. When, for example, Moja was asked, WHERE GO? she replied, OUT ME. Accordingly, this reply was classified as a locative verb phrase, of the form P + VL, and entered as a VLP. Further, if any locative was combined with a verb, the reply was also classified as a VLP. When, for example, Dar was asked, WHAT YOU WANT? he replied, GROOM THERE. Accordingly, this reply was classified as a locative verb phrase (VLP). Locatives that occurred alone, and locative phrases that could not become VLP's by the above rules, were entered as L,LP. The combination of a temporal marker with at least one verb, or with a noun that could designate action, such as DRINK, or with a locative that could designate action, such as OUT, was classified as a Temporal Verb Phrase (TVP).

The few remaining cases of phrases that did not fall into any of the major classifications already described were entered into the column labelled "Other," which was divided into two subcolumns: "Appropriate" and "Inappropriate." Multiple sign replies that did not fall into any of the major classifications, but nevertheless contained a sign from the target category, were tabulated as "Appropriate Other." Multiple sign replies that neither fell into any of the above major classifications nor contained signs from the target category were tabulated as "Inappropriate Other."

When more than one sign appeared in the replies of Moja, Pili, Tatu, and Dar, some of the signs were interesting but orthogonal to this analysis. Because they were orthogonal, they could not alter the scoring of the replies. The following set of rules were used to identify these cases.

Incorporations. Human children often incorporate into their replies words found in the eliciting question. This is an important aspect of discourse in that it is an early indicator of topic maintenance in the development of human children (Keenan, 1977; Keenan & Klein, 1975). Washoe, Moja, Pili, Tatu, and Dar used incorporation in a similar way. For example, when Moja was asked, WHERE GRAPES? she replied, GRAPES THERE. While incorporations may serve important pragmatic functions, they are redundant with the eliciting question and for this analysis incorporated signs were not scored. Brown (1968, p. 280) took a similar position in his study of children's replies to Wh-questions.

Reiterations. Speaking children (Keenan, 1977; Nelson, 1980; Scollon, 1979), signing children (Hoffmeister, Moores, & Ellenberger, 1975, p. 123), and signing chimpanzees (Drumm, Gardner, & Gardner, 1986; Chapter 2 this volume) often reiterate words and signs within an utterance. Reiteration seems to function as a pragmatic device indicating emphasis or assent (Drumm, Gardner, & Gardner, 1986). When, for example, Tatu was asked, WHO YOU? she replied, TATU TATU. Since signs that reiterate earlier signs must be from the same sentence constituent category, these signs were scored as a unit.

Duplications. As in the case of human children, the replies of Washoe, Moja, Pili, Tatu, and Dar sometimes included more than one example of the same sentence constituent. When, for example, Naomi Rhodes asked Tatu, WHO ME? Tatu replied, MARTI, MARK, NAOMI. All the signs in her reply repeated the same sentence constituent and were scored as a unit. Perhaps Tatu was guessing, but what is important, for this analysis is that only name signs (N) were used in the reply.

Indexical Signs. In ASL, the pronouns YOU and ME are from a class of signs known as indexical signs. For example, the sign ME is an extended index finger pointing to the signer's chest; whereas, the sign YOU is an extended index finger pointing to the addressee's chest. When YOU or ME occurred in both the question and the reply, the direction of the point determined whether the sign was counted as an incorporation. When, for example, Naomi Rhodes asked Moja, WHO TICKLE YOU? Moja replied, ME. The sign ME in this reply is an incorporation of the sign YOU in the eliciting question because the direction of the point is the same. When Robert Lindsay asked Moja, WHO ME CHASE? Moja replied, CHASE YOU. The sign YOU in this reply is an incorporation of the sign ME in the eliciting question.

The indexical demonstrative sign THIS/THAT/HERE/THERE was incorporated in many of the replies of Moja, Pili, Tatu, and Dar. When, for example, Thomas Van Cantfort asked Dar, WHAT THAT? for a bib, Dar replied, THAT BIB. Only the BIB sign was scored; the sign THAT in this reply was an incorporation and was not scored. When Richard Rosenborg asked Moja, WHOSE THAT COAT? Moja replied, THAT THAT. The signs THAT in this reply were incorporations and were not scored. The sign WHOSE has two components: in the first component, the thumb touches the chin and the index finger makes small circles around the mouth; in the second component, a flat hand indicates the item with the palm directed towards the item. This second component of the WHOSE sign seems related to the indexical signs. Similarly, Hoffmeister (1977) suggested that "the POINT is involved in the more sophisticated operations of ASL: the modulations of verbs and the possessive, reflexive, and plural pronous. All of these operations are directly derived from the system of pointing in ASL" (p. 2). When Naomi Rhodes asked Tatu, WHOSE BLANKET? Tatu replied, THAT THAT MINE. The signs THAT In this reply were incorporations and were not scored.

Markers. The signs listed as markers in Tables 5.3-5.6 serve important functions in the modulation of meaning. Nevertheless, with the exception of the temporal markers, these signs could not alter the appropriateness or inappropriateness of the reply with respect to sentence constituency. Thus, in answer to the question WHO DRINK? Dar replied, DRINK PLEASE YOU. In the scoring of this reply, only YOU was scored; PLEASE, while contextually appropriate, was from the category Marker and was not scored. DRINK was not scored because it was an incorporation. Temporal markers were the only markers scored in this analysis.

Traits. The signs listed as traits in Tables 5.3-5.6 serve important functions in the modulation of meaning. Throughout the day, the human companions asked Moja, Pili, Tatu, and Dar questions that called for GOOD, SORRY, and other trait signs. Nevertheless, in this sample, none of the questions called for a trait reply. Thus, in answer to the question WHO DRINK? Moja replied, GOOD ME. In the scoring of this reply, ME was scored and GOOD, from the category Trait, while highly appropriate to the context, was not called for by the question and hence not scored.

Orthogonals Only. Finally, replies that were entirely comprised of markers or traits, or incorporated signs from the eliciting question were scored as "Inappropriate Other" for this analysis. When for example, Pili was asked WHO TICKLE? he replied, TICKLE. The reply TICKLE was scored as "Inappropriate Other" in this analysis.

Summary

The above rules allowed each reply to be assigned to one and only one sentence constituent category. These categories are proper nouns, pronouns, possessives, attributes, common nouns, verbs, locatives, quantitatives, locative phrases, locative verb phrases, temporal verb phrases, appropriate others and inappropriate others. Once each reply had been assigned to one of this set of mutually exclusive categories, a question frame by target category contingency chi-square analysis was performed on each of the 15 samples of replies.

Interscorer Reliability

Thomas Van Cantfort and James Rimpau used the rules presented in the previous section to assign the 1,297 replies to categories. Thomas Van Cantfort had three years of experience as a member of the foster families of Tatu and Dar, while James Rimpau had four years of experience as a member of the foster families of Moja and Dar; both had been involved in gathering samples of replies for this study. The interscorer agreements range from 93.3% to 100% with an interscorer agreement across all subjects and all samples of 96.8% Those few cases of disagreements between the scorers were clerical errors; that is, one of the two scorers failed to follow the rules. All disagreements were resolved by the two scorers before the statistical analyses were performed. The high level of interscorer reliability that was achieved provides evidence that the rules assign the replies to one and only one sentence constituent category.

Distributional Analyses of the Replies

Inclusive Analyses

The hypothesis that Wh-questions exert control over the replies and that sentence constituents are distributed in an exclusive manner was tested with a question frame by target category contingency chi-square analysis. The hypothesis was tested separately for each sample and for each subject. To perform valid chi-square analyses, there have to be at least as many observations as there are cells in the matrix. In two cases, Moja at 74 months of age and Dar at 37 months of age, there was one less observation than cells. The missing observations were due to experimenter error and were discovered when it was too late to make up for the missing observations. Since the target categories for Where action and Where nominal are both locatives, these question frames were combined in analyzing Moja's sample at 74 months and Dar's sample at 37 months.

Tables 5.7–5.10 show that the question frames exerted a high degree of control over the replies in these samples. The chi-square analysis for Dar's first sample, at 21 months of age, was statistically significant at $p = .0217$. For all the remaining samples, the chi-square analyses were statistically significant beyond the $p < .0005$ level.

The results are also evidence of the power of the original rules in the classification of replies and demonstrate that these rules are constrained by the task and the possible set of replies. Thus, the rules developed for Washoe are cross-validated in the present study.

Restrictive Analyses

A more restrictive assignment of replies to categories was used in constructing Tables 5.11–5.14, which show the distribution of categories for replies that contain only one sign or that contain signs from only one of the categories of Tables 5.3–5.6. Although many of the most interesting replies of the chimpanzees in these samples must be sacrificed in the analyses of Tables 5.11–5.14, the method of inclusion has considerable merit. That is, if the analysis is confined to those replies that contain a single category of signs, then it must be the chimpanzee subject rather than the human experimenter who decided which was the single most important category in each case.

The rules for assigning individual signs to target categories that had been used for the inclusive analyses were used for the restrictive analyses also, with two exceptions. First, in the inclusive analyses, replies from the category "Trait" were assigned to the category "Inappropriate Others." In the restrictive analyses, replies from the category "Trait" were assigned to the target category "Trait (Tr)" (see Tables 5.11–5.14), but were still scored as inappropriate for all 13

Table 5.7

Distribution of Sentence Constituents in All Replies

Moja 32 Months

Question frame	N				Other		Total
	N+P	n	V	L,LP	inapp.	Total	app.
Who demonstrative	4*	2			2	8	4
Who subject/object	2*	1			5	8	2
What demonstrative		6*			2	8	6
What want		2*	1*	3		6	3
Where action/nominal				8*		8	8

chi-square = 54.409, df = 16, p < .0005

Moja 38 Months

Question frame	N		PS							Other		Total	
	N+P	P	PS+n	A	n	TVP	V	VLP	L,LP	app.	inapp.	Total	app.
Who demonstrative	5*				3					2*	2	12	7
Who subject/object		1*	2		3					1*	5	12	2
Who trait	1*				2					2*	7	12	3
Who possessive		2	3*	1	1						5	12	3
What quality				10*	1						1	12	10
What demonstrative					9*					2*	1	12	11
What want		1			2*	1*	2*		3	1*	2	12	6
What predicate/now					4		2*	1*	3	2*		12	5

Top table (continued)

Question frame	N+P	P	PS+n	A	n	TVP	V	VLP	L,LP	app.	inapp.	Total	app.
Where action		1			1				7*	1*	2	12	8
Where nominal		1	1	1	2				2*		5	12	2

chi-square = 240.701, df = 90, p < .0005

Moja 43 Months

	N		PS							Other		Total	
Question frame	N+P	P	PS+n	A	n	TVP	V	VLP	L,LP	app.	inapp.	Total	app.
Who demonstrative	7*									4*	1	12	11
Who subject	1*	6*	1							1*	3	12	8
Who object	2*	4*			1						5	12	6
Who trait	1*	5*			1					1*	4	12	7
Who possessive		2	7*							2*	1	12	9
What quality				9*	3							12	9
What demonstrative			1	1	10*							12	10
What want					4*		3*	1*	1	2*	1	12	10
What predicate		1			6		4*			1*		12	5
Where action		1				1	2	1*	4*		3	12	5
Where nominal		1					2	1*	5*		7	12	5

chi-square = 374.790, df = 100, p < .0005

Cells for appropriate constituents are marked with an asterisk. N = proper noun, P = pronoun, PS = possessive, A = attribute, n = common noun, TVP = temporal verb phrase, V = verb, VLP = locative verb phrase, L = locative, LP = locative phrase, app. = appropriate, inapp. = inappropriate

Table 5.7 (continued)

Moja 62 Months

Question frame	N		PS		n	V	L,LP	Q	Other		Total	
	N+P	P	PS+n	A					app.	inapp.	Total	app.
Who demonstrative	5*	1			3				1*		10	6
Who subject	1*	8*								1	10	9
Who object	5*	1*							1*	3	10	7
Who trait	3*	1*			1					5	10	4
Who possessive		4	6*								10	6
What quality				4*	3				2*	1	10	6
What demonstrative					8*	1				1	10	8
What want					8*	1*	1				10	9
What predicate					5	4*				1	10	4
Where action					1		7*			2	10	7
Where nominal					1		9*				10	9
How many								9*	1*		10	10

chi-square = 476.699, df = 99, $p < .0005$

Moja 74 Months

Question frame	N N+P	P	PS PS+n	A	n	V	VLP	L,LP	Other app.	Other inapp.	Total Total	Total app.
Who demonstrative	8*					1				1	10	8
Who subject		9*							1*		10	10
Who object	1*	3*						1		5	10	4
Who trait	1*	5*							1*	3	10	7
Who possessive		3	4*							3	10	4
What quality				8*	2						10	8
What demonstrative					9*					1	10	9
What object of action				1	7*		1			1	10	7
What want					5*	2*		1		2	10	7
What predicate					4	6*					10	6
Where action/nominal		1			1	1		14*		2	19	14

chi-square = 424.123, df = 90, p < .0005

Cells for appropriate constituents are marked with an asterisk. N = proper noun, P = pronoun, PS = possessive, A = attribute, n = common noun, TVP = temporal verb phrase, V = verb, VLP = locative verb phrase, L = locative, LP = locative phrase, app. = appropriate, inapp. = inappropriate

Table 5.8
Distribution of Sentence Constituents in All Replies

Pili 20 Months								
	N				*Other*			*Total*
Question frame	*N+P*	*n*	*V*	*L,LP*	*app.*	*inapp.*	*Total*	*app.*
Who demonstrative	1*	1	3			3	8	1
Who subject/object	2*	1				5	8	2
What demonstrative		8*					8	8
What want		4*	1*	2	1*		8	6
Where action/nominal		1		3*		4	8	3

chi-square = 47.452, *df* = 20, *p* = .0005

Cells for appropriate constituents are marked with an asterisk. N = proper noun, n = common noun, P = pronoun, V = verb, L = locative, LP = locative phrase, app. = appropriate, inapp. = inappropriate

Wh-question frames. Second, in the inclusive analyses, replies that were entirely comprised of incorporated signs from the eliciting questions were scored as "Inappropriate Others," whereas in the restrictive analyses incorporated replies were omitted.

Because the restrictive analyses were based on a subset of replies, it was necessary to combine several of the Wh-question frames. Since the target categories for Who demonstrative, Who subject, Who object, and Who trait were proper nouns and pronouns, these question frames were combined. The same reasoning holds for combining Where action and Where nominal; both of these question frames call for locatives, so they also were combined.

The more restrictive classification of replies in Tables 5.11–5.14 yields results that are highly similar to the results of Tables 5.7–5.10. For all the subjects and all of the samples, the chi-square analyses were statistically significant. Statistical significance ranged from a probability of .0117 to probabilities below .0005. These results support the hypothesis that Wh-questions exert control over the replies given by the four chimpanzee subjects. In general, the method used in Tables 5.7–5.10 to assign replies to categories is comparable to methods used with children except that, for the chimpanzees, this method assigns verbal units to categories in advance, independently of any contextual information (cf. Brown, 1968; Ervin-Tripp, 1970).

Replication at Age Five

In addition to demonstrating that Moja, Pili, Tatu, and Dar provide the sentence constituents specified by the different Wh-questions, these results also replicate the results of an earlier study with Washoe. The results of Moja

Table 5.9
Distribution of Sentence Constituents in All Replies

Tatu 18 Months

Question frame	P	n	V	L,LP	Other app.	Other inapp.	Total	Total app.
Who subject/object/trait	3*		1	3		3	10	3
What demonstrative		6*			1*	3	10	7
What want		8*		2			10	8
Where action/nominal				6*		4	10	6

chi-square = 36.990, df = 15, p = .0005

Tatu 28 Months

Question frame	N N+P	P	n	V	VLP	L,LP	Other inapp.	Total	Total app.
Who subject/object/trait	3*		1	1			5	10	3
Who possessive	4	1	1			2	2	10	0
What demonstrative			9*				1	10	9
What want			9*		1*			10	10
Where action/nominal	1	1		1		3*	4	10	3

chi-square = 54.417, df = 24, p = .0004

Cells for appropriate constituents are marked with an asterisk. N = proper noun, P = pronoun, PS = possessive, A = attribute, n = common noun, V = verb VLP = locative phrase, L = locative, LP = locative phrase, app. = appropriate, inapp. = inappropriate

Table 5.9 (continued)

Tatu 34 Months

Question frame	N		PS		V		L,LP	Other		Total	
	N+P	P	PS+n	n	V	VLP		app.	inapp.	Total	app.
Who demonstrative	8*				1			1*		10	9
Who subject/object	3*	1*						1*	5	10	5
Who trait	3*	2*							5	10	5
Who possessive	2	1	2*	1	1				3	10	2
What demonstrative				9*	1					10	9
What object of action				3*				1*	5	10	4
What want				6*	2*	1*	1			10	9
What predicate				2	3*	2*	1	1*		9	6
Where action				2			7*		1	10	7
Where nominal				2	2		6*		2	10	6

chi-square = 194.064, df = 72, p < .0005

Tatu 49 Months

Question frame	N		PS	A	n	V	VLP	L,LP	Other		Total	
	N+P	P	PS+n						app.	inapp.	Total	app.
Who demonstrative	7*	2							1*		10	8
Who subject/object	2*	3*						1	1*	3	10	6
Who trait	1*	1*			1					7	10	2
Who possessive		1	7*							2	10	7
What quality				8*					2*		10	10
What demonstrative				1	8*				1*		10	9
What object of action					5*				1*	3	10	6

Question frame	n	V	VLP	L,LP	Other app.	Other inapp.	Total	Total app.
What want	7*			3			10	7
What predicate	1	6*		1		2	10	6
Where action		2	1*	7*			10	8
Where nominal		1		6*		3	10	6

chi-square = 375.660, df = 90, p < .0005

Tatu 61 Months

Question frame	N		PS	A	n	V	VLP	L,LP	Other		Total	Total
	N+P	P	PS+n						app.	inapp.	Total	app.
Who demonstrative	9*								1*		10	10
Who subject	4*	3*				1				2	10	7
Who object	4*	2*				1				5	10	4
Who trait	4*	1							1*	3	10	7
Who possessive	3		6*								10	6
What quality		1		7*					1*		10	8
What demonstrative				1	9*						10	9
What object of action					9*				1*		10	10
What want					2*	1*	1*				10	4
What predicate					1	7*	1*			1	10	8
Where action					1			5*		4	10	5
Where nominal					1			7*		3	10	7

chi-square = 412.288, df = 99, p < .0005

Cells for appropriate constituents are marked with an asterisk. N = proper noun, P = pronoun, PS = possessive, A = attribute, n = common noun, V = verb, VLP = locative verb phrase, L = locative, LP = locative phrase, app. = appropriate, inapp. = inappropriate

Table 5.10
Distribution of Sentence Constituents in All Replies

Dar 21 Months

Question frame	PS		n	V	L,LP	Other inapp.	Total	Total app.
	P	PS+n						
Who subject/object/trait	1*		1			8	10	1
What demonstrative		1	6*			3	10	6
What want			6*	1*		2	10	7
Where action/nominal					2*	8	10	2

chi-square = 27.985, df = 15, p = .0217

Dar 26 Months

Question frame	N		PS+n	n	V	L,LP	Other inapp.	Total	Total app.
	N+P	P							
Who subject/object/trait	1*	1*					8	10	2
What demonstrative				7*	1		2	10	7
What want				3*	3*	3	1	10	6
What predicate				2	5*	3		10	5
Where action						8*	2	10	8
Where nominal				1	1	4*	4	10	4

chi-square = 66.755, df = 25, p < .0005

Dar 37 Months

Question frame	N		A	PS	n	V	VLP	L,LP	Other		Total	
	N+P	P		PS+n					app.	inapp.	Total	app.
Who demonstrative	5*	1						2	2*		10	7
Who subject/object	2*	5*			1			1		1	10	7

	N	PS		A	n	V	VLP	L, LP	Other app.	Other inapp.	Total	app.
Who trait	3*	1*		1*		1			1	1*	3	5
Who possessive	3	1								5	10	1
What quality					8*				1		10	8
What demonstrative						9*			1		10	9
What want						4*	1*		3	1*	10	6
What predicate						2	3*	3	3	1*	9	4
Where action/nominal						3	3	8*	8*	6	20	8

chi-square = 222.456, df = 72, p < .0005

Dar 49 Months

Question frame	N (N+P)	PS	PS+n	A	n	V	VLP	L, LP	Other app.	Other inapp.	Total	Total app.
Who demonstrative	6*			1					1*		10	7
Who subject					2				2*	6	10	2
Who object			2		1					7	10	2
Who trait	4*				2				1*	1	10	5
Who possessive			5*						2*	2	10	7
What quality				6*					1*	2	10	7
What demonstrative				1	7*			1		1	10	7
What want						1*		3			10	6
What predicate					4	3*	1*	2			10	4
Where action					1			8*		1	10	8
Where nominal					1	2				6	10	0

chi-square = 251.594, df = 80, p < .0005

Cells for appropriate constituents are marked with an asterisk. N = proper noun, P = pronoun, PS = possessive, A = attribute, n = common noun, V = verb, VLP = locative verb phrase, L = locative, LP = locative phrase, app. = appropriate, inapp. = inappropriate

Table 5.11
Distribution of Sentence Constituents in Single Category Replies

Moja 32 Months								
Question frame	*N,P*	*n*	*V*	*L*	*Tr*	*Total*		
Who questions	6*	3				9		
What demonstrative		6*			1	7		
What want		2*	1*	1		4		
Where action/nominal				7*		7		

chi-square = 43.608, *df* = 12, *p* < .0005

Moja 38 Months								
Question frame	*N,P*	*PS*	*A*	*n*	*V*	*L*	*Tr*	*Total*
Who questions	7*	1		7			1	16
Who possessive	2	3*	1	1		1		8
What quality			10*	1				11
What demonstrative				9*				9
What want	1			2*	2*	2		7
What predicate				4	2*	3		9
Where action/nominal	1	1	1	3	1	8*		15

chi-square = 122.717, *df* = 36, *p* < .0005

Moja 43 Months								
Question frame	*N,P*	*PS*	*A*	*n*	*V*	*L*	*Tr*	*Total*
Who questions	26*	1		2			1	30
Who possessive	2	7*						9
What quality			9*	3				12
What demonstrative		1	1	10*				12
What want				4*	3*			7
What predicate	1			6	4*			11
Where action/nominal	1			1	2	9*		13

chi-square = 254.579, *df* = 36, *p* < .0005

Moja 62 Months								
Question frame	*N,P*	*PS*	*A*	*n*	*V*	*L*	*Q*	*Total*
Who questions	24*			4				28
Who possessive	4	6*						10
What quality			4*	3				7
What demonstrative				8*	1			9

Table 5.11 (continued)

	N,P	PS	A	n	V	L	Tr	Total
What want					8*	1*	1		10
What predicate					5	4*			9
Where action/nominal					2		15*		17
How many								9*	9

chi-square = 370.350, df = 42, p < .0005

Moja 74 Months								
Question frame	N,P	PS	A	n	V	L	Tr	Total
Who questions	26*				1	1	1	29
Who possessive	3	4*						7
What quality			8*	2				10
What demonstrative				9*				9
What object of action				1	7*			8
What want					5*	2*	1	8
What predicate					4	6*		10
Where action/nominal	1				1	1	14*	17

chi-square = 296.738, df = 42, p < .0005

Cells for appropriate constituents are marked with an asterisk. N = proper noun, P = pronoun, PS = possessive, A = attribute, n = common noun, V = verb, L = locative, Q = quantity, Tr = trait.

Table 5.12
Distribution of Sentence Constituents in Single Category Replies

Pili 20 Months					
Question frame	N,P	n	V	L	Total
Who questions	3*	2	3		8
What demonstrative		8*			8
What want		4*	1*	1	6
Where action/nominal			1	3*	4

chi-square = 28.213, df = 9, p = .0009

Cells for appropriate constituents are marked with an asterisk. N = proper noun, P = pronoun, n = common noun, V = verb, L = locative.

Table 5.13
Distribution of Sentence Constituents in Single Category Replies

Tatu 18 Months					
Question frame	*N,P*	*n*	*V*	*L*	*Total*
Who questions	3*		1	3	7
What demonstrative		6*			6
What want		8*		2	10
Where action/nominal				6*	6

chi-square = 33.519, *df* = 9, *p* = .0001

Tatu 28 Months					
Question frame	*N,P*	*n*	*V*	*L*	*Total*
Who questions	3*	1			4
Who possessive	5	1			6
What demonstrative		9*			9
What want		9*			9
Where action/nominal	2		1	3*	6

chi-square = 44.058, *df* = 12, *p* < .0005

Tatu 34 Months						
Question frame	*N,P*	*PS*	*n*	*V*	*L*	*Total*
Who questions	17*			1		18
Who possessive	3	2*	1	1		7
What demonstrative			9*	1		10
What object of action			3*			3
What want			6*	2*		8
What predicate			2	3*		5
Where action/nominal			2	2	13*	17

chi-square = 136.263, *df* = 24, *p* < .0005

Tatu 49 Months								
Question frame	*N,P*	*PS*	*A*	*n*	*V*	*L*	*Tr*	*Total*
Who questions	16*						1	1	18
Who possessive	1	7*							8
What quality			8*						8
What demonstrative			1	8*					9
What object of action	1			5*					6

Table 5.13 (continued)

What want				6*		1		7
What predicate				1	6*			7
Where action/nominal					3	13*		16

chi-square = 301.592, *df* = 42, *p* < .0005

Tatu 61 Months								
Question frame	*N,P*	*PS*	*A*	*n*	*V*	*L*	*Tr*	*Total*
Who questions	24*				2			26
Who possessive	4	5*						9
What quality	1		7*					8
What demonstrative			1	9*				10
What object of action				9*				9
What want				2*	1	5		8
What predicate				1	7*		1	9
Where action/nominal				1		12*		13

chi-square = 321.136, *df* = 42, *p* < .0005

Cells for appropriate constituents are marked with an asterisk. N = proper noun, P = pronoun, PS = possessive, A = attribute, n = common noun, V = verb, L = locative, Tr = trait

and Tatu at five years of age were compared with Washoe's results at the same age. Washoe's estimated age was ten months when she arrived in Reno, and the Wh-question sample was gathered in the 50th and 51st month of Project Washoe. Washoe's replies to the question frames Who, What, Where, and Whose contained the appropriate sentence constituents 84% of the time (B. Gardner & Gardner, 1975). The question frame by target category contingency chi-square for Washoe was 1,196.5 with 90 degrees of freedom. With 90 degrees of freedom, a chi-square of 140.8 is required for significance at *p* < .0005. These results demonstrate that Wh-questions exerted a high degree of control over Washoe's replies.

In his study of children's replies to Wh-questions, Brown (1968) concluded that children demonstrate mastery of a Wh-question when they provide the appropriate sentence constituent about half the time. Using Brown's criterion of mastery of Wh-questions, Washoe had reached or surpassed this criterion for Who, What, Where, and Whose (see Table 5.15). Washoe's percentage of appropriate replies to the ten Wh-question frames formed by combining these major interrogatives with other signes ranged from 56% to 100%.

Table 5.14
Distribution of Sentence Constituents in Single Category Replies

Dar 21 Months					
Question frame	*N,P*	*n*	*V*	*L*	*Total*
Who questions	1*	1			2
What demonstrative		6*			6
What want		6*	1*	1*	8
Where action/nominal				2*	2

chi-square = 21.231, *df* = 9, *p* = .0117

Dar 26 Months					
Question frame	*N,P*	*n*	*V*	*L*	*Total*
Who questions	2*				2
What demonstrative		7*	1		8
What want		3*	3*	3	9
What predicate		2	5*	3	10
Where action/nominal		1	1	12*	14

chi-square = 70.132, *df* = 12, *p* < .0005

Dar 37 Months							
Question frame	*N,P*	*PS*	*A*	*n*	*V*	*L*	*Total*
Who questions	16*			2		3	21
Who possessive	4	1*					5
What quality			8*	2			10
What demonstrative				9*			9
What want				4*		3	7
What predicate				2	3*	3	8
Where action/nominal				3	3	6*	12

chi-square = 148.893, *df* = 30, *p* < .0005

Dar 49 Months								
Question frame	*N,P*	*PS*	*A*	*n*	*V*	*L*	*Tr*	*Total*
Who questions	12*	1	1	7				21
Who possessive		5*	1					6
What quality	1		6*					7
What demonstrative			1	7*				8

Table 5.14 (continued)

Dar 49 Months								
Question frame	N,P	PS	A	n	V	L	Tr	Total
What want	1			5*	1*	3		10
What predicate				4	3*	2		9
Where action/nominal			1	2		6*	1	10
chi-square = 150.355, df = 36, p < .0005								

Cells for appropriate constituents are marked with an asterisk. N = proper noun, P = pronoun, PS = possessive, A = attribute, n = common noun, V = verb, L = locative, Tr = trait.

Washoe's sample can be compared with Moja's sample at 62 months of age and Tatu's sample at 61 months of age. The Wh-question samples for Washoe, Moja, and Tatu were very similar (see Tables 5.7, 5.9, and 5.15). Both samples of replies to the question frames for Moja and for Tatu contained the appropriate sentence constituents 71% of the time. The question frame by target category contingency chi-square for Moja and Tatu was 476.7 and 412.3, respectively, with 99 degrees of freedom. With 99 degrees of freedom, a chi-square of 151.9 is required for significance at $p < .0005$. Like Washoe, Moja and Tatu reached Brown's criterion of mastery for the interrogatives Who, What, Where, and Whose (see Table 5.16). Both for Moja and for Tatu, 10 of the 12 individual Wh-question frames that can be formed with Who, What, Where, and Whose had reached Brown's criterion of mastery (see Tables 5.7, 5.9 and 5.17).

Beyond replicating the Washoe study, this study with Moja and Tatu expanded the analysis by including several additional Wh-question frames. Tatu provided the appropriate sentence constituents for What object of action 100% of the time, while Moja provided the appropriate sentence constituents for How many 100% of the time. In the earlier study, Washoe was asked Who action questions. In the present study, this ambiguous question was refined, and Moja and Tatu were asked Who subject questions (e.g., WHO CHASE TATU?), which call for an agent reply, and Who object questions (e.g., WHO MOJA CHASE?), which call for a patient reply. These questions turned out to be unequal in difficulty. Both for Moja and for Tatu, the Who subject questions yielded a higher percentage of appropriate replies than the Who object questions (90% vs. 70% in the case of Moja and 70% vs. 40% in the case of Tatu).

Developmental Trends

Replies to Questions

As children grow older, they are more and more likely to respond to questions by adults (Bloom, Rocissano, & Hood, 1976; Cairns & Hsu, 1978; Ervin-

Table 5.15
Distribution of Sentence Constituents in All Replies

Washoe 61 Months

Question frame	N		PS		C	n	TVP	V	VLP	L,LP	Other		Total	Total
	N+P	P	PS+n								app.	inapp.	Total	app.
Who pronoun	48*					1					1*		50	49
Who action	10*	29*					1*		2*	1*	2*	5	50	45
Who trait	11*	20*				5	1				1*	12	50	32
Whose demonstrative	2	1	44*			1					1*	1	50	45
What color					43*	3					4*		50	47
What demonstrative						50*							50	50
What now	1	2				1	35*	4*	4*	1	1*	1	50	44
What want	3					17*	4*	7*	7*	3	6*	3	50	41
Where action	1	1				1	1		5*	33*		8	50	38
Where object@	1	2				3	1	3	1	24*		9	43	24

chi-square = 1,196.5, df = 90, p < .0005

Cells for appropriate constituents are marked with an asterisk. N = proper noun, P = pronoun, PS = possessive, C = color, n = common noun, TVP = temporal verb phrase, V = verb, VLP = locative verb phrase, L = locative, LP = locative phrase, app. = appropriate, inapp. = inappropriate

@ This row only contains 43 cases, see original article for explanation.

From: Gardner, B.T. and Gardner, R.A. Evidence for sentence constituents in the early utterances of child and chimpanzee. *Journal of Experimental Psychology: General*, 1975, *104*, 3, 244-267.

Tripp, 1970; Parnell, Patterson & Harding, 1984; Toler & Bankson, 1976; Tyack & Ingram, 1977). For example, Bloom, Rocissano and Hood (1976, p. 538) reported the percentage of replies to Wh- and Yes/No questions ranged from a low of 53% at stage 1 to a high of 97% at stage 5. Just like children, Moja, Tatu, and Dar showed a similar developmental pattern in their replies to Wh-questions asked by adults (see Figure 5.1). The percentage of replies to Wh-questions, for the chimpanzee subjects, ranged from a low of 53% in the early samples to a high of 96% in the later samples.

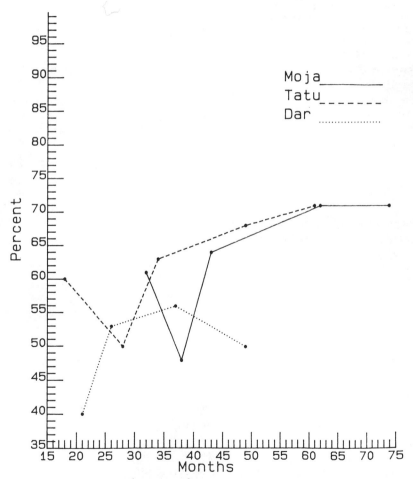

Fig. 5.1 Percent of replies to Wh-questions by age.

As Moja, Tatu, and Dar grew older, the number of question frames increased, and the percentage of replies to Wh-questions increased (see Table

Table 5.16

Percent Appropriate Replies to Who, What, Where, and Whose Questions by Age for Moja, Tatu, and Dar

Moja/Age in months	32	38	43	62	74
What questions	64*	67*	71*	68*	74*
Where questions	100*	42	42	80*	74*
Who questions	38	33	67*	62*	73*
Whose questions	—	25	75*	60*	40
How many	—	—	—	100*	—
Tatu/Age in months	*18*	*28*	*34*	*49*	*61*
What questions	75*	95*	74*	76*	78*
Where questions	60*	30	65*	70*	60*
Who questions	30	30	63*	53*	70*
Whose questions	—	0	20	70*	60*
Dar/Age in months	*21*	*26*	*37*	*49*	
What questions	65*	60*	69*	60*	
Where questions	20	60*	40	40	
Who questions	10	20	63*	40	
Whose questions	—	—	10	70*	

*The appearance of words from the appropriate category in half the replies is the criterion used to attribute mastery of a question form to children (Brown, 1968; Ervin-Tripp, 1970).

5.2). There was also an increase in the number of different signs recorded in the replies to Wh-questions. When Moja was first tested, at 32 months of age, 19 different signs were recorded in her replies, while in her last test, at 74 months of age, 47 different signs were recorded. Similarly, when Tatu was first tested, at 18 months of age, 15 different signs were recorded in her replies, while in her last test, at 61 months of age, 43 different signs were recorded. And also when Dar was first tested, at 21 months of age, 15 different signs were recorded in his replies, while in his last test, at 49 months of age, 48 different signs were recorded.

As children grow older, more of their replies to adults' questions are grammatically appropriate. Tyack and Ingram (1977, p. 219) reported, in their cross-sectional study, an increase in the percent of appropriate replies starting from a low of 53% for children of the youngest group (36–41 months) and increasing to a high of 67% for children of the oldest group (60–65 months). Just like children, Moja, Tatu, and Dar showed a similar developmental pattern in their appropriate replies to Wh-questions asked by adults (see Figure 5.2). Although the early results from this study were collected from chimpanzee subjects that were younger than the youngest children in Tyack and Ingram's study, the pat-

Table 5.17
Percent of Appropriate Replies to Different Wh-question Frames by Age for Moja, Tatu, and Dar

Moja/Age in months	32	38	43	62	74
What demonstrative	75*	92*	83*	80*	90*
Who demonstrative	50*	58*	92*	60*	80*
What want	50*	50*	83*	90*	70*
Where action/nominal	100*	42	42	80*	74*
What quality	—	83*	75*	60*	80*
Who subject/object/trait	25	21	58*	67*	70*
Who possessive	—	25	75*	60*	40
How many	—	—	—	100*	—
What object of action	—	—	—	—	70*
What predicate	—	42	42	40	60*

Tatu/Age in months	18	28	34	49	61
What want	80*	100*	90*	70*	40
What demonstrative	70*	90*	90*	90*	90*
Where action/nominal	60*	30	65*	70*	60*
Who demonstrative	—	—	90*	80*	100*
What predicate	—	—	67*	60*	80*
Who subject/object/trait	30	30	50*	40	60*
What quality	—	—	—	100*	80*
Who possessive	—	0	20	70*	60*
What object of action	—	—	40	60*	100*

Dar/Age in months	21	26	37	49	
What demonstrative	60*	70*	90*	70*	
What want	70*	60*	60*	60*	
Where action/nominal	20	60*	40	40	
What predicate	—	50*	44	40	
What quality	—	—	80*	70*	
Who demonstrative	—	—	70*	70*	
Who subject/object/trait	10	20	60*	30	
Who possessive	—	—	10	70*	

*The appearance of words from the appropriate category in half the replies is the criterion used to attribute mastery of a question form to children (Brown, 1968; Ervin-Tripp, 1970).

tern is similar. The percent of appropriate replies, for the chimpanzee subjects, ranged from a low of 40% in the early samples to a high of 71% in the later samples.

Types of Wh-questions

Table 5.16 lists the percent of appropriate replies, for Moja, Tatu, and Dar, to Who questions (the sum of Who demonstrative and Who subject, object, trait), What questions (the sum of What quality, What demonstrative, What object of action, What want, and What predicate), Where questions (the sum of Where action and Where nominal), and Whose questions. Moja, Tatu, and Dar showed a similar order in the of mastery of Wh-questions among themselves, but just like children (Ervin-Tripp, 1970, p. 89), there was variability in the specific sequence in which each of the chimpanzees mastered the Wh-question frames (Table 5.16). Using the same criterion for mastery as has been used with children (Brown, 1968; Ervin-Tripp, 1970), Moja, Tatu, and Dar were replying appropriately to questions containing What and Where in their early samples, but not yet to questions containing Who and Whose. It was only in the later samples that Moja, Tatu, and Dar used proper nouns and pronouns in over half their replies to Who questions, and possessive pronouns (MINE and YOURS) in over half their replies to Whose questions. In the sample taken when Moja was 62 months old, she was replying appropriately to Who, What, Where and Whose, as before. In addition, she was replying with number signs to most of the questions containing How many. Similarly, in the case of children, both Brown (1968) and Ervin-Tripp (1970) agreed that stage 3 children should be credited with mastery of Who, What, and Where questions. In addition, the children studied by Brown responded appropriately to What do (our What predicate) questions, while Ervin-Tripp's subjects responded appropriately to Whose questions. Neither Brown nor Ervin-Tripp found evidence for mastery of Why, How, or When.

Table 5.17 shows the percent of appropriate replies to each Wh-question frame for each subject by age. Again, using Brown's (1968) 50% criterion of mastery as a convenient benchmark, Tatu, at 18 months of age, met or surpassed the 50% criterion for replies to What want, What demonstrative, and Where action/nominal. It was not until Tatu was 34 months of age that she met or surpassed the 50% criterion for replies to Who demonstrative, What predicate, and Who subject/object/trait. And it was still later, at 49 months of age, that Tatu met or surpassed the 50% criterion for replies to What quality, Who possessive, and What object of action. In Moja's first sample, at 32 month of age, replies to What demonstrative, Who demonstrative, What want, and Where action/nominal met or surpassed Brown's criterion. It was not until Moja was 43 months of age that she met or surpassed the 50% criterion for replies to What quality, Who subject/object/trait, and Who possessive. And it

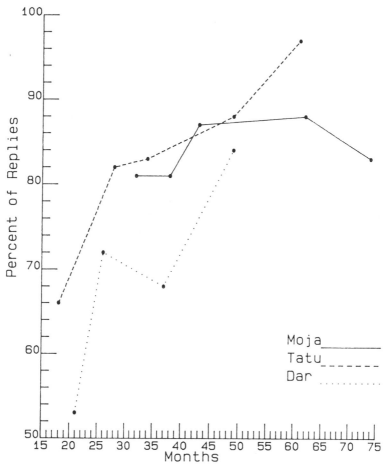

Fig. 5.2 Percent of appropriate replies to Wh-questions.

was still later, at 74 months of age, that Moja met or surpassed the 50% criterion for replies to How many, What object of action, and What predicate. Table
5.17 also shows a similar pattern for Dar.

The individual question frames were formed by combining a major interrogative sign with other signs. The interrogatives Who and What were combined with either a demonstrative sign (e.g., WHO THAT? or WHAT THAT?)
or with an action sign (e.g., WHO CHASE YOU? WHAT PLAY?). Moja, Tatu,
and Dar showed a developmental pattern in providing appropriate replies to
these different Wh-question frames. Table 5.17 shows that when questions
were formed by combining Who and What with a demonstrative sign, the subjects gave appropriate replies at an earlier age than when these major interrogatives were combined with an action sign. The subjects gave appropriate replies
to What demonstrative questions before What predicate questions, and gave

appropriate replies to Who demonstrative questions before Who subject/object/trait questions. The major interrogative Where was combined with either an action sign (e.g., WHERE GO? WHERE TICKLE?) or a nominal sign (e.g., WHERE COW? WHERE YOUR SHIRT?). Moja, Tatu, and Dar showed a developmental pattern for these two types of Where questions. For all subjects, the Where action question in the early samples yielded a higher percentage of appropriate replies than the Where nominal question (see Tables 5.7, 5.8, 5.9 and 5.10).

DISCUSSION

Both in Project Washoe, and in its sequel with the chimpanzees Moja, Pili, Tatu, and Dar, we tried to avoid the problem of devising a priori definitions of language that might satisfy linguists, psycholinguists or behaviorists, either individually or collectively. Our strategy has been to obtain observations on the acquisition of sign language by young chimpanzees that can be compared with the observations of the acquisition of spoken languages or sign languages by young human children. Any theoretical interpretations that can be applied to the early utterances of children can also be applied to the early utterance of chimpanzees. If the children can be said to have acquired some aspect of language on the basis of their performance, then the chimpanzees can be said to have acquired that aspect of language to the extent that their performance matches that of children.

The longitudinal samples of replies to Wh-questions by cross-fostered chimpanzees revealed a developmental pattern comparable to that reported for human children. As children grow older, the percent of replies to questions asked by adults increases, and furthermore, the percent of appropriate replies also increases. Moja, Tatu, and Dar showed a similar developmental pattern in their replies to questions asked by adults (see Figures 5.1 and 5.2). Just like human children, these chimpanzees followed a rough order in the types of Wh-questions that they answered appropriately. Both children and chimpanzees, initially, provide nominals for What questions and locatives for Where questions, followed by verbs for What do/predicate questions and proper nouns and pronouns for Who questions, and followed still later by appropriate replies to How questions. Appropriate answers to the other types of Wh-questions, such as When questions, appear much later in the developmental patterns for children and have not yet been studied for chimpanzees (for children see Ervin-Tripp, 1970, p. 105; for chimpanzees see Tables 5.16 and 5.17). Within the different kinds of questions that can be formed with the major interrogatives, we also found a comparable pattern for children and for chimpanzees. For example, both children and chimpanzees provide appropriate replies to Who subject questions earlier than Who object questions (for children see Ervin-Tripp, 1970, p. 89; for chimpanzees see Tables 5.7 and 5.9).

In the case of children, replying to Wh-questions has been considered evidence of grammatical competence—that children categorize the words that they use as constituents of sentences, such as agents, actions, and objects of actions (Brown, 1968; Veneziano, 1985). At the same time, the question-and-answer process exhibits a basic coordination between participants in discourse. For children, answering questions and providing only the information that is requested by the Wh- interrogative is taken as evidence of pragmatic or conversational competence (Ervin-Tripp, 1970; Anselmi, Tomasello, & Acunzo, 1986).

In this view, the study of replies to Wh-questions by chimpanzees builds upon and expands the findings on the semantically appropriate use of individual signs, reported in Chapters 3 and 4 of this volume. The acquisition of signs by chimpanzees—just as the acquisition of words and signs by children—can be characterized by three networks of connections that develop concurrently. The first of these networks develops between signs and their referents; the second develops among the signs themselves, and governs the ways in which they can be combined; and the third develops between the signing of participants in discourse, and makes possible conversational interchanges.

References

Anselmi, D., Tomasello, M., & Acunzo, M. (1986). Young children's responses to neutral and specific contingent queries. *Journal of Child Language, 13,* 135–144.

Bloom, L., Lahey, J., Hood, L., Lifter, K., & Fiess, K. (1980). Complex sentences: Acquisition of syntactic connectives and relations they encode. *Journal of Child Language, 7,* 235–261.

Bloom, L., Rocissano, L., & Hood, L. (1976). Adult-child discourse. *Cognitive Psychology, 8,* 521–552.

Brown, R. (1968). The development of Wh questions in child speech. *Journal of Verbal Learning and Verbal Behavior, 7,* 277–290.

Brown, R. (1970). The first sentences of child and chimpanzee. In R. Brown (Ed.), *Selected psycholinguistic papers,* (pp. 208–281). New York: Macmillan.

Brown, R. (1973). *A first language: The early stages.* Cambridge, MA: Harvard University Press.

Cairns, H., & Hsu, J. (1978). Who, why, when and how: A development study. *Journal of Child Language, 5,* 477–488.

de Villiers, J., Tager-Flusberg, H., Hakuta, K., & Cohen, M. (1979). Children's comprehension of relative clauses. *Journal of Psycholinguistic Research, 8,* 499–518.

Drumm, P., Gardner, B.T., & Gardner, R.A. (1986). Vocal and gestural response by cross-fostered chimpanzees. *American Journal of Psychology, 99* (1), 1–29.

Ervin-Tripp, S. (1970). Discourse agreement: How children answer questions. In J. Hayes (Ed.), *Cognition and the development of language*, (pp. 79–107). New York: John Wiley & Sons.

Ervin-Tripp, S., & Miller, W. (1977). Early discourse: Some questions about questions. In M. Lewis & L. Rosenblum (Eds.), *Interaction, conversation and the development of language*, (pp. 9–25). New York: John Wiley & Sons.

Gardner, B.T., & Gardner, R.A. (1971). Two-way communication with an infant chimpanzee. In A. Schrier & F. Stollnitz (Eds.), *Behavior of nonhuman primates*. (Vol. 4, pp. 117–184). New York: Academic Press.

Gardner, B.T., & Gardner, R.A. (1975). Evidence for sentence constituents in the early utterances of child and chimpanzee. *Journal of Experimental Psychology: General, 104*, 244–267.

Gardner, B.T., & Gardner, R.A. (1985). Signs of intelligence in cross-fostered chimpanzees. *Philosophical Transactions of the Royal Society, B 308*, 159–176.

Gardner, R.A., & Gardner, B.T. (1978). Comparative psychology and language acquisition. *Annals of the New York Academy of Science, 309*, 37–76.

Goodluck, H., & Tavakolian, S. (1982). Competence and processing in children's grammar of relative clauses. *Cognition, 11*, 1–27.

Hoffmeister, R. (June, 1977). The influential POINT. Paper presented at the National Symposium on Sign Language Research and Training, Chicago.

Hoffmeister, R., Moores, D., & Ellenberger, R. (1975). Some procedural quidelines for the study of the acquisition of sign languages. *Sign Language Studies, 7*, 121–137.

Keenan, E. (1977). Making it last: Repetition in children's discourse. In S. Ervin-Tripp and C. Mitchell-Kernan (Eds.), *Child discourse*, (pp. 125–138). New York: Academic Press.

Keenan, E., & Klein, E. (1975). Coherency in children's discourse. *Journal of Psycholinguistic Research, 4*, 365–380.

Muchmore, E., & Socha, W. (1976). Blood transfusion therapy for leukemic chimpanzee. *Laboratory Primate Newsletter, 15*(3), 13–15.

Nelson, K. (1980). First words of the chimp and child. Paper presented at the Southeastern Psychological Association, Washington, D.C.

Parnell, M., Patterson, S., & Harding, M. (1984). Answers to Wh-questions: A developmental study. *Journal of Speech and Hearing Research, 27*, 297–305.

Scollon, R. (1979). A real early stage: An unzippered condensation of a dissertation on child language. In E. Ochs and B. Schieffelin (Eds.), *Developmental pragmatics*, (pp. 215–227). New York: Academic Press.

Stokoe, W., Casterline, D., & Croneberg, C. (1976). *A dictionary of American Sign Language on linguistic principles.* (New edition). Silver Spring, MD: Linstok Press.

Tager-Flusberg, H. (1982). The development of relative clauses in child speech. *Papers and Reports on Child Language Development, 21,* 104–111.

Toler, S., & Bankson, N. (1976). Utilization of an interrogative model to evaluate mothers' use and children's comprehension of question forms. *Journal of Speech and Hearing Disorder, 41,* 301–314.

Tyack, D., & Ingram, D. (1977). Children's production and comprehension of questions. *Journal of Child Language, 4,* 211–224.

Van Cantfort, T. (1986). Developmental trends in the replies of chimpanzees to Wh-questions. Unpublished doctoral dissertation. University of Nevada - Reno.

Veneziano, E. (1985). Replying to mother's questions: A way to lexical acquisition. *Journal of Pragmatics, 9,* 433–452.

6. Expression of Person, Place, and Instrument in ASL Utterances of Children and Chimpanzees*

James B. Rimpau, R. Allen Gardner and Beatrix T. Gardner

E ach language uses a mixture of devices such as markers, inflections and word order to modulate meaning. English is unusual in its heavy reliance on word order for the modulation of meaning; ASL, like most human languages, relies more heavily on inflectional devices (Klima & Bellugi, 1979, pp. 299 & 314). Dictionaries of ASL and books that teach vocabulary describe signs in citation form—the form that is seen when an informant is asked "What is the sign for X?" Descriptions of inflected forms can be found in books that teach conversational usage such as Fant's (1972) introduction to ASL. Fant's objective was to teach hearing persons "how to put signs together the way deaf people do" (p. vi) and his lessons include many examples of modulated signs. The sign LIKE is shown with two hands and with one hand; the two-handed version expresses that you like something very much (p. 35). The sign EAT, when made with both hands moving alternately and repeatedly, indicates a banquet or a big meal (p. 46). Normally, the sign ALL-RIGHT is made with just one movement, but in excusing a minor social error, such as someone forgetting your name, two small quick movements are used to emphasize that it is a casual, unimportant circumstance (p. 7).

As Fant (1972) points out, an important set of modulations for ASK, GIVE, MEET, and many other verbs make use of the *sight line*:

This is an imaginary line between signer and observer, i.e. "speaker" and "listener." Whenever a sign such as SEE moves along the sight line toward the observer, the pronouns "I" and "you" are implied, thus they need not be signed. That is to say, instead of signing I SEE YOU, you need to sign only SEE. Since the sign moves from "I" towards

---

*Based on a dissertation submitted by James Rimpau to the University of Nevada-Reno, in partial fulfillment of the requirements for the PhD degree.

"you", the pronouns are built into the movement (p. 2). . . . The sign ASK-QUESTION is extremely versatile. When you sign it toward the observer, it means "I ask you." When the signer signs it toward himself, coming from the observer, it means "You ask me." When the signer signs it toward himself coming from an angle to the sight line, it means "(a third person or persons) ask me." To convey the idea, "I asked several people," move the sign in an arc as you repeat it, as if the people you asked were standing there in front of you. (p. 75)

As is evident in these examples from Fant, changes in the form of a sign can produce semantic, pragmatic, and grammatical effects. Indeed, a given change in form, such as reiteration, can be used for all three. Reiteration makes HOUSE into TOWN and TREE into FOREST which is a semantic effect. Reiteration also makes HOPE emphatic which is a pragmatic effect, and reiteration changes the verbs SIT and FLY into the nouns CHAIR and AIRPLANE which is a grammatical effect. Recent research on ASL has concentrated on the grammatical effects, particularly on the line-of-sight inflection described by Fant, in which reference to participants is incorporated into signs for action (Wilbur, 1980, p. 19).

Human Signers: Adults and Children

In studies of ASL, adult signers are treated as informants. They are asked to convey in gestures, English words or sentences that employ critical distinctions: for example, distinctions of degree, as in Fant's case of "like" and "like very much," distinctions in person reference, as in "I give you," "I give them," "I give to each of them," "They each give me," and so on. Video records of these productions are examined to see whether each inflectional process changes the appearance of classes of signs in a characteristic way (Klima & Bellugi, 1979, pp. 299–315).

In studies conducted with children, more naturalistic methods are used. Investigators examine film and other records of conversations between children and familiar adults, and search for signs that vary in appearance from citation form. Two variations often mentioned as characteristic of 'baby sign' are reiteration of signs (Hoffmeister, Moores, & Ellenberger, 1975) and making signs on the body of the adult addressee (Schlesinger & Meadow, 1972). Schlesinger and Meadow noted that parents frequently make signs on infants as well, just as we did with the cross-fostered infant chimpanzees (see Chapter 1 this volume). They suggested that this is a device for getting a young child's attention, and also a warm, approving or playful way of signing (pp. 67–68). Signs placed on the addressee are not limited to 'baby sign.' Stokoe (personal communication to B. Gardner, February, 1988) noted that "such signing is not restricted to young children but to intimate register; lovemaking deaf couples, for example, feel free to use each other's body for sign placing."

The adult use of inflectional devices is the product of a long developmental process (Cokely and Gawlik, 1974). Ellenberger and Steyaert (1978) studied how participants and places are incorporated into signs for actions by a child learning ASL as his first language. They noted that:

While one might expect spatial modifications to appear earlier because of their pictorial nature, they are, in fact, relatively late acquisitions, perhaps because such representations may require a fairly advanced mastery of cognitive skills involving spatial relationships. (p. 268)

Ellenberger and Steyaert produced and analyzed a longitudinal series of films of a child between the ages of 43 and 71 months. They found that inflections indicating participants and places appeared in childish, immature forms when their subject, the deaf child of deaf parents, was between four and five years old. Before that, action signs such as BITE and BREAK occurred rarely and only in citation form. Beginning at 54 months, the deaf boy indicated the participants in an action sometimes by placing the action sign on the body of a person or on an object, and sometimes by merely moving the action sign toward the person or object, as adult signers do (Ellenberger & Steyaert, 1978, p. 265).

Nonhuman Signers: Chimpanzees

In the cross-fostering laboratory a human member of the foster family was with Washoe, Moja, Tatu, and Dar from the time that these chimpanzees awakened in the morning until they fell asleep at night. One of the responsibilities of the human adults was to describe, in the daily field records, what went on while they were with the subjects: meals, naps, chores, games that were played, and, of course, sign language conversations. Detailed descriptions of perceptual-motor, social, and communicative behavior as well as notes on food intake and toileting were included in the daily field records.

In these field records, descriptions of the form of signs (see Chapter 3 this volume) were based on the system developed by Stokoe (1960). The Stokoe system uses three sets of symbols that refer to distinctions within three aspects of a gesture. The first aspect is the place (P) on the body or in space where the sign is made—e.g., the cheek, the chest, in front of the signer. The second aspect is the configuration (C) of the hand—e.g., whether the hand is fisted or open, which fingers are extended, and how the hand is oriented toward the place. The third is the type and direction of movement (M)—e.g., contact or grasp, or rub up or down or in a circle.

The field notes also contain detailed descriptions of deviations from citation forms. From these descriptions, we can detect types of modifications that have parallel effects on many different signs. For example, there were reports that COME, DOG, SORRY, and a number of other signs normally made with one hand were duplicated with both hands making the same sign at the same time. At least 20 different types of form modifications appear in the field descriptions. Each type can be characterized by an aspect of sign form—e.g., place or movement—and by the way in which this aspect differs from citation form.

Many of the form modifications that were reported for the cross-fostered chimpanzees—e.g., making a sign on the adult or with the hands of the adult or making it very large—produced conspicuous changes in the appearance of the sign. Yet all the modifications (except for blended signs in phrases) preserved the basic place, configuration and movement of the sign that enabled the observer to identify it. In this respect, these form modifications are very different from errors in diction (R. Gardner & Gardner, 1984, pp. 393–397).

A commonly reported modification involved place: the young chimpanzees placed signs on the body of the adult addressee instead of on their own body. Thus, SWALLOW, for which the citation place is the throat, and TICKLE, for which the citation form is the back of the hand, were placed on the corresponding body part of the addressee. The following entry comes from the field records for 58-month-old Dar (observer's initials and date of entry in parentheses):

Greg was hooting and making other sounds, to prevent Dar from falling asleep. Dar put his fist to Greg's lips and made kissing sounds. Greg asked, WHAT WANT? and Dar replied, QUIET, placing the sign on Greg's lips. (GRG 5/19/81)

There were other types of place modification. In one of these, the chimpanzees placed signs on or near the referent, as when OPEN was placed on various doors, containers, or on the addressee's mouth, and when HURT was placed on various cuts and bruises, or on the signer's head, after a fall. In a different type of place modification, the sign was shifted beyond the normal signing space, either further away from the body, or lifted unusually high, as in the following entry for Dar at 36 months:

After Dar eats his breakfast cereal, I feed him banana. Dar signs with his hands under the table. I tell Dar, CAN'T SEE and then Dar signs SEE BANANA, making the BANANA sign over his head. (VC 7/7/79)

Other types of modification involved configuration. Instead of forming the sign with their own hand, the chimpanzees molded the hand of the addressee, as in the following for Washoe at 28 months:

After her nap, Washoe signed OUT. I was hoping for Washoe to potty herself and did not comply. Then Washoe took my hands and put them together to make OUT, and then signed OUT with her own hands, to show me how. Again today, Washoe signed UP and then took my hand and signed UP with it. (NR 11/15/67)

The most commonly reported modification in movement was to make the movement of the sign more vigorous or emphatic, as in the following for Moja at 26 months:

Moja signed DOG on Ron and me, and looked at our faces, waiting for us to "woof". After several rounds, I made a "meeow" instead. Moja signed DOG again, I repeated "meeow" again, and Moja slapped my leg harder. This went on. Finally, I woofed and Moja leapt on me and hugged me. (TT 1/4/75)

There were additional ways in which the young chimpanzees modified movement; for example, by enlarging the movement and also by prolonging the sign. Two commonly reported modifications involve the sign as a whole rather than its place or its configuration or its movement. Signs were reiterated one or more times, and there were also two-handed versions of signs normally made with one hand, as in the following for Moja at 45 months:

Moja just does one no-no after another as soon as we get out in yard. She even jumps the fence. Finally, I retrieve her, tell Moja she must play in garage. Moja signed, SORRY SORRY. I then sign, YOU SURE SORRY? NOW GOOD? and she replies SORRY SORRY. The first three SORRY are in the standard, one hand form, but she uses both hands for the last SORRY. (SW 9/6/76)

Several of the modifications that were described involved whole utterances rather than individual signs. Both signs of a phrase were involved in blended signs. The following entry is for Moja at 56 months (ICECREAM is made by rubbing the index edge of the fist down over the lips, NO by shaking the head):

Moja stares longingly at Dairy Queen, as we drive by. Then for a minute or more signs, NO ICECREAM many times, by shaking head while holding fist to mouth, index edge up. (RAG 7/9/77)

The modification in which a gaze is prolonged is known as the "questioning look" in ASL (Covington, 1973; Van Cantfort & Rimpau, 1982, pp. 36–38). Like the rising pitch in a spoken question, this type of gaze distinguishes questions from statements. The following is for Tatu at 12 months:

Tatu takes a picture book and looks through it. I join her. Seems to be especially interested in pictures of flowers and of chimpanzees. Tatu points to flowers, THERE?, with raised eyebrows and prolonged eye contact. I sign FLOWER then Tatu turns back to another page. (KW 12/23/76)

The field notes showed that each of the different types of modification was used by all the subjects. The modifications were also productive, in that each type of modification was used with different signs. Thus, as early as month 11, Pili was placing HEAR, QUIET, TICKLE, SLEEP, and three other signs on the body of the adult as well as on his own body. Other types of modification also appeared early, before the end of the first year. The chimpanzee Dar signed OPEN on such referents as the refrigerator, the cap on a bottle of soda pop, and his trailer door. In that first year, however, only a few types of modification were used regularly and productively, with several different signs. Thus, the field records also indicate that there were developmental trends, in the number and types of modifications used by the cross-fostered chimpanzees (B. Gardner & Gardner, in preparation).

Numerous examples of modified signs were reported in the daily records of Washoe, Moja, Pili, Tatu and Dar. The signing of the young chimpanzees has also been recorded on video tape, and these tapes provide a means of studying in detail their use of form modifications as a modulation of meaning.

METHODS

Video-Taped Records

Between September, 1979 and August, 1980, Moja, Tatu and Dar were video taped in 58 different sessions°. This chapter is based on a set of eight video tapes of Dar together with Tony McCorkle, who had been a member of Dar's foster family for eight months at the beginning of the sessions. This particular set of video tapes was selected for analysis because they all involve the same chimpanzee interacting with the same companion in the same setting over a period of many months. In each tape, Dar and Tony are sitting on a sofa, signing to each other while engaging in quiet activities like looking at magazines, food sharing, grooming or tickling. These eight video tapes span the time from Dar's 40th to his 49th month and are the entire sample of Dar signing with Tony. The video-taped sessions range in length from 7 to 25 minutes, for a total of approximately 105 minutes.

Transcripts

The transcripts of the eight tapes of Dar's signing were recorded in a four-column format (see Table 6.1). The first column contained general context notes, for example, "Tony opens a small box of cereal." The second column contained Tony's utterances and the third column contained Dar's utterances. Tony and Dar's signs were recorded by using the nearest word equivalent in (adult)

°G.R. Gaustad was in charge of the production of the video-taped records, and the authors acknowledge gratefully his vital contribution to the research in this chapter.

Table 6.1
Excerpt from Transcript

Context	TM Utterance	D Utterance	Form Notes
D and TM sitting on sofa. D playing with shoe.	WHAT THAT (shoe)/ WHAT THAT (diff. shoe)/ WANT . . . . GROOM/ WHERE GROOM/	SHOE/ SHOE/ GROOM GROOM* GOOD/ DAR/	*P = back of TM's hand
D and TM on sofa again. TM has 2 shoes in his lap.	OK/ signed to camera. WHAT THIS (shoe)/ YOURS/ WHOSE (TM's shoes)/	DRINK/ SHOE DAR THAT (shoe) MINE THAT (shoe) SHOE/ YOURS*/	*Signed toward TM's shoes
D and TM back on sofa.	WHOSE (TM's shoes)/	MINE/	
D tries to leave sofa.	THIS (shoe) MINE/	YOU POTTY*/	*P = TM's nose
Picture breaks up.		bad pix — CAN'T/	
New scene.	WHAT THIS (shoe)/ WHOSE (TM's shoe)/	SHOE/ GOOD MINE/ POTTY*/	*P = TM's nose

English. When translating signs into English, the procedure used in the cross-fostering research was to consult sign language dictionaries and informants fluent in ASL in order to decide on a suitable gloss for a given sign, and then to write that gloss every time that sign was observed (cf. B. Gardner and Gardner, 1971, pp. 144–145). These glosses were never altered to make the transcript read like good English. Rather, the single word glosses served as shorthand or speed writing system for recording signed utterances. The fourth column contained form notes that usually referred back to the signs made by Dar or Tony and miscellaneous notes. Whenever signs occurred in something other than the citation form, the gloss for the sign was marked with an asterisk and the variation was described in English words in column 4. For example, for the utterance by Dar that was glossed as YOU GUM°, column 4 contains the entry "place = Tony's cheek."

The syntactic and grammatical devices of ASL are analogous to those of vocal languages but are adapted to a visual mode of transmission. To modulate the meaning of signs, adult human signers use devices such as establishing loci, facial expression, eye gaze, repetition and modifications of movement (Klima & Bellugi, 1979). Because these sign modifications are so different from spoken word modifications, researchers have often overlooked their existence. For those who are unfamiliar with ASL inflections, many of the glossed utterances in the transcripts might seem highly telegraphic, even though they are actually well-formed ASL utterances.

RESULTS

Reliability

Before analyzing the use of modified and citation form signs by Dar, it is necessary to demonstrate that the transcripts of the video tapes were reliable. As Mohay (1982) has noted, this has often been overlooked.

In the literature on the acquisition of spoken language by hearing children there is a lamentable lack of study of the reliability of data transcription. Therefore, detailed analyses and sophisticated theories frequently rest on one person's interpretation of the child's spoken utterances (e.g. Halliday 1975, Bloom 1970, Greenfield & Smith 1976). There are good reasons for this. It is essential that the second transcriber be as familiar with the child, the home environment, and the type of data being analyzed as is the experimenter, if high levels of agreement are to be reached. Such personnel are not readily available; extensive training programs may be needed to produce them, making reliability studies time-consuming and expensive to conduct. (p. 76)

James Rimpau, who had been a member of the foster families of both Moja and Dar, served as the first transcriber. Both Beatrix Gardner and Susan Nichols had been members of the foster families of Washoe, Moja, Pili, Tatu and Dar and they acted as second transcribers. Susan Nichols transcribed one 13-minute video-taped session of chimpanzee Dar, and, to demonstrate that tapes of other chimpanzees could be reliably transcribed, Beatrix Gardner transcribed one 12-minute video-taped session of chimpanzee Tatu. These independently prepared transcripts were compared to those produced by the first transcriber to determine agreement on: (a) content; (b) reiteration of signs; and (c) segmentation of utterances. Because the place component of a sign was of primary interest in this research, an additional segment of tape, in which Dar modified the place of signs frequently, was transcribed by Susan Nichols, and compared to Rimpau's transcript of the same tape.

Gloss

Gloss agreement was calculated by comparing the first observer's transcript with the second observer's transcript, on a sign by sign basis. The two written transcripts were aligned by comparing the context notes in column 1 and the glosses for Tony's signing in column 2. For example, the first observer recorded "Tony and Dar sitting on sofa in playroom" in column 1 of the transcript, and "WHAT (repeated) THIS (hat)" in column 2. The second observer recorded "Dar sits on couch in playroom with Tony" in column 1, and "WHAT (repeated) THIS (hat)" in column 2. Once the transcripts were aligned the following rules applied to Dar's utterances: (1) score agreement of gloss X; (2) go to the next gloss in the record that is different from X, and score that gloss. Agreement was reported as a percent and was calculated by the formula A/ (A + D), where A was the number of glosses in agreement and D was the number of glosses that disagreed.

For Tatu, the two observers agreed on 83 (80.6%) of the 103 glosses recorded in the first observer's transcript. (The gloss agreement for the human companion's signing in this reliability sample was roughly equivalent, 86 of the 114 or 75.4%.) For Dar, the two observers agreed on 227 (84.1%) of the 270 glosses recorded in the first observer's transcript. The agreement on the glosses in these reliability samples for Tatu and Dar fall within the acceptable range for children.

Extensive reliability studies showed the percentage of communicative units identified by both transcribers ranged from 71 to 92, depending on the complexity of the material in the taped record. These were felt to be acceptable levels of agreement. (Mohay, 1982, p. 76)

Reiteration

We refer to repetition of a sign within an utterance as *reiteration*. For example, in response to the statement TIME ICECREAM NOW, Tatu signed ICECREAM ICECREAM ICECREAM ICECREAM ICECREAM ICE-

CREAM (Drumm, Gardner and Gardner, 1986, p. 19; see Chapter 2 this volume). When examining similar occurrences in samples of child speech, researchers (Keenan, 1977; Keenan and Klein, 1975) have suggested that reiteration should be interpreted as a device for indicating assent or emphasis. In calculating *reiteration agreement*, only those signs that were already scored as gloss agreements were used. The observers agreed on reiterations on 88% of the cases in the reliability sample for Tatu and on 85% of the cases in the reliability sample for Dar.

Segmentation

Segmentation agreement refers to the observers' agreement in identifying utterance boundaries. When, for example, Dar signed THAT RED BIRD, should this be considered a single three-sign utterance or three one-sign utterances or some combination of these? Segmentation agreement is of primary importance to investigators who use measures like Mean Length of Utterance (MLU), but it is considered here as another means of demonstrating that the transcribers were in substantial agreement.

Segmentation agreement was scored by the following rules: (1) score whether or not sign X is the last sign of an utterance; (2) go to the next gloss in the record that is different from X, and score whether or not that gloss is the last of an utterance. The transcribers agreed on the location of 85% of the utterance boundaries for Tatu, and on 80% of those for Dar. Experimenters analyzing audio tapes of children's speech have reported similar levels of agreement for the identification of utterance boundaries (Siegel, 1962; Shatz & Gelman, 1973; Rondal & Defays, 1978).

Place

Signs that were not made in the place listed in the description of their citation form will be referred to as *place-modified signs*. A segment of the transcript of Dar's eighth taped session contained many examples of place-modified signs and therefore was selected as a sample. This transcript was retyped omitting the fourth column (see Table 6.1), which had included the descriptions of place-modified signs. The retyped transcript was given to a second person (Susan Nichols) who was asked to watch the relevant segment of the taped session and identify and describe those signs that had place modifications. The second transcriber, working independently, was to recreate the fourth column of the sample transcript. If Susan Nichols disagreed with the first transcriber's gloss for a particular sign, she could cross it out and replace it with what she believed to be the correct gloss.

In the original transcript of this sample, 56 signs were described as place-modified signs. Ten different signs, including TICKLE, GROOM and GUM, were represented in this group. The two transcribers agreed that all these 56 signs were place-modified. Although gloss agreement is of secondary importance in this sample, the two transcribers agreed on 83.9% of the 56 glosses. Indeed, the gloss agreement on this sample was almost identical to the gloss agreement calculated earlier, on a different sample of Dar's signing. It is notable that for the nine exceptional cases there was agreement on the place of contact, even though there was disagreement on the gloss. For example, the first transcriber reported the sign GUM made on Tony's cheek and Susan Nichols reported the sign APPLE made on Tony's cheek. With regard to place, and without regard to gloss agreement, the two transcribers agreed on the place of contact for 98.2% of the 56 signs. If only those glosses that were agreed on by both transcribers are considered, then the two agreed on the place of contact for 97.9% of the 47 signs.

Analysis by Sign Category

During the ten-month period in which this sample of Dar's signing was taped (November, 1979 to August, 1980), his reliable sign vocabulary grew from 93 to 106 signs (see Chapter 3 this volume). Table 6.2 is an alphabetized list of the signs reported in the eight taped samples of Dar's signing. In these eight taped samples, 71 different signs were reported, of which 29.6% occurred in a place other than the place given as the citation form of that sign.

Table 6.3 shows the 71 signs in the video-taped samples of Dar's signing, categorized as names/pronouns, locatives, nouns, verbs, modifiers and markers. The classification is based on that used in earlier studies of replies to Wh-questions (B. Gardner and Gardner, 1975; Van Cantfort, 1986; see Chapter 5, this volume).

As in many spoken languages, there are signs in American Sign Language, such as DRINK and BRUSH, that can be used as either nouns or verbs (a noun/verb category was not used in the studies of replies to Wh-questions because it was necessary to sort vocabulary items into mutually exclusive categories; when such items occurred they were always listed as common nouns). In the video-taped sample of Dar's signing, 12 signs were reported that are categorized as both nouns and verbs in ASL dictionaries (Stokoe, Casterline & Croneberg, 1976; Sternberg, 1981). They have been listed as noun/verbs in Table 6.3. Two signs were included in the noun/verb category based on our observations of Dar's usage, even though they are classified as verbs only in the ASL dictionaries. PEEKABOO was used by Dar to name Halloween masks, and SEE as a name for eyeglasses, binoculars, telescopes, etc. (R. Gardner and Gardner, 1984). Table 6.3 shows the number of occurrences of each of the 71 signs, as well as the number of times each sign occurred in a place-modified form.

"In American Sign Language (ASL), there are clues different from those in English for deciding that something is a verb. One major clue is inflection

Table 6.2
Signs Reported in Eight Taped Samples of Dar's Signing

APPLE	CRY*	KEY	SEE
BALL	DAR	LISTEN	SHIRT*
BED	DOG*	ME	SHOE
BERRY*	DRINK	MEAT	SODAPOP
BIRD	EARRING	MILK	SWALLOW*
BLACK	EAT*	MINE	SWEET*
BOY	FLOWER	MORE	THAT
BRUSH*	FRUIT	NUT	THINK
BUG	GIMME	OIL	TICKLE*
CAN'T	GO	OPEN*	TM
CARROT	GOOD	ORANGE	TOOTHBRUSH
CAT	GROOM*	OUT	TOOTHPASTE
CEREAL	GUM*	PEACH*	VACUUM
CHASE	HANKY*	PEEKABOO	WRISTWATCH*
CHEESE	HAT*	PLEASE*	WIPER
COMB*	HEAR	POTTY*	YOU
COOKIE	HOME*	QUIET*	YOURS
COW	HURT	RED	

* = Place modifications reported for these items.

for person" (Fischer and Gough, 1978, p. 17). If the place modifications in this sample of Dar's signing were being used as pronominal inflections (i.e., to incorporate reference to persons and places into signs for action), they should be found most frequently in the verb and noun/verb categories. Tables 6.4a and 6.4b show that this was indeed the case. Six of nine signs (66.7%) classified as verbs and 5 or 13 (38.5%) signs classified as noun/verbs were found to have place-modified forms. Taken together, 50% of the signs in these two categories were found to have place-modified forms. Signs in the other categories—locatives, markers and common nouns—were less likely to be modified in this way and none of the names/pronouns or modifiers in this sample were found to have place-modified forms. Taken together, only 20.4% of the signs from outside the verb and noun-verb categories were found to have place-modified forms. When the actual number of modified occurrences (tokens rather than types) within each category was counted (Table 6.4b), this same pattern was evident and the difference between verbs plus noun/verbs and all other categories was even more pronounced. Over one quarter (28.4%) of the 352 occurrences of signs from the noun/verb and verb categories were place-modified signs. In contrast, only 4.3% of the 1,179 occurrences of signs from all other categories were place-modified signs. This difference between verbs plus noun/verbs and all other signs is highly significant (chi-square = 93.99, $df = 1$, $p < .001$).

Table 6.3
Signs Reported in Taped Sample Classified into General Categories

Names/ Pronouns	Common nouns		Nouns/Verbs	Verbs
153 DAR	17 APPLE	67 GUM(17)	1 BED	1 CHASE
60 ME	1 BALL	77 HAT(2)	34 BRUSH(25)	4 CRY(1)
31 TM	1 BERRY(1)	20 HURT	23 COMB(8)	3 GO
73 YOU	19 BIRD	8 KEY	61 DRINK	3 OPEN(3)
	2 BOY	1 MEAT	93 EAT(2)	19 GROOM(16)
Locatives	1 BUG	2 MILK	10 HANKY(2)	9 QUIET(6)
16 HOME(9)	6 CARROT	2 NUT	3 HEAR	10 SWALLOW(3)
6 OUT	9 CAT	11 OIL	8 LISTEN	1 THINK
64 THAT	1 CEREAL	2 ORANGE	1 PEEKABOO	29 TICKLE(27)
	4 CHEESE	16 PEACH(3)	17 POTTY(7)	
Markers	47 COOKIE	14 SHIRT(7)	8 SEE	Modifiers
7 CAN'T	30 COW	19 SHOE	2 TOOTH-	7 BLACK
6 GIMME	6 DOG(1)	51 SODAPOP	BRUSH	65 GOOD
39 MORE	1 EARRING	31 SWEET(1)	2 VACUUM	70 MINE
68 PLEASE(4)	2 FLOWER	2 TOOTH-		18 RED
	1 FRUIT	PASTE		12 YOURS
		3 WIPER		
		10 WRISTWATCH		

Number preceding item is number of reports in taped samples. Number in ( ) following item is number of times the sign was reported in a modified form.

Analysis by Context

Place-modified signs occurred more frequently in some grammatical categories than others. Is it possible that they also occurred more frequently in replies to some types of questions than others?

B. Gardner and Gardner (1975) and Van Cantfort (1986; see Chapter 5 this volume) demonstrated that Wh-questions exert a high degree of control over the replies of the chimpanzees. They found, for example, that What demonstrative questions were answered with common nouns (e.g., Q: WHAT THAT? A: BOOK) while Who pronoun questions were answered with proper names (e.g., Q: WHO YOU? A: ME WASHOE) and Where action questions were typically answered with locatives or locative phrases (e.g., Q: WHERE SHALL SUSAN BITE YOU? A: SUSAN BITE THERE).

Because the earlier studies were designed to analyze different Wh-question types, they used prescripted, well-formed Wh-questions which were presented in a counterbalanced order. In the video-taped samples, Tony also asked Dar many Wh-questions. Tony, however, was ad-libbing his role in the dialogue,

Table 6.4a
Number of Different Signs by Grammatical Category

Category	Total signs	Modified signs	Modified signs(%)
Names/Pronouns	4	0	0.0
Locatives	3	1	33.3
Markers	4	1	25.0
Modifiers	5	0	0.0
Common nouns	33	8	24.2
Nouns/Verbs	13	5	38.5
Verbs	9	6	66.7
Total	71	21	29.6

Table 6.4b
Frequency of Occurences of Signs by Grammatical Category

Category	Total occurrences	Modified occurrences	Modified occurrences (%)
Names/Pronouns	317	0	0.0
Locatives	86	9	10.5
Markers	120	4	3.3
Modifiers	172	0	0.0
Common nouns	484	38	7.9
Nouns/Verbs	263	44	16.7
Verbs	89	56	62.9
Total	1,531	151	9.9

and consequently his Wh-questions were not prescripted or asked in a counter-balanced order. Moreover some of Tony's questions were not complete and well-formed (e.g., WHAT?) and other questions were of mixed types (e.g., WHO BRUSH WHERE?).

Of the many types of questions that Tony asked Dar, there was on type of question that should have excluded reference to person, place, or instrument, and that was the What demonstrative type (cf. B. Gardner and Gardner, 1975; Van Cantfort, 1986). The What demonstrative category contains WHAT THIS? and NAME THIS? questions.In this analysis, it also included seven questions that were all variants of WHO MAKE SOUND? These questions occurred during a game in which Tony made animal sounds (moo, meow, etc.), and Dar named the animal associated with the sound. Although Tony signed these as Who questions, the appropriate reply was clearly a common noun (COW, CAT, etc.) and so, for this analysis, these questions were included with the What demonstrative questions.

Since verb signs are not appropriate replies to What demonstrative questions, indicators of person, place, or instrument should be absent, also. But, appropriate replies to other types of questions could contain verbs or nouns or still other categories of signs. For example, What want questions could be answered with either nouns or verbs or locative verb phrases such as YOU ME OUT. Many of Tony's questions, such as Who questions and Where questions, fell outside of the What demonstrative type; in addition, his questions were sometimes mixed types, sometimes incomplete or ill-formed, and sometimes difficult to classify. If Tony's questions are divided into two types, then reference to person, place or instrument should appear less often in replies to What demonstrative questions than in replies to Other questions.

Table 6.5 shows the results of dividing Dar's replies to the 435 Wh-questions asked by Tony into "What demonstrative" and "Other" categories, and then scoring whether or not the utterance contained an indication of person, place or instrument. As in the systematically controlled studies by B. Gardner and Gardner (1975) and Van Cantfort (1986), the question types in these videotaped conversations exert a high degree of control over the replies (chi-square for Table 6.5 is 53.88, $df = 1$, $p < .001$). Dar rarely used modificatons of signs or additional signs to indicate person, place or instrument in response to questions in the What demonstrative category, but often used such signs or modifications in response to the Other questions.

Thus Dar did indeed indicate persons, places and instruments in the expected question contexts. A second, more specific analysis was made, using only signs in citation form from the verb and noun/verb categories (see Table 6.3). When one of these signs occurred in a reply, the question was categorized as either a "What demonstrative" or "Other." We predicted that when the citation form occurred in replies to What demonstrative questions they were being used as nouns, and did not need to be accompanied by a second sign to indicate person, place or instrument. However, when the citation forms occurred in replies to other types of questions, they could have been used as verbs and therefore could be accompanied by a second sign to indicate person, place or instrument.

The 13 most frequently occurring items in the noun/verb and verb categories (see Table 6.3) served as the sample for this analysis. We examined replies that contained the citation form of these items, and classified replies as containing the citation form alone, or the citation form together with a second sign to indicate person, place or instrument. The distribution of the 178 citation forms that occurred in replies to Tony's questions is shown in Table 6.6. This yields a chi-square of 8.08, corrected for continuity, $df=1$. A chi-square of 6.64 is required for significance at $p < .01$. Table 6.6 shows that Dar rarely added a second sign that indicated person, place or instrument to these citation forms when they were used as nouns, but often added such a sign when the citation forms could have been used as verbs.

Table 6.5
Distribution of Replies that
Indicate Person, Place or Instrument
All replies

	With person, place or instrument	Without person, place or instrument	Total
What demon. questions	41	80	121
All other questions	228	86	314
Total	269	166	435

Table 6.6
Distribution of Replies with Signs
Indicating Person, Place or Instrument
for 13 Verbs & Nouns/Verbs
in Citation Forms

	With person, place or instrument	Without person, place or instrument	Total
What demon. questions	9	24	33
All other questions	82	63	145
Total	91	87	178

Dar modified the place of signs in three distinct ways: by making them on his own body, but in a place different from the citation form; by making them on the addressee; and by making them on an object. Does each modified form mean something different? The distributional analysis technique was used to test two hypotheses about specific types of place modifications. First, when Dar modified a sign by placing it on the addressee, was he indicating the pronoun "YOU"? Second, when he modified a sign by placing it somewhere on his own body (but not in the citation place) was he indicating the locative "THERE"?

To test these two hypotheses we compared replies to three types of Wh-questions: Who/Whose questions, which call for signs indicating persons; Where questions, which call for signs indicating places; and What demonstrative questions which, as noted before, do not call for indicators of person, place or instrument. For this analysis, only signs which frequently occurred in place-modified forms were of interest, so replies containing the nine most commonly modified nouns, noun/verbs and verbs (see Table 6.3) were selected as the sample.

Whenever one of these nine signs occurred in a reply to a Who/Whose question (Who pronoun, Who action or Who trait), a Where question (Where action or Where object) or a What demonstrative question, the form of the sign (i.e., citation; place = body; place = addressee; place = object) was noted. Dar often used several modified signs together in a single utterance; when this happened, the form of the final sign of his utterance was counted for this classification. The results are shown in Table 6.7. An "On Object" row does not appear in Table 6.7 because modified signs with place = object only occurred twice in responses to these three question types.

Table 6.7
Distribution of Three Different Forms:
Citation, On Body, On Addressee

	What demon.	Where	Who/ Whose	Total
Citation	11	8	14	33
On body	3	8	1	12
On addressee	4	6	17	27
Total	18	22	32	72

As can be seen in Table 6.7, the three question types control the form of the signs in the replies (chi-squares = 13.84, $df = 4$, $p < .01$). Two-thirds of the place-modified signs that were made on Dar's own body (but different from the citation place) occurred in replies to Where questions. This is exactly where we expected the locative THERE to be used. Nearly two-thirds of the place-modified signs made on the addressee were in response to Who/Whose questions, where we expected a proper name or a pronoun. Citation forms occurred in replies to all three types of questions. This was also an expected outcome, since citation forms, when combined with name signs or with signs like YOU, ME and THAT/THERE become appropriate replies to Who/Whose and Where questions.

Detailed Analysis of Frequently Modified Signs

In all there were 1,531 signs in this taped record and 151 (9.9%) of these were place-modified signs. Some of these place-modified signs occurred infrequently and therefore were difficult to interpret. Four vocabulary items accounted for slightly over half (85 or 56%) of the 151 place-modified signs in this sample. The most commonly modified items, TICKLE, BRUSH, GUM, and GROOM, with 27, 25, 17, and 16 occurrences respectively, will be analyzed in detail.

Verbs and Noun/Verbs

Tickle. Tickling was an activity that nearly always evoked laughter from Dar, and tickling with a hard object resulted in an even more enthusiastic response. The sign TICKLE was one of the first signs that Dar and the other chimpanzees learned, and they used it to ask their companions to tickle them, both with their hands and with hard objects. Two toys that Dar offered most often for these games were a hard plastic bull and a slightly softer plastic dinosaur. Dar often signed TICKLE on one of these toys as he brought it to his companion. He also signed TICKLE on the hand of his addressee apparently as a request to be tickled.

Dar had been using the sign TICKLE since he was about seven months old. The citation form of the sign TICKLE is:

P: Back of hand.
C: Index extended.
M: Index rubs to side.

The records from the fifteen-day period in which TICKLE met the criterion of reliability (see Chapter 3) included five reports of Dar making TICKLE in citation form (i.e., on the back of his own hand) and ten reports of Dar making the sign on the back of an addressee's hand. Within his first year, Dar used the sign TICKLE in more than one form. Before Dar was two years old, he was also placing the TICKLE sign on inanimate objects (toys).

In the video-taped sample, Dar used still another variation of the TICKLE sign. He signed TICKLE on himself, but not in the place listed in the citation form. Several times in the video-taped sessions Dar signed TICKLE on his neck, which was a favorite spot on which to be tickled. Adult human signers move some verbs around in a similar fashion. Fischer and Gough (1978) remarked that when signing a verb that includes a body part as an argument, the sign is placed on the part of the body involved so that, for example, "If one describes a mosquito bite, one shows where the victim has been bitten, and so on" (p. 27).

All four forms of the TICKLE sign appear in the taped samples. Dar signed the citation form of TICKLE twice (6.9%). He signed TICKLE on his toys eleven times (37.9%) and on his addressee's hand eight times (27.6%). Finally, he signed TICKLE somewhere on his own body (excluding the back of the hand) eight times (27.6%).

Brush. Dar was just under one year old when the sign BRUSH was added to his vocabulary of reliable signs. The citation form of the sign BRUSH is:

P: Back of forearm.
C: Fist, palm to P.
M: Rubs to and fro.

In all reports from the fifteen-day reliability run, Dar signed BRUSH on his own forearm. Subsequent reassessment records (see SOD procedure, Chapter 3 this volume) indicate that, by the time Dar was two years old, he was moving the sign around to different places on his own body. In the video-taped samples, Dar added a third form of BRUSH, placing the sign on the addressee's forearm. In these video tapes, Dar signed BRUSH 34 times. Of these BRUSH signs, 9 (26.6%) were the citation form, 14 (41.2%) were signed somewhere on his own body (other than his forearm) and 11 (32.4%) were signed on the addressee's forearm.

Groom. Dar was just over two years old when the sign GROOM became part of his reliable sign vocabulary. The citation form of the sign GROOM is:

P: Forearm.
C: Pincer hand.
M: Index and thumb grasps and pulls.

Dar signed GROOM on the addressee's hand from the time he first learned the sign. The reports from the fifteen-day reliability run indicated that Dar made the sign on his addressee's forearm 11 times and on his own arm 4 times. The reassessment records also confirm that, for Dar, the most common place for the sign GROOM was on the wrist and forearm of the addressee. In the video-taped sample Dar signed GROOM 19 times. Of these, 13 (68.4%) were made on his companion's wrist. Dar used the citation form of GROOM three times (15.8%), and three times (15.8%) he signed GROOM on himself but in a place other than his wrist or forearm.

Place = Addressee. Most of Dar's utterances in the video-taped sample are replies to Tony's questions. Consequently, it is possible to look for a relationship between the forms of signs used by Dar and the immediately preceding utterance of his companion. If Dar signed TICKLE, BRUSH or GROOM on his addressee when he was asking the addressee to perform the appropriate action, then these modified signs should occur in replies to questions where some form of "YOU action" would be appropriate. In the sample, Dar signed TICKLE on Tony eight times and all eight were in replies to questions. Each of these questions was some form of WHAT ME DO?, WHAT WANT? or WHO TICKLE—that is, questions to which "you tickle" would be an appropriate answer. Dar signed GROOM on Tony 13 times and 12 of these were in replies to questions. Of the 12 questions, 7 were some form of WANT GROOM? or WHAT NOW? Additionally, one WHERE GROOM? question was answered with the reply GROOM (on Tony's hand) GROOM (on the top of Dar's head). Thus Dar signed GROOM on his addressee's hand when "you groom" would be appropriate. Dar signed BRUSH on Tony 11 times and all 11 were in replies to questions. Only 2 of the 11 were WHO BRUSH? questions. Seven others were questions that Dar answered appropriately and then went on to add BRUSH (on the companion's arm) to his reply. For example, when Tony stopped brushing Dar, pretended to cry and asked WHAT ME DO?, Dar replied CRY BRUSH (on his own shoulder) BRUSH (citation form) BRUSH (on the companion's arm). When Tony asked WHAT THIS? of the brush, Dar answered BRUSH (citation form) BRUSH (on the companion's arm).

Place = Object. Dar often signed on his toys or other objects. In this sample he signed TICKLE on a toy 11 times. Nine of these were replies to questions. Of these nine, seven were some form of WHAT THIS (toy) DO? or WHICH (companion or toy) TICKLE?

Place = Body. Two of the three times that Dar signed GROOM somewhere on his own body, he was responding to the question WHERE GROOM? Dar signed TICKLE on himself eight different times, five of which were responses to questions. Although it was a common question in many situations, WHERE TICKLE? did not happen to occur in this sample. All five times that Dar signed TICKLE somewhere on himself in reply to a question, the sign was part of a phrase that contained a second TICKLE sign indicating an agent. For example, he answered the question WANT TICKLE? with BOY TICKLE (on Dar's neck) TICKLE (on his companion's hand). Dar replied to WHERE BRUSH? or WHERE (with BRUSH implied) questions six times. Four of these replies included a BRUSH sign somewhere on his own body.

As a group, nearly two-thirds of these place-modified signs were used according to the following pattern: place = addressee is used when "you X" would be appropriate; place = object is used when "X with that" would be appropriate; place = body is used when "X there" would be appropriate.

The establishment of loci is a sophisticated use of place and direction of movement. Placing signs on persons and objects appears to be a developmental stage on the way to the adult use of the establishment of loci. In the case of signs for action, that is, signs from the verb and noun/verb categories, Dar used this device to incorporate reference to person, place and instrument.

Nouns

Unlike verbs, noun signs rarely occurred in place-modified forms. In this sample, only 8 of the 31 items classified as common nouns in Table 6.3 occurred in modified forms—in all cases in the form place = addressee. Altogether, common nouns occurred 484 times in the video tapes but only 38 of these were made on the addressee. In the following sections we will examine the contexts in which these modified forms occurred.

Inedibles. Five of the common nouns that occurred in modified forms, DOG, HAT, WRISTWATCH, SHIRT and PEACH, were used to refer to inedible items. (The peach in this case was an artificial, plastic fruit.) Dar made one of these five signs on Tony 19 times in this sample. Of these 19 (57.9%) occurrences, 11 were answers to WHOSE questions, which Tony occasionally shortened to WHO.

Four of six times that Dar signed WRISTWATCH on Tony's wrist he had been asked WHOSE WRISTWATCH? The other two times, Tony had signed WRISTWATCH? Without introducing additional specific criteria it would be difficult to specify appropriate replies to such single-sign questions. Four of seven times that Dar signed SHIRT on Tony's chest, he had been asked some form of WHOSE SHIRT? The remaining three times were replies to Tony's single-sign question, SHIRT?

Dar signed place = addressee forms of HAT, PEACH, SHIRT and WRISTWATCH in replies to well-formed questions 12 times. Of these, 10 (83.3%) were replies in which "your + noun" would have been appropriate. In many vocal languages, the form of a noun is modified to indicate possessor. In a discussion of the prefixes used in the Washo Indian language, Jacobsen (1979) wrote, "In the first and second persons the same prefixes indicate subject of verb and possessor of noun" (p. 146; cf. Jacobsen, 1977).

Dar made the sign DOG as follows:

P: Thigh.
C: Open hand.
M: Palm contacts repeatedly.

He used the sign readily when questioned about actual dogs, toy dogs, and pictures of dogs (R. Gardner and Gardner, 1984). The chimpanzee Moja invented a game in which she signed DOG on the thigh of her human addressee and the person would then act like a dog, barking and running on all fours and jumping over furniture (see Chapter 1 this volume). Pili, Tatu and Dar learned this game from Moja and it was a favorite pastime in the cross-fostering laboratory. It appeared once in these tape records. Tony was making animal sounds, and when he barked like a dog, Dar signed DOG on Tony's leg. In this context, Dar seemed to be signing "you act like a dog."

Edibles. The other three common nouns that occurred in place = addressee forms in this sample were GUM, SWEET and BERRY. All refer to favorite food items, since SWEET was used to refer to gum, cookies, candy, etc.

Dar was 19 months old when the sign GUM became part of his reliable sign vocabulary. The citation form of the sign GUM is:

P: Cheek.
C: Index extended or open hand.
M: Tip of index finger contacts or rubs down.

During the fifteen-day reliability run for the sign GUM, Dar made the sign on his own cheek 13 times and on the addressee's cheek twice. In subsequent Sign of the Day samples, Dar continued to make the sign both on himself and on the addressee. In the video-taped samples, Dar signed GUM 67 times. Seventeen (25.4%) of the GUM signs were on his companion's cheek, and 50 (74.6%) were made in the citation form. Fifteen of the 17 modified GUM signs were in response to questions, and 6 of the 15 questions were some form of WHO? Dar and his companion were sharing some gum, and it is notable that in these six replies Dar included his own name sign and/or the signs GUM or SWEET made on his own cheek.

Dar seemed to be using the place-modified form of the GUM sign in a broader range of contexts than any other common noun sign. Occasionally an explanation seems obvious. When his companion began to chew a piece of gum and asked, WHERE? Dar responded with, GOOD GUM (on Tony's cheek) THERE (on Tony's lips) SEE—a modification that makes the location of the gum very clear.

All of the modified GUM signs occurred in two of the taped sessions. In repeatedly viewing these two sessions, it became apparent that Dar was signing on Tony's cheek in order to ensure that the sign was perceived by Tony. Consider the circumstances in which the modified GUM signs occurred. In both these taped sessions, Tony had some gum which he was willing to share but apparently hoped to dole out slowly, between rounds of other activities. Dar, on the other hand, seemed to want to postpone all other activities until the supply of gum was completely consumed. The resulting interaction consisted primarily of Dar pestering Tony for gum, while Tony tried to ignore the requests and introduce new topics for discussion. Unlike spoken conversations, where it is difficult to ignore someone sitting just inches away, the addressee in a signed conversation can effectively ignore a signer by simply looking the other way. These place-modified GUM signs might be a result of Dar's trying to make sure that Tony attended to the sign (cf. Schlesinger and Meadow, 1972, p. 67).

Dar only made a single SWEET and a single BERRY sign during the video-taped sessions. Both seem to fit the favored food item pattern established by GUM. The one time that Dar signed SWEET on Tony's lips, Tony had a cookie that Dar had asked for several times before by signing COOKIE COOKIE, DAR COOKIE, and MINE GOOD.

Dar made the sign BERRY as follows:

P: Tip of thumb or index, extended from fist or open hand.
C: Pincer hand or contracted hand.
M: Grasps or grasps and pulls.

The single modified BERRY sign in the video-taped records appears to fit the GUM and SWEET pattern (as do other reports of modified BERRY, in the field records). In this case, however, Dar was using one hand to support himself from a railing. Thus, for this particular BERRY sign, he might have used Tony's hand as the place because his own hand was occupied.

DISCUSSION

Vocabulary Size

We have reviewed the evidence for sign inflections in video tapes of chimpanzee Dar's conversations with Tony, a familiar human adult. The directional changes that Dar made in his verb signs to indicate person reference are systematic and express distinctions in meaning. Unlike the familiar English suffixes and prefixes, the inflectional changes that Dar made affected the *internal* structure of signs, and produced sets of related signs, such as the four forms of TICKLE and the three forms of BRUSH. While Klima and Bellugi (1979, pp. 272–315) and Wilbur (1980, pp. 15–28) emphasize the grammatical implications of inflections, Stokoe brings out the lexical implications.

There is no way to compare the lexicon of American Sign Language and the lexicon of English directly . . . The total number of all ASL signs recorded in all the handbooks and dictionaries in print cannot be much above four thousand (p. 63). . . . While other languages package some part of meaning in a fixed discrete unit ‹called a word and modify this by substituting different units, by attaching other units to make phrases, or by affixing still other units, American Sign Language operates with a flexible package, the sign, and it can modify its meaning over a continuum by manner changes in the SIG [movement or direction]. Thus many signs have a semantic range comparable to that of a fairly large number of related words or of a whole repertoire of phrases. (1972, p. 54)

The system we have used to gloss signs into English in this volume is a sort of shorthand. A single word gloss is applied each time a particular sign is observed, and that same gloss is used for all forms of the sign. It follows that the vocabulary lists in Chapter 3, this volume, and list of glosses in Table 6.2 will always underestimate the size of a subject's vocabulary. For example, Table 6.2 lists 71 signs that occurred in the eight video-taped samples of Dar's signing. Signs like TICKLE and GUM each have one entry on this table. If a different gloss was used for each different form of a sign, TICKLE would have four entries: (1) TICKLE (citation form); (2) TICKLE (place = addressee); (3) TICKLE (place = object); and (4) TICKLE (place = body). GUM would have two entries: (1) GUM (citation form); and (2) GUM (place = addressee). Overall Table 6.2 would grow from 71 signs to 97 signs, an increase of 36.6%. To some extent, dictionaries of spoken language recognize this and provide separate entries for related words (e.g., eat/ate or buy/bought).

We can list reliable items for Dar and for other cross-fostered chimpanzees, and at any point in time estimate that vocabulary size would be the number of reliable items, plus some value. It is unlikely that we can ever calculate this value exactly, but based on the video-taped sample of Dar, there are at least one-third more signs than items in his vocabulary.

Methods for Studying Children

The place modifications that we studied with young chimpanzees are also regarded as extremely important in the grammar of ASL:

The key to understanding ASL syntax, particularly word order, is the recognition that locations in space are used for inflectional purposes. Within the "signing space" (the allowable area in which signs are made), signs may be moved from one location to another to indicate differences in subject and object. (Wilbur, 1980, p. 19)

In view of the importance of place modifications, there has been surprisingly little systematic study of the acquisition of this inflection by young children. Schlesinger and Meadow reported that the deaf infant, Ann, produced immature variants of signs that included placing the signs on the mother and father, in addition to producing signs in standard form. This deaf child of deaf parents was studied when she was 8 to 22 months old, and the illustrative examples of her place modifications show that signs of several grammatical types were modified (Schlesinger and Meadow, 1972, pp. 65–68). Schlesinger and Meadow (1972), as well as other investigators (Maestas y Moores, 1980), report that parents also commonly place signs on infants—CUTE, TIRED, BOY, BABY, BREAD. Perhaps a form modification that is commonly used by infants and their parents is the precursor to the inflection that indicates participants in action.

Another deaf child of deaf parents, first filmed at age 43 months, began to modify action signs by placing them on or near relevant people and objects when he was between four and five years old (Ellenberger and Steyaert, 1978). Only his action signs were examined and this report, too, relies on illustrative examples to document the child's progress. A possible course of development is that this form modification gradually becomes restricted to the appropriate classes of signs and to the appropriate contexts and can then be considered an inflection. To establish whether or not this is the case, more information is required, for children who are between two years and five years old, and for all types of signs, not action signs alone.

An important contribution that comparative psychology can make is in the application of rigorous principles of experimental method to the problems of developmental psycholinguistics. Several cases where comparative psychologists have added experimental rigor to procedures of existing research with children (e.g., Fouts, Shapiro and O'Neil, 1978; R. Gardner and Gardner, 1975; Van Cantfort, Gardner and Gardner, Chapter 5 this volume), and cases in which comparative psychologists applied experimental methods where none were used before (cf. R. Gardner and Gardner, 1984) are discussed in Van Cantfort and Rimpau (1982, pp. 47–64). Instead of relying on illustrative examples and anecdotes on the language used by young children, the methods developed for the study of place modifications with young chimpanzees can be applied to obtain the relevant information.

As in the Ellenberger and Steyaert study and many other recent studies of children, our records consisted of a series of video tapes of the young chimpanzees using signs in conversations with a familiar adult. These unstructured conversations contained a great many questions from the adult, as is also the case for adults in dialogue with young children (Holzman, 1972, p. 314).

The key to our method was to compare the use of citation forms and modified forms of signs. The comparisons were made for signs from different grammatical classes (Tables 6.4a, 6.4b), and for the linguistic contexts that were generated by different types of questions (Tables 6.5, 6.6, and 6.7). Some of the questions in unstructured conversations, such as the single-sign questions, were not useful to the analysis of modified forms. In follow-up studies, it is possible to increase the precision of the technique by instructing the adults to insert a series of prescripted, well-formed questions in the course of the conversation, as has been done in other work with children (Brinton and Fujiki, 1986) and chimpanzees (Van Cantfort, Gardner & Gardner, Chapter 5 this volume). However, it is important to recognize that we will only get probabilistic answers to questions about the use of inflected forms in required linguistic contexts. Nowhere in the signed conversations between Tony and Dar is there a context in which a place-modified sign, and only a place-modified one, is required since a phrase in which the citation form in combination with added lexical items can express the same meaning. Conversely, a place-modified sign could be an effective addition to any utterance. For example, Tony stopped brushing Dar, pretended to cry and asked, WHAT ME DO? Dar replied, CRY BRUSH BRUSH BRUSH. The first BRUSH sign was made on Dar's shoulder, the second in citation form and the third on Tony's arm. The use of three distinct BRUSH signs seems sensible and appropriate in this utterance.

For the Future

The complete set of video tapes of Dar signing with Tony has been transcribed. There are also nine sessions of Dar signing with other human companions, and samples of Moja (27 sessions) and Tatu (15 sessions) signing with their companions. This is certainly a rich source of data for future research. In addition to extending the study of place modifications to Moja and Tatu, other types of sign modifications can be examined in detail. Almost all the modifications noted in the daily field records appeared in the video-taped conversations. There were numerous occurrences recorded in the video transcripts in which Dar modified the movement component (speed or size) in what appears to be a means of adding emphasis to an utterance. Reiteration of signs was recorded frequently also. Comparison of citation and modified forms for other subjects and other types of modifications is clearly a promising avenue for future research.

References

Bloom, L. (1970). *Language development: Form & function in emerging grammars.* Cambridge, MA: MIT Press.

Bolinger, D. (1975). *Aspects of language.* New York: Harcourt Brace Jovanovich.

Brinton, B., Fujiki, M., Winkler, E., & Loeb, D. F. (1986). Responses to requests for clarification in linguistically normal and language-impaired children. *Journal of Speech and Hearing Disorders, 51,* 370–378.

Brown, J.L. (1975). *The evolution of behavior.* New York: W.W. Norton & Co. Inc.

Brown, R. (1970). The first sentences of child and chimpanzee. In R. Brown (Ed.), *Selected psycholinguistic papers,* (pp. 208–281). New York: Macmillan.

Cokely, D., & Gawlik, R. (1974). Childrenese as pidgin. *Sign Language Studies, 5,* 72–81.

Covington, V. (1973). Juncture in American Sign Language. *Sign Language Studies, 2,* 29–38.

Drumm, P., Gardner, B.T., & Gardner, R.A. (1986). Vocal and gestural responses of cross-fostered chimpanzees. *American Journal of Psychology,* *99,* (1), 1–29.

Ellenberger, R., & Steyaert, M. (1978). A child's representation of action in ASL. In P. Siple (Ed.), *Understanding language through sign language research.* New York: Academic Press.

Fant, L. (1972). *Ameslan: An introduction to American Sign Language.* Northridge, CA: Joyce Motion Picture Co.

Fischer, S., & Gough, B. (1978). Verbs in American Sign Language. *Sign Language Studies, 18,* 17–48.

Gardner, B.T., & Gardner, R.A. (1971). Two-way communication with an infant chimpanzee. In A.M. Schrier and F. Stollnitz (Eds.), *Behavior of nonhuman primates,* (Vol. 4, pp. 117–184). New York: Academic Press.

Gardner, B.T., & Gardner, R.A. (1975). Evidence for sentence constituents in the early utterances of child and chimpanzee. *Journal of Experimental Psychology: General, 104,* 244–267.

Gardner, B.T., & Gardner, R.A. (1980). Two comparative psychologists look at language acquisition. In K.E. Nelson (Ed.), *Children's language,* (Vol. 2, pp. 331–369). New York: Gardner Press.

Gardner, B.T., & Gardner, R.A. (1985). Signs of intelligence in cross-fostered chimpanzees. *Philosophical Transactions of the Royal Society, B 308,* 159–176.

Gardner, R.A., & Gardner, B.T. (1969). Teaching sign language to a chimpanzee. *Science, 165,* 664–672.

Gardner, R.A., & Gardner, B.T. (1978). Comparative psychology and language acquisition. *Annals of the New York Academy of Sciences, 309,* 37–76.

Gardner, R.A., & Gardner, B.T. (1984). A vocabulary test for chimpanzees (*Pan troglodytes*). *Journal of Comparative Psychology, 98,* (4), 381–404.

Greenfield, P., & Smith, J. (1976). *The structure of communication in early language development.* New York: Academic Press.

Halliday, M. (1975). *Learning how to mean: Explorations in the development of language.* London: Arnold Press.

Hewes, G.W. (1973). Pongid capacity for language acquisition: An evaluation of recent studies. *Symposia of the Fourth International Congress of Primatology, 1,* 124–143.

Holzman, M. (1972). The use of interrogative forms in the verbal interaction of three mothers and their children. *Journal of Psycholinguistic Research, 1,* 311–335.

Jacobsen, W.H., Jr. (1977). A glimpse of the pre-Washo pronominal system. *Proceedings of the 3rd annual meeting of the Berkeley Linguistics Society, 3,* 55–73.

Jacobsen, W.H., Jr. (1979). Why does Washo lack a passive? In Frans Plank,

Ergativity: Towards a theory of grammatical relations, (pp. 145–160). New York: Academic Press.

Keenan, E. (1977). Making it last: Repetition in children's discourse. In S. Ervin-Tripp and C. Mitchell-Kernan (Eds.), *Child discourse*, (pp. 125–138). New York: Academic Press.

Keenan, E., & Klein, E. (1975). Coherency in children's discourse. *Journal of Psycholinguistic Research, 4,* 365–380.

Kellogg, W.N. (1968). Communication and language in the home-raised chimpanzee. *Science, 162,* 423–427.

Klima, E.S., & Bellugi, U. (1979). *The signs of language.* Cambridge, MA: Harvard University Press.

Laird, L. (1972). A nonhuman being can learn language. *College Composition and Communication, 23* (2), 142–154.

Lieberman, P. (1984). *The biology and evolution of language.* Cambridge, MA: Harvard University Press.

Lyons, J. (1978). *Semantics*, (Vol. 1). New York: Cambridge University Press.

Maestas y Moores, J. (1980). Early linguistic environment: Interactions of deaf parents with their infants. *Sign Language Studies, 26,* 1–13.

Markowicz, H. (1980). Myths about ASL. In H. Lane and F. Grosjean (Eds.), *Recent perspectives on American Sign Language*, (pp. 1–6). Hillsdale, NJ: Lawrence Erlbaum Associates.

Marschark, M., & West, S.A. (1985). Creative language abilities of deaf children. *Journal of Speech and Hearing Research, 28,* 73–78.

Mohay, H. (1982). A preliminary description of the communication systems evolved by two deaf children in the absence of a sign language model. *Sign Language Studies, 34,* 73–90.

Muchmore, E., & Socha, W. (1976). Blood transfusion therapy for leukemic chimpanzee. *Laboratory Primate Newsletter, 15* (3), 13–15.

Robinson, C. (1979). Development of hand preference in children and young chimpanzees. Unpublished doctoral dissertation. University of Nevada-Reno.

Rondal, J.A., & Defays, D. (1978). Reliability of mean length of utterance as a function of sample size in early language development. *The Journal of Genetic Psychology, 133,* 305–306.

Schlesinger, H.S., & Meadow, K.P. (1972). *Deafness and mental health: A developmental approach.* Berkeley: University of California Press.

Shatz, M., & Gelman, R. (1973). The development of communication skills: Modifications in the speech of young children as a function of listener. *Monographs of the Society for Research in Child Development, 38* (5), pp. 1–38.

Siegel, G.M. (1962). Interexaminer reliability for mean length of response. *Journal of Speech and Hearing Research, 5,* 91–95.

Sternberg, M.L.A. (1981). *American Sign Language: A comprehensive dictionary.* New York: Harper & Row.

Stokoe, W.C. (1960). Sign language structure: An outline of the visual communication systems of the American deaf. *Studies in Linguistics*, Occasional Papers. Buffalo, NY: University of Buffalo.

Stokoe, W.C. (1972). *Semiotics and human sign languages.* The Hague: Mouton & Co.

Stokoe, W.C. (1978). *Sign language structure*, revised edition. Silver Spring, MD: Linstok Press.

Stokoe, W., Casterline, D., & Croneberg, C. (1976). *A dictionary of American Sign Language.* Silver Spring, MD: Linstok Press.

Van Cantfort, T.E. (1986). Developmental trends in the replies of chimpanzees to Wh-questions. Unpublished Dissertation. University of Nevada-Reno.

Van Cantfort, T.E., & Rimpau, J.B. (1982). Sign language studies with children and chimpanzees. *Sign Language Studies, 34*, 15–72.

Wilbur, R. (1980). The linguistic description of American Sign Language. In H. Lane and F. Grosjean (Eds.), *Recent perspectives on American Sign Language*, (pp.7–32). Hillsdale, NJ: Lawrence Erlbaum Associates.

Wood, S., Moriarty, K.M., Gardner, B.T., & Gardner, R.A. (1980). Object permanence in child and chimpanzee. *Animal Learning and Behavior, 8* (1), 3–9.

7. Communicative Context and Linguistic Competence: The Effects of Social Setting on a Chimpanzee's Conversational Skill

Chris O'Sullivan and Carey Page Yeager

A problem familiar to anyone who has attempted behavioral research with young children or chimpanzees is that it is essential, and not always easy, to gain the cooperation of the subject when testing. An implication is that testing conditions may affect the performance elicited. In the domain of measurement of language skills, effects of the interlocutor's behavior on children's performance have been noted. Brown (1973, p. 178), for example, explained deficient performances by two children in a study as being due to their mothers' attempts to elicit speech by asking the names of things, rather than conversing in a natural way. According to Brown, this sort of exchange results in lower linguistic productivity by children.

Labov (1972) dealt with the effect of social context on linguistic performance in much greater detail in a book-length study of a sociolinguistically special population: lower class black American children. Studies using standardized tests and elicitation procedures had led some linguists and educators to conclude these children had a language "deficit." Yet Labov observed that, in informal settings, they engaged in competitive verbal games with each other. With some difficulty, a black associate of Labov's created a social context that elicited such a display of verbal skill. He had to make the children feel comfortable and free to participate actively in a game of "showing off," in spite of social inhibitions or prohibition against such behavior with an adult. Labov (1972, pp. 205–213) claims that it was a question of setting up the right sort of language game to elicit the behavior to be measured.

In the research presented here, our hypothesis was that the social context may also influence the linguistic performance of a signing chimpanzee. The linguistic skill we were interested in measuring was mastery of the rules of conversation. This skill is considered an essential component of linguistic competence by child language researchers (cf. Bateson, 1975; Bloom, Rocissano, and Hood, 1976). Conversational skills include turn-taking during discourse, making spontaneous contributions, and giving novel (as opposed to imitative) responses. Mastery of the rules of conversation also includes the ability to vary the mode of discourse with the communicative context.

To test the hypothesis that the interactional context may affect a chimpanzee's conversational behavior, we video taped several sessions of human interactions with Nim, a chimpanzee who had been trained in sign language at Columbia University (Terrace, 1979). The samples were collected under two social conditions, training and conversational. In the training sample, we followed the protocol used during Nim's training sessions in his classroom at Columbia (Sanders, 1985). In the conversational sample, we followed the more relaxed protocol of human-chimp interactions that was the norm at the Institute for Primate Studies (IPS) at the University of Oklahoma, where Nim was then residing. According to Sanders (1985, p. 200), this interaction style was also familiar to Nim from his extracurricular time at his previous home in New York.

METHOD

Experimental Design

In the training sample, the mode of interaction was similar to a drill in which Nim was asked to name objects. Terrace had been observed to use this method with Nim during a brief (less than an hour) visit at IPS ten months before. Chris O'Sullivan attempted to adopt this method in weekly interactions with Nim for a month after the visit. The result was a series of threats from Nim, culminating in a bite. With that reaction, the drill sessions ceased.

In the conversational sample, unlike the training sample, there was no direction imposed by the human interlocutor. The mode of interaction was similar to the usual sessions with Nim during the three years following his return to IPS from New York. Sitting outside or walking on a lead, Nim typically asked for and received tickling and participated in other nonverbal play. He tended to request whatever people around him had that was desirable (a soda, a hat, or shoes—Nim was particularly attracted to shoes). In this context, the caretaker might point out things in the environment and ask Nim to identify them. Generally, the interactions were unstructured and had no particular communicative goals other than companionship. As these typical interactions were primarily social in nature, they seemed to constitute the appropriate context in which to assess Nim's conversational skills.

Subject

Nim, a male chimpanzee, was six years and ten months old when the study was conducted. From shortly after his birth in November, 1973, he had received sign language training at Columbia University, under conditions described by Terrace (1979; Terrace et al., 1979). When he was three years and ten months old, he was returned to his birthplace, the Institute for Primate Studies, where he lived with other chimpanzees on an island or in a cage. There is no record of the frequency of Nim's signing interactions with humans after his return to IPS. He probably saw some signs nearly every day, and engaged in sign interactions three times a week. Twice a week on the average (at least in warm months), students took him for outings on the farm where IPS was located.

Procedure

The data consisted of video tapes of interactions between Nim and two human companions familiar to him, Dave Autry and Bob Ingersoll. Both were psychology students at the University of Oklahoma who had often taken Nim for outings over the three years prior to this study. Both had experience with other signing chimpanzees as well, before and after Nim's return, and had taken sign language classes from R. S. Fouts.

The study was conducted over a three-day period in August, 1980, at IPS. Video tapes were made of six interactions, with two video tape sessions per day. Nim's human companions alternated sessions. Prior to each video tape session, Nim was taken from his cage, put on a lead and taken for a short walk, then brought to a grassy open area where the taped interactions took place. For all sessions, Nim remained on the lead and a box containing toys and articles of clothing was placed nearby.

The first five sessions constituted the *conversational sample* and averaged 16 minutes each. During these sessions, the human companion was instructed to interact with Nim in a relaxed way, according to custom. They tickled and wrestled with each other, and played with different items from the box, to which Nim had free access. No food was introduced during the five conversational sessions with one exception: On one occasion, the human interactor arrived with half a can of soda, which he and Nim shared, finishing it a few minutes into the session.

The sixth session constituted the *training sample*. During this session, the box was placed beside the human and Nim was not permitted to take objects from it, nor to grab the objects from the human. The human removed the items one at a time and asked Nim to name them, demanding Nim's attention by signing emphatically if he failed to respond, or by turning Nim's head back to face the human if he looked away. During this session, Nim was given an orange and some raisins. The training session was terminated after eight minutes because of increasing irritation and volatility on the part of both participants, although the procedure was not unfamiliar to Nim. As mentioned earlier, this procedure had been adopted in an abbreviated series of training sessions at IPS the previous year, in our attempt to follow the procedures used in training Nim during his early years. A recent article by Sanders corroborates the similarity of the training session to Nim's classroom sessions at Columbia University (Sanders, 1985, pp. 198 & 200). In our experience with preadolescent Nim at IPS, this approach invariably triggered an aggressive response.

Analysis

A transcript of each video tape was made by the second author assisted by the human participant for that session. The conversational analysis closely followed the methodology and operational definitions of Terrace et al. (1979), and the more complete account of these methods in Sanders (1985). Yeager had learned these methods and applied them to an extensive corpus of the orangutan Chantek's sign interactions while working with Lyn Miles in Tennessee. The purpose of this analytic system is to determine the level of conformity of a conversational sample to the rules of conversation, specifically the caveats against interruption (following turn-taking rules), and the requirement of making spontaneous and novel contributions to the conversation.

Nim's utterances were analyzed for adjacency vs. spontaneity: A sign sequence was considered *adjacent* if it occurred within five seconds after the end of a sign sequence by the human interlocutor; it was considered *spontaneous* if the human had not signed within the five seconds preceding Nim's sign. Interruption rate was also temporally determined: Utterances were counted as *interruptions* when the signer began to sign after the other primate had started to sign and before he had finished signing.

Nim's adjacent utterances were further analyzed on the basis of content. The three exhaustive categories of adjacent signs were novel, expansion, and imitation, following the terminology and definitions of Sanders (1985). A sign or sign sequence was *novel* only if it contained none of the signs used by the caretaker in his preceding adjacent utterance. It was an *expansion* if it contained one or some of the signs used by the human in his prior adjacent utterance, but included an additional sign or signs. It was an *imitation* if all the signs were used by the human in his prior adjacent utterance. Table 7.1 gives an example of dialogue and utterance classification. [Editors' Note: In order to be comparable to Sanders' earlier analyses of Nim's conversations (Sanders & Terrace, 1979), the authors of this chapter have followed his definitions for novel utterances, expansions and imitations. For an improved terminology, and a discussion of definitions of novel, expansion and imitation as used in studies of children and in other sign language studies of chimpanzees, see Chapters 2 and 5 this volume.]

RESULTS

In order to make observations about the effect of the social context on Nim's performance, the conversational sample was compared with the training sample. The results of the analyses for spontaneity and adjacency are shown in

Table 7.2 as percentages of utterance types. In the training sample, a small percentage of Nim's sign sequences (14%) were spontaneous; in the conversational sample, most of Nim's sign sequences (60%) were spontaneous.

Table 7.1
Sample of Prior Context Analysis of Nim's Utterances

Time	Human	Nim	Classification
:13	WANT TICKLE NIM?/		
:14	WHAT THIS?/		
:15		HAT/	Novel
:17	WANT TICKLE?/		
:18		TICKLE NIM/	Expansion
.			
.	(tickling in progress)		
.			
:33		MORE/	Spontaneous
:34	COME HERE,		
:35	NIM,		
:36			
:37	PLAY/		
.			
.	(more tickling)		
.			
:47		GO THERE?/	Spontaneous

When adjacency rates are high, the proportion of expansions and imitations combined is also high. Thus, in the training sample, 86% of Nim's sign sequences were adjacent, and 31% of his total utterances were expansions and imitations. In the conversational sample, 40% of Nim's sign sequences were adjacent, and expansions and imitations combined accounted for only 11% of all the utterances.

The two samples present a strong contrast in interruption rates, as well: In the training sample, Nim's interruption rate was 31% but in the conversational sample it was only 9% (see Table 7.3). Interruptions by Nim and by his human interlocutor were calculated on the basis of Nim's total utterances for each sample.

DISCUSSION

The data show that Nim did modify his conversational style according to the social context. In the drill session, he imitated his interlocutor twice as often as he did in the social/play session. Nim made more than four times as many spontaneous linguistic contributions to the interaction when the setting was social than he did when it was didactic. Nim behaved as if he understood that "the rules of the game" were different in these two types of interactions, even though his interlocutor was the same. These results suggest that an assessment of the performance of a signing chimpanzee will reflect the subject's response to the situation as well as the skill that is being measured.

Table 7.2
Classification of Nim's Utterances in Training and Conversational Contexts

	Sample	
	Training	Conversational
Number of utterances	65	149
Spontaneous	13.8%	59.7%
Adjacent		
Novel	55.4%	29.5%
Expansion	16.9%	4.7%
Imitation	13.8%	6.0%

Table 7.3
Interruptions by Nim and His Human Interlocutor in Training and Conversational Contexts as Percentages of Nim's Total Utterances

	Sample	
	Training	Conversational
By Nim	31%	9%
By human	6%	6%

Two questions are raised by these results. First, why are the results different in the two social contexts? Second, what are the implications of these results for the interpretation of past research, based on observations of linguistic performance in a single type of setting?

Starting with the question of Nim's responses to the different contexts, Nim's performance in the training sample seems parallel in some respects to children's performances in similar contexts. As noted earlier, Brown (1973) observed that children's performance declined when their mothers asked them to name objects. Similarly, Shatz (1983, p. 873) states that redundancy is characteristic of children's responses to tests involving object identification (object identification was the primary task in the training sample). Thus, in testing situations, chimpanzees may adopt some of the strategies shown by young children, specifically lack of elaboration (Brown, 1973), repetitiveness, and imitation (Shatz, 1983). Brown cites Kernan's explanation that the child who was at ease made spontaneous contributions, while the child who was uneasy merely answered questions (1973, p. 178).

Shatz (1983) also describes children as drawing on common routines in their verbal interactions. The mode of interaction in the training sample was purposely modelled on the procedures used during the four years that Nim was trained and tested at Columbia University. In many respects, Nim's response was also similar to that reported by Terrace et al. (1979) in their analysis of Nim's conversational behavior in video tapes made in Nim's classroom at Columbia. The adjacency rate in our training sample, 86%, is nearly identical to the adjacency rate of 87% reported by Terrace et al. (1979). Thus, the percent of Nim's utterances that were spontaneous was 13–14% in both cases.

When Bloom, Rocissano, and Hood (1976, p. 527) reported novelty, expansion, and imitation rates for children, they calculated rates as percentages of the children's total utterances. Accordingly, we have used Nim's total utterances in our samples whenever we calculated percentages. Terrace et al. (1979, pp. 896–897), however, reported Nim's novelty, expansion, and imitation rates as percentages of Nim's *adjacent* utterances, resulting in higher percentages.[*] In order to draw comparisons across the three data sets, we have recalculated the rates given by Terrace et al. as percentages of Nim's total utterances in their sample (672). We then found that his novelty rates were comparable to our training sample: 55% of his utterances in our training sample, and 46% in Terrace's sample, were novel. Given similar adjacency rates, imitation and expansion rates combined are not extremely different: 31% for our training sample and 41% for Terrace et al.'s. Nim's imitation rate alone (excluding expansions) was much lower in our training sample (14%) than in Terrace et al.'s data (34% of his total utterances), however. Indeed, our figure is slightly lower than the imitation rate of 18% reported by Bloom, Rocissano, and Hood (1976, p. 527) for children at stage 1 of language development.

Nim's history is informative as to how this sort of conversational repertoire might have developed, and how the sample analyzed by Terrace et al. (1979) was obtained. According to Sanders (1985), most of Nim's sign language training took place in his classroom at Columbia, where "in the typical training situation, the trainer would begin in control of some object that Nim would like to obtain . . . Nim's use of the sign [was] instrumental in his obtaining these rewards" (p. 200).

Sanders also described the conditions under which fifteen video tapes (a subset of which constituted Terrace et al.'s sample) were made of Nim's

---

[*]Editors' Note: This way of calculating rates inflates the percentage of imitation and expansion and distorts all of the comparisons that Terrace made between Nim's imitation rate and that of children.

interactions. Teachers prepared lesson plans for these video-taped interactions, and "some recordings included explicit training of new signs, with the use of molding, guidance, and imitation," but more often tried to create situations in which Nim would use familiar signs (p. 200). Nonetheless, "the videotape recordings captured a variety of situations in which the trainer was keen to elicit signing from Nim . . . the videotaped sessions were not representative of the more relaxed sessions at home" (p. 201). Thus it appears that imitation was sometimes an appropriate response in such a context, and adjacent signing (responding to questions or prompts) was nearly always an appropriate response. It also appears that the training session we video taped was similar to many previous video-taped sessions for Nim, except that we did not attempt to teach him new signs. (This difference might account for the lower imitation rate we obtained.)

Turning to the second question, how do our results reflect on the interpretation of earlier sign language studies of chimpanzees and conclusions about the linguistic capacities of apes? Terrace et al.'s 1979 article presented conversational analyses of three and a half hours of the video-tape sample described by Sanders (1985). The conversational analysis revealed that a high percentage of Nim's utterances were repetitions of his interlocutors' prior utterances and that his spontaneous contributions were extremely rare. Such a pattern of conversational interaction cast doubt on the achievements of all signing chimpanzees. It presented a picture of chimpanzees simply "aping" signs, and perhaps performing other tricks of the hand for rewards. Yet the entire corpus on which this conclusion was based consisted of training and testing situations. No relaxed conversational interactions were included. Our conversational sample indicated that Nim's conversational behavior under such conditions does not reflect his entire repertoire. The evidence presented here demonstrates that Nim's conversational behavior in a relaxed conversational social interaction was very different from his behavior in a training or testing situation. We question whether conclusions about conversational skills can be drawn from an analysis of interactions that are more didactic than sociable.

According to Terrace et al. (1979):

> Sequences of signs, produced by Nim and other apes, may resemble superficially the first multiword sequences produced by children. But unless alternative explanations of an ape's combination of signs are eliminated, in particular the habit of partially imitating teachers' recent utterances, there is no reason to regard an ape's multisign utterances as a sentence. (pp. 900–901)

It is in this context that out findings of relatively low imitation rates on Nim's part in both our training and conversational samples—rates comparable to the human standard—assume particular importance.

Another basis of Terrace et al.'s (1979) critique of chimpanzee sign language use was Nim's high interruption rate across the three and a half hours of video tape, which was given as 70% (p. 897). To obtain figures that could be compared to the interruption rate in the present experiment, we recalculated this interruption rate as a percentage of Nim's total utterances in the sample, rather than as a percentage of the "overlapping" utterances. Using this method, Nim's interruption rate was 51% in Terrace et al.'s sample. Nim's interruption rate in our training sample, 31%, was considerably lower. [Editors' Note: A degree of temporal overlap between the signs of two persons engaged in conversation is a common feature of fluent signing by human adults. In order to be parallel to Terrace, the authors of this chapter have followed his definition of *interruption*, which does not take such normal overlaps into account. For a discussion of overlap and turn-taking, see Baker and Covington, cited in Van Cantfort and Rimpau, 1982.] Moreover, the percent of Nim's utterances interrupted by the caretaker in Terrace et al.'s sample may also have been higher than in our samples: Extrapolating from figures given by Terrace et al. (p. 897), it appears that 22% of Nim's utterances were interrupted by his interlocutor, while only 6% of Nim's utterances were interrupted in our samples (see Table 7.3).

In accounting for the human's interruptions, Terrace et al. (1979) refer to the human's efforts to "hold the floor," (p. 897). The difference between Nim's interruption rates in our training and conversational samples is even greater than that between Terrace et al.'s sample and our training sample. When Nim interrupted his interlocutor in our training sample, he was often responding to the human's repeated question, to which he had previously failed to respond or had responded by changing the topic. Thus, in Terrace's training/drill situation and in ours, interruptions seem to indicate a lack of cooperation between the interlocutors and attempts to assert conversational dominance.

Van Cantfort and Rimpau (1982, p. 24; see also Gaustad, 1981, p. 90) questioned whether Nim's performance was generalizable to other chimpanzees. They speculated that his deficiencies might be due to the means of instruction and to other aspects of Nim's upbringing. Our data support this view only to the extent that our training sample, like the sample reported by Terrace et al. (1979), elicited interactional behaviors in Nim that he may have developed during his early classroom instruction. Our data provide more support for questions raised by Van Cantfort and Rimpau (1982, pp. 21–22) about the restriction of the analysis to discourse during training sessions.

In contrast, Savage-Rumbaugh, Pate, Lawson, Smith, and Rosenbaum (1983) concluded that the differences found between the chimpanzees trained by the Gardners and Fouts and those trained by Rumbaugh (1977) and Terrace are "more reflective of ways in which different experimenters have interpreted the behaviors of the chimpanzees than of true differences in the capacities of the apes themselves" (p. 459). Although we acknowledge that observer bias is always a problem, we feel that one must be particularly cautious in drawing conclusions that skill deficits exist. What is being measured in any set of observations of chimpanzee language use (or anything else) are behaviors, not capacities. It is quite possible that the researchers' diverse interpretations are based on observations of behaviors that are, in fact, different. If the social ambiance or task elicits different behaviors, different inferences in regard to capacity will follow.

A comment that seems highly apropos is Shatz's (1983) summation: "Thus, many of the explanations proposed over the years to account for children's lack of ability have to be revised as the employment of different tasks often revealed the presence of knowledge or a skill thought to be lacking" (p. 872). As evidence that we need constant reminders of the importance of settings and tasks when drawing conclusions about abilities, statements similar to Shatz's can be found in the writing of psychologists and linguists many years before. In 1970, Cazden devoted an article to admonishing her colleagues for neglecting context in child language research, and drawing negative conclusions from negative evidence.

An underlying problem in scientific philosophy often seems to be raised by attempts to assess linguistic ability. As Edwards (1976) articulated the problem, with reference to the deficit theory of child language:

Was the speech so constrained by the situation or the context that generalizations beyond that context would be misleading? . . . some accounts of verbal deprivation rest on a premature assumption that what is not done is never done, or *cannot* be done. (p. 117)

All of these comments apply to sign language research with chimpanzees, except that child language researchers are not discouraged from further investigation if their subjects seem deficient.

Other important requisites of studying language behavior, as Labov (1972) demonstrated, are gaining the cooperation of one's subject, and ascertaining that the goals are mutually understood. Cooperation assumes particular importance in measuring conformity to the rules of conversation. From this perspective, one might argue that Nim's alleged failure to understand the very basis of linguistic communication, social exchange, was in part an appropriate response to the task at hand.

In our study, Nim demonstrated different conversational behaviors in different contexts. The evidence that his apparent conversational ability varied across social settings should challenge researchers to create new and involving tasks to explore the range of knowledge and skills their subjects may possess. Prematurely proclaiming the limits of chimpanzees' cognitive or linguistic capacities does little to advance our own knowledge.

References

Bateson, M.C. (1975). Mother-infant exchanges: The epigenesis of conversational interaction. In D. Aaronson and R.W. Rieber (Eds.), *Developmental psycholinguistic and communication disorders*, (Vol. 263). New York: New York Academy of Sciences.

Bloom, L., Rocissano, L., & Hood, L. (1976). Adult-child discourse. *Cognitive Psychology, 8*, 521–552.

Brown, R. (1973). *A first language*. Cambridge, MA: Harvard University Press.

Cazden, C. (1970). The neglected situation in child language research and education. *Journal of Social Issues, 25*, 35–60.

Edwards, A.D. (1976). *Language in culture and class: The sociology of language and education*. London: Heinemann Educational Books, Ltd.

Gaustad, G.R. (1981). Review of *Nim*, by H.S. Terrace. *Sign Language Studies, 30*, 89–94.

Labov, W. (1972). *Language in the inner city: Studies in the black English vernacular*. Philadelphia: University of Pennsylvania Press.

Sanders, R.J. (1985). Teaching apes to ape language: Explaining the imitative and nonimitative signing of a chimpanzee (*Pan troglodytes*). *Journal of Comparative Psychology, 99*, 197–210.

Sanders, R.J., & Terrace, H.S. (September, 1979). Conversations with a chimpanzee: Language-like performance without competence. Paper presented at the American Psychological Association Meeting, New York.

Savage-Rumbaugh, E.S., Pate, J.L., Lawson, J., Smith, S.T., & Rosenbaum, S. (1983). Can a chimpanzee make a statement? *Journal of Experimental Psychology: General, 112*, 457–492.

Shatz, M. (1983). Communication. In J.H. Flavell and E.M. Markman (Eds.), *Handbook of Child Psychology*, (Vol. 3, pp. 841–889). New York: Wiley.

Terrace, H.S. (1979). *Nim*. New York: Knopf.

Terrace, H.S., Petitto, L.A., Sanders, R.J., & Bever, T.G. (1979). Can an ape create a sentence? *Science, 206*, 891–902.

Van Cantfort, T.E., & Rimpau, J.B. (1982). Sign language studies with children and chimpanzees. *Sign Language Studies, 34*, 15–72.

8. The Infant Loulis Learns Signs from Cross-Fostered Chimpanzees

Roger S. Fouts, Deborah H. Fouts
and *Thomas E. Van Cantfort*

I n October, 1970, Roger Fouts brought Washoe to the Institute for Primate Studies (IPS), University of Oklahoma, where he had been appointed as Research Associate. The University of Oklahoma maintained a colony of 18 chimpanzees at IPS, and Fouts planned to continue the research with Washoe there, with new objectives and new questions. Would Washoe sign to the other chimpanzees? If Washoe signed to them, what would she sign? Would the other chimpanzees learn signs, either from human caregivers or from Washoe herself? The long range goal of the continuation of Project Washoe was to explore the cultural transmission of ASL: Would Washoe pass on her signing skills to an offspring?

Washoe at Oklahoma

At IPS, Washoe was housed with other chimpanzees of the colony, inside a laboratory building, in a complex of interconnected enclosures. As part of her introduction to the colony, she also spent considerable time with other juveniles, on a one-third acre island in a lake, several hundred feet from the laboratory building. The Oklahoma students who were members of Roger Fouts' research team used both ASL and spoken English when interacting with Washoe. Although none of the students were native or fluent signers, they all attended classes in ASL throughout their participation in the research.

Washoe was observed to sign to the other IPS chimpanzees shortly after her arrival. At that time, the other chimpanzees had no experience with ASL, and did not appear to understand what she was signing, nor to answer her. Washoe often signed COME HUG to other juvenile chimpanzees when they became upset. Once, when she was with three juveniles on the island, she signed this phrase in a somewhat different context. While Washoe was grooming a young colony-born male in the middle of the island, two female chimpanzees discovered something that frightened them at the east end of the island (most probably a snake) and began giving alarm calls. Washoe stood up bipedally and watched the two females move toward the other end of the island, while they continued to give occasional alarm calls. Wahsoe started in that direction also, but her young friend remained lounging on the ground. When Washoe was approximately four meters away, she turned and signed to him, COME HUG COME HUG, but he remained where he was. Washoe then went back to him, took his hand, and led him to the west end of the island.

On another occasion, when she was in a group of chimpanzees who were being given fruit, Washoe indicated a water spigot in a corner and signed GO DRINK to one of her competitors. She often signed HUG to the young chimpanzees, but after Washoe was introduced to the adult population, the sign she used most was TICKLE. If, as was often the case, the other chimpanzees did not respond to her sign, Washoe pursued them until a tickle game was started.

Booee, Bruno, Cindy, and Thelma were the first of the IPS chimpanzees to learn signs from their human caregivers (Fouts, 1973). Booee and Bruno, and later, Lucy and Ally (a.k.a. Ali), went on to acquire sizable vocabularies and sophisticated signing skills (Fouts, 1975; Fouts, Chown & Goodin, 1976; Fouts, Shapiro & O'Neil, 1978). At least one of the young chimpanzees, Manny, learned COME HUG from Washoe, and used it in appropriate contexts, such as when greeting or when comforting another chimpanzee (Fouts & Rigby, 1977). Washoe, herself, continued to learn new signs, adding items such as MONKEY and ROCK to her vocabulary. She participated in a study comparing the effectiveness of two specific procedures, modelling and molding, for introducing new signs (Fouts & Goodin, 1974). In this follow up of Fouts' dissertation research (1972), modelling and molding were equally effective procedures for nine-year-old Washoe (and eight-year-old Lucy). Washoe also continued to produce phrases, and some of her phrases were novel combinations of signs, describing objects that were not represented by a sign in her vocabulary, such as WATER BIRD for the swans on the lake, and ROCK BERRY for Brazil nuts (Fouts & Rigby, 1977).

Washoe's Babies

In August, 1976, Washoe gave birth to her first infant, a baby with a congenital heart defect who lived for four hours only. In January, 1979, she gave birth to her second infant, Sequoyah, fathered by Ally. Unfortunately, this infant was sickly also, and died of pneumonia when he was two months old. Throughout Sequoyah's short life, Washoe displayed excellent maternal behavior (for details see Fouts, Hirsch & Fouts, 1982).

Several primate facilities around the country were contacted in hopes of finding an infant that could replace Washoe's dead baby. The Yerkes Regional Primate Research Center kindly agreed to provide the project with a ten-month-old male, and on March 24, 1979, 15 days after the death of Sequoyah, Loulis arrived at IPS. Fouts went to see Washoe first, and signed to her, I HAVE BABY FOR YOU. Washoe became very excited. Every hair on her body stood on end. She began to hoot and swagger bipedally while signing, BABY MY BABY repeatedly. Fouts then went out to fetch Loulis. When he returned carrying Loulis and entered Washoe's enclosure her high excitement disappeared immediately. Fouts had expected Washoe to take and hold Loulis, but instead she only looked at him and signed a very calm, BABY. Loulis, meanwhile, clung tightly to Fouts while watching Washoe. When Fouts left the two in their enclosure, they were sitting next to each other, looking out, and, in Washoe's case, interacting with the human observers.

After an hour, Washoe began to approach Loulis playfully, touching him gently and then moving away, in an attempt to start tickle or chase play. Loulis did not respond. He continued to sit on the floor and look at the humans. When night came, Washoe tried to get Loulis to sleep in her arms, as her own infant had done. Loulis refused, and slept alone, on the same bench as Washoe. At 4:00 A.M. the next morning, Washoe woke up, stood bipedally, swaggered, and signed COME BABY to Loulis, slapping her arms loudly as she signed. This commotion woke Loulis, and no doubt frightened him. He jumped into Washoe's arms and they both went back to sleep, and from then on, they have slept together at night. Thus, within 24 hours, Washoe had begun to care for Loulis as if she were his mother, and he, too, began to depend on her mothering. According to plan, the human caregivers restricted their signing to Washoe, and the present study was initiated.

PROJECT LOULIS

Signing to Loulis

To show that Loulis could learn signs from chimpanzees, human beings did not use ASL signs in his presence (with the exception of seven question signs, WHO, WHAT, WHERE, WHICH, WANT, SIGN and NAME). Instead, Fouts and his associates used vocal English and the rich repertoire of human and chimpanzee nonverbal gestures, postures, and calls to interact with Washoe and Loulis. When Washoe signed to them, they responded appropriately: for example, if she signed DRINK, she was given a drink, or told, in English, that she would get a drink in a little while. If anyone erred and signed when Loulis was present, the instance was recorded. Over the five years of the experiment, there were fewer than 40 such instances.

While humans refrained from signing to Loulis, chimpanzees were not bound by this rule. In addition to his adoptive mother Washoe, three other signing chimpanzees interacted with Loulis, in the course of the five-year-three-month experiment. In December, 1979, seven-year-old Moja, who had been reared in the Gardners' cross-fostering laboratory (see Chapter 1 this volume) joined Washoe and Loulis at IPS. The following year, Washoe, Loulis, and Moja, along with the Foutses, moved to Central Washington University.

Fig. 8.1 Washoe (15.5 years) with her adopted son Loulis (3 years).

The three chimpanzees were housed in a new complex of interconnected en-closures. In May, 1981, Washoe, Loulis and Moja were joined by five-and-a-half-year-old Tatu and five-year-old Dar, who had also been cross-fostered in the Gardners' laboratory.

Criteria of Form and Usage

In order to qualify as a sign, a gesture that Loulis made had to resemble the form of an actual ASL sign in place, configuration, and movement. In addition, before it was counted as a sign in Loulis' vocabulary, the gesture had to be reported by three different observers as occurring in an appropriate context. The observers recorded the gesture, the context, and the accompanying non-verbal behavior. They also noted whether Loulis was oriented toward someone (e.g., toward Washoe, or Dar, or a human caregiver), and whether he was look-ing someone in the face, when he made the sign. Either or both these be-haviors were used to determine the addressee. In addition, level of arousal was scored as high, medium, or low by noting the degree to which his hair was pilo-erected. Loulis' body postures and facial expressions were recorded as well, as were any vocalizations (e.g., laughs, screams, or pant-hoots). If the sign and the nonverbal behaviors were consistent with each other and with the referent, then the sign was judged to have been used appropriately by Loulis.

Gestures developed into signs gradually, as in the case of COME/GIMME, which Loulis started to make soon after he joined Washoe. In early COME/GIMMEs, Loulis extended his arm in front of himself, palm up, for one to three seconds. In the following months, the form of the sign improved, as Loulis began to flex the extended hand. He also began to babble or play with this sign, making it in a variety of unrelated contexts. By August, 1980, he was using COME/GIMME almost entirely in appropriate contexts, and at this time, his nonverbal behavior started to complement the COME/GIMME signs. For example, when offered a highly preferred food or drink, Loulis now looked di-rectly at the object while he food-grunted and signed GIMME. He began to orient the sign toward humans or chimpanzees, and he gazed at the face of the addressee. During the second meeting of Loulis and Moja, when the connect-ing cage door was opened, Loulis oriented toward Moja and signed COME directly to her. Moja approached the signing infant, and initiated a play interac-tion. COME/GIMME became a distinct sign for Loulis, quite separate from reaching or the natural chimpanzee begging gesture. In approximately 25% of the COME/GIMME signs that Loulis made, he used one hand to sign and the other hand to reach or to make the begging gesture.

In a number of cases, such as the signs TICKLE, DRINK, and HUG, there was an initial period during which Loulis used the correct form in a vari-ety of contexts before he restricted their use to appropriate contexts. Loulis was not credited with these signs until there were three observations, by different observers, of his use of the sign in appropriate contexts. In the case of TICKLE, for example, Loulis had many opportunities to observe Washoe soliciting tickling from the human caregivers. Washoe would first sign TICKLE, then press her side against the caging so that the person could tickle her. Initially, Loulis imitated Washoe by pressing his body to the caging, without making the sign, and usually the caregiver would tickle him when he did this. Later, Loulis began to make TICKLE signs, but did not press his body to the caging. Then he went through a period of signing TICKLE repeatedly to himself, without approaching the human caregiver. Finally, he began to incorporate the nonverbal elements that Washoe used in signing TICKLE. Thus, he would approach persons with a play-face, slightly bipedal, and sign TICKLE either on himself or on the person, and then press his side or bottom against the caging for tickling. Thirteen of Loulis' first 22 signs went through a transition of this sort, before he began to use them in their appropriate contexts (Fouts, Hirsch & Fouts, 1982).

Signs in Loulis' Vocabulary

The first sign to appear in Loulis' vocabulary was the name sign that Washoe used for George Kimball. Loulis was first observed to use this sign eight days after his introduction to Washoe. George's name sign was originally made by moving the open hand down the back of the head, indicating the long hair, fashionable for men in the 1970s. However, Washoe changed the form of the sign in a very effective way. George was in charge of serving Washoe and Loulis breakfast, so his attention was much in demand. If George had his back turned, he could not tell that Washoe was signing. So Washoe made his name sign into a noisy sign, by slapping the top of her head. The sign proved to be so effective in getting George's attention, that Washoe began to use it to refer to persons who did not have name signs, and finally, to anyone who was not looking at her. We glossed this noisy attention-getting sign as the PERSON (or "Hey you!") sign. In addition to Loulis, Moja, Tatu, and Dar also acquired this unusual sign from Washoe, and all used it in the same way as Washoe did.

At 15 months of age, Loulis started to use combinations of two signs, such as HURRY GIMME and PERSON COME. By age 29 months, Loulis was using at least 17 different signs (Fouts, Hirsch & Fouts, 1982). By age 63 months, his vocabulary had grown to 47 signs (Fouts, Fouts & Schoenfeld, 1984). On June 24, 1984, after five years and three months of the experimental procedure, the restriction on human signing in Loulis' presence was ended, because, in essence, it was a form of deprivation for Loulis as well as for the other chimpanzees. At that time, Loulis was 73 months old, and his vocabulary consisted of the 51 signs shown in Table 8.1. A few of his signs, such as FLOWER/DEB and HAT/PERSON, appeared to be homonyms, and the form described in the table was assigned two different English glosses, for the two distinct contexts in which it was used.

Table 8.1 shows that the vocabulary of Loulis included signs from several different categories: names (e.g., ALAN, DAR), pronouns (ME, YOU), nouns (e.g., BALL, BIRD), verbs (e.g., CHASE, HUG), locatives (e.g., IN, OUT) and such markers and traits as NO, SORRY, and WANT. This last sign has two distinct forms in ASL—a one-handed version, placed on the signer's chest, and a two-handed version, made in the space before the signer's body (cf. DESIRE and WANT in Stokoe, Casterline, & Croneberg, 1976, *Dictionary of American Sign Language*). Washoe used the first of these forms (see Table 3.2), while one of the few signs used by human signers in Loulis' presence was the other form of WANT. Even though Loulis was exposed to both forms of the sign, the WANT that he acquired was the one used by his mother.

In June 1986, the policy of speaking and signing in the presence of the chimpanzees was changed. From that time on, only signing was used in the presence of the chimpanzees°, and vocal speech was used only outside the chimpanzee living area. As of October, 1987, the vocabulary of Loulis had increased to 70 signs.

Washoe as Teacher

When she was an infant in Reno, Washoe's human foster family taught her signs by modelling, molding, and signing on her body the way human parents teach deaf infants (Maestas y Moores, 1980; Schlesinger & Meadow, 1972; Chapter 1 this volume). She used all of these methods with her own infant, Loulis.

During the first three days that they were together, Washoe often turned toward Loulis, signed COME, approached, and then grasped his arm and retrieved him. During the next five days, she signed COME, and only approached Loulis. Then, after the first eight days, Washoe no longer approached but only signed COME while orienting and looking at Loulis until he responded by coming to her. COME was among the first signs that Loulis came to use.

Parents of deaf children often mold the infant's hand into the configuration and then put the hand through the movement of a sign (Maestas y Moores, 1980, pp. 5–6; Chapter 1 this volume). Washoe also molded Loulis' hands. For example, while waiting for a candy bar that a human friend was bringing to her, Washoe signed FOOD repeatedly with much excitement and food-grunts. Loulis was sitting next to her, watching. Washoe stopped signing, took Loulis' hand, molded it into the FOOD configuration, and put it through the FOOD movement several times (see Table 3.2 this volume). In a similar context,

---

°With the exception of occasional tests, to demonstrate that the chimpanzees continued to understand spoken English.

Table 8.1

Form of Signs in Loulis' Vocabulary

ALAN P: Temple C: Fist M: Index edge contacts	BOOK P: Palms C: Both curved hands, palms facing M: Palms of opposite hands grasp
APPLE/FRUIT P: Cheek C: Curved hand, palm to P M: Knuckles rub down	BRUSH P: Arm or other place on body to be brushed C: Open hand or fist, palm to Signer M: Rubs to and fro
BALL P: Fingertips C: Both curved hands, palms facing M: Fingertips of opposite hands contact	CATCH P: Palm, of curved hand C: Fist M: Back of fist contacts

BANANA
P: Tip of index, extended from fist
C: Hooked index extended from fist
M: Index grasps then pulls toward
   Signer
	CHASE
	P: Inside of wrist, of open hand,
	   forearm extended
	C: Fist
	M: Knuckles contact repeatedly

BIB P: Chest C: Both open hands, palms to Signer M: Fingertips rub down	CLEAN P: Palm, of open hand, palm up C: Fist M: Knuckles rub repeatedly in circle
BIRD P: Lips C: Pincer hand, palm to Signer M: Index and thumb grasp repeatedly	COMB P: Temple C: Open hand or claw hand, palm to P M: Rubs down

BLANKET
P: Underside of chin
C: Both fists, palms to Signer and
   forearms vertical
M: Knuckles contact
	COME/GIMME*
	P: Space in front of Signer
	C: Curved hand or pincer hand, palm
	   down or palm to side
	M: Arm extends toward Addressee or
	   object, then wrist or fingers beckon

Table 8.1 (continued)

DAR
P: Ear
C: Index extended from fist
M: Tip of index contacts or rubs forward

DIANA
P: Nose
C: Thumb extended from open hand,
    palm to side
M: Thumb contacts

DIRTY
P: Underside of chin
C: Open hand or fist, palm down
M: Back of wrist contacts repeatedly,
    often forcefully so that teeth click
    together audibly (the audible
    component is characteristic
    of Washoe also)

DRINK*
P: Lips or mouth
C: Thumb extended from fist
M: Tip of thumb contacts or inserts

FLOWER/DEB
P: Nose
C: Curved hand, palm to Signer
M: Fingertips contact

FOOD/EAT
P: Lips
C: Curved hand or pincer hand,
    palm to Signer
M: Fingertips contact

FRIEND
P: Indexes
C: Both hooked indexes extended from
    fists, one palm up and other palm
    down
M: Indexes of opposite hand interlock

GO*
P: Space in front of Signer
C: Index extended from fist or from
    open hand
M: Arm extends away from Signer
    then wrist rotates to point index
    toward location

GOOD*
P: Lips
C: Open hand
M: Palm contacts repeatedly

GUM
P: Cheek
C: Index extended from fist or from
    open hand
M: Tip of index contacts then
    bends and straightens

HAT/PERSON*
P: Top of head
C: Open hand
M: Palm contacts repeatedly

HOSE
P: Space in front of Signer
C: Index extended from fist
M: Index or hand wiggles up and down

HOT/COFFEE
P: Space in front of lips
C: Open hand
M: Approaches then turns to palm down
    while extending arm away from Signer

HUG*
P: Upper arms
C: One curved hand or both curved
    hands, forearms crossed
M: Palms contact

Table 8.1 (continued)

HURRY P: Space in front of Signer C: Spread hand, bent at wrist M: Shakes	**PAINT** P: Palm of hand C: Open hand, palm to Signer M: Fingertips contact then fingers bend and straighten
IN P: Palm, of curved hand, index edge up C: Open hand or curved hand, palm to Signer and fingers point down M: Fingers insert	**PEEKABOO/MASK** P: Both eyes C: Open hand M: Palm contacts
ME/MINE* P: Chest C: Open hand M: Palm contacts repeatedly	**PLEASE** P: Chest C: Open hand, palm to P M: Rubs to side
MILK P: Space in front of Signer C: Fist, index edge up M: Squeezes repeatedly	**ROGER** P: Ear C: Pincer hand M: Index and thumb grasp
MORE P: Fingertips C: Both pincer hands M: Fingertips of opposite hands contact repeatedly	**SANDWICH** P: Back, of open hand, palm to Signer C: Curved hand, palm to P and crossing P M: Palm contacts and hand grasps
NO P: Head C: N/A M: Shakes side to side	**SHOE*** P: On object or space below Signer C: One fist, or both fists, side by side and palms to Signer M: Knuckles contact object or ground
NUT* P: Teeth C: Thumb extended from fist, palm down M: Tip of thumb rubs away from Signer	**SORRY** P: Chest C: Open hand, palm to Signer M: Rubs down

OUT
P: Palm, of curved hand, palm to
    Signer
C: Open hand, fingers point down
M: Back of hand contacts then moves
    up out of grasp
	SWALLOW
	P: Throat
	C: Index extended from fist or from
	    open hand
	M: Tip of index rubs down

	THAT/THERE P: On object or in space in front of Signer C: Index extended M: Tip of index contacts or points toward object or location

Table 8.1 (continued)

TICKLE* P: Back of hand or place on body to be tickled C: Hooked index extended M: Tip of index rubs to side	WANT P: Chest C: Curved hand, palm to Signer M: Rubs down
TIME P: Back of wrist C: Hooked index extended M: Tip of index contacts sometimes repeated	WASHOE P: Contralateral ear C: Curved hand M: Fingertips rub
TOOTHBRUSH P: Lips or teeth C: Index extended from fist or from open hand, finger points to side M: Edge of index rubs side to side	YOU P: Addressee C: Index extended M: Index points

P = Place, C = Configuration, and M = Movements
*Indicates first ten signs acquired by Loulis

Washoe formed the sign GUM, but with her hand on Loulis' cheek (see Table 3.2 this volume). During the first few months after his arrival, Washoe was also observed to place DRINK on Loulis' lips and HAT on his head, the way parents of deaf children place signs on their infants (Maestas y Moores, 1980, p. 5; Schlesinger & Meadow, 1972, pp. 67–68; see also Chapters 1 and 6 this volume).

Sometimes the first observation of a new sign involved direct imitation. For example, Loulis first used DRINK during a meal after Washoe used this sign in answer to a human caregiver who had asked WHAT about a drink. As Washoe was signing DRINK, Loulis watched her and signed DRINK, himself. Washoe also modelled directly for Loulis. For example, she signed BRUSH and then brushed Loulis with a hairbrush. On another occasion, Washoe placed a small plastic chair in front of Loulis, and then signed CHAIR/SIT to him several times in succession, watching him closely throughout.

It is important to remember that Washoe and Loulis were not under constant observation. Funds available in those critical early days permitted only four hours per day of scheduled observation by trained observers. In only a handful of cases could we be sure that we had observed the events surrounding the first use of a sign by Loulis. In most cases Loulis' signs appeared to be delayed imitations of signs that he had seen Washoe or another signing chimpanzee using in similar context (Fouts, Hirsch & Fouts, 1982).

Nonverbal Skills

In addition to signs, Loulis acquired other skills from the cross-fostered chimpanzees. He learned to use bowls and spoons as feeding implements, just as Washoe, Moja, Tatu, and Dar used them. He learned to build a sleeping nest with blankets in Washoe's unique way. Washoe builds a nest by taking her blanket and swirling it around herself on the floor, and sometimes she wraps herself in it. Then she collects toys and other objects and places them in her nest. For many months, Loulis simply watched Washoe, or played by himself, although occasionally he helped by giving her a toy. Then, Washoe began to hold Loulis as she built her nest. Eventually, Loulis learned Washoe's nesting methods and when given his blanket at night, he swirled it around himself as she did.

Washoe Learns From the Younger Chimpanzees

Washoe herself has learned new signs from Moja, Tatu, and Dar. Because the Gardners could not find the BLANKET sign in the sign language manuals then available, Washoe was taught to use the noun/verb COVER for blankets (see Chapter 3 this volume, pp. 60–61). Later in Reno, Moja, Tatu, and Dar were taught BLANKET, which differs in place, configuration, and movement from COVER (see Table 3.2). After these younger chimpanzees joined her, Washoe came to use both signs for blankets. From Moja, Washoe acquired a more precise form of the sign APPLE, and used it for apples, only. She continued to use the earlier form of her sign for several different kinds of fruits (cf. B. Gardner & Gardner, 1975, p. 261).

CONCLUSION

The findings presented in this chapter show that Loulis acquired signing and other skills from Washoe and the younger chimpanzees in his community. As in human language acquisition (Mocrk, 1976), the chimpanzee mother actively taught her offspring, and the infant actively learned. The laboratory environment provided interesting events and an enriched social atmosphere, "interesting things to talk about . . . and good friends to talk to" (R. Gardner & Gardner, 1974). Data collection by trained observers was a matter of course—as much a part of the routine as serving meals and cleaning. Because of this we have been able to examine the development of social behavior, communication, and other skills in Loulis without disrupting them, and in this way, obtained a comprehensive record of cultural transmission.

REFERENCES

Fouts, R.S. (1972). Use of guidance in teaching sign language to a chimpanzee. *Journal of Comparative and Physiological Psychology, 80,* 515–522.

Fouts, R.S. (1973). Acquisition and testing of gestural signs in four young chimpanzees. *Science, 180*, 978–980.

Fouts, R.S. (1975). Communication with chimpanzees. In G. Kurth & I. Eibl-Eibesfeldt (Eds.), *Hominisation und verhalten*, (pp. 137–158). Stuttgart: Gustav Fischer Verlag.

Fouts, R.S., Chown, B., & Goodin, L. (1976). Transfer of signed responses in American Sign Language from vocal English stimuli to physical object stimuli by a chimpanzee (*Pan*). *Learning and Motivation, 7*, 458–475.

Fouts, R.S., Fouts, D.H., & Schoenfeld, D. (1984). Sign language conversational interaction between chimpanzees. *Sign Language Studies, 42*, 1–12.

Fouts, R.S., & Goodin, L. (November, 1974). Acquisition of signs in chimpanzees: A comparison of training methods. Paper presented at the Annual Meeting of the Psychonomic Society, Boston, MA.

Fouts, R.S., Hirsch, A.D., & Fouts, D.H. (1982). Cultural transmission of a human language in a chimpanzee mother-infant relationship. In H.E. Fitzgerald, J.A. Mullins & P. Page (Eds.), *Psychobiological perspectives: Child nurturance*, (Vol. 3, pp. 159–193). New York: Plenum Press.

Fouts, R.S., & Rigby, R. (1977). Man-chimpanzee communication. In T. Sebeok (Ed.), *How animals communicate*, (pp. 1034–1054). Bloomington: Indiana University Press.

Fouts, R.S., Shapiro, G., & O'Neil, C. (1978). Studies of linguistic behavior in apes and children. In P. Siple (Ed.), *Understanding language through sign language research*, (pp. 163–185). New York: Academic Press.

Gardner, B.T., & Gardner, R.A. (1975). Evidence for sentence constituents in the early utterances of child and chimpanzee. *Journal of Experimental Psychology: General, 104*, 244–267.

Gardner, R.A., & Gardner, B.T. (1974). Teaching sign language to the chimpanzee, Washoe. *Bulletin D'Audio Phonologie, 4* (5), 145–173.

Maestas y Moores, J. (1980). Early linguistic environment: Interactions of deaf parents with their infants. *Sign Language Studies, 26*, 1–13.

Moerk, E.L. (1976). Processes of language teaching and training in the interactions of mother-child dyads. *Child Development, 47*, 1064–1078.

Schlesinger, H.S., & Meadow, K.P. (1972). *Deafness and mental health: A developmental approach*. Berkeley: University of California Press.

Stokoe, W., Casterline, D., & Croneberg, C. (1976). *A dictionary of American Sign Language*. Silver Spring, MD: Linstok Press.

9. Loulis in Conversation with the Cross-Fostered Chimpanzees

Roger S. Fouts and Deborah H. Fouts

T he cross-fostered chimpanzees learned ASL signs from familiar adult human beings. Soon they were initiating conversations with familiars and also addressing signs to strangers, nonhuman beings such as dogs and cats, and even to toys. They had to learn that only some people would sign back. Other signing chimpanzees made good conversational partners (R. Gardner & Gardner, 1978, pp. 44–46; Gorcyca, Garner, and Fouts 1975; 1982). When human signing was restricted to see if Loulis would learn signs from the cross-fosterlings, other chimpanzees were virtually the only source of conversational partners. Gradually, Loulis joined the conversations.

This chapter is concerned with Loulis' conversational development, the topics and the addressees of his conversations with other chimpanzees, and the social relations revealed in his signed interactions with Washoe, Moja, Tatu, and Dar. We began the systematic study of signed interaction between chimpanzees in May, 1981, when Dar and Tatu, each about five years old, came to the Ellensburg laboratory to be integrated into the social group which consisted of sixteen-year-old Washoe, her three-year-old adopted son Loulis, and eight-year-old Moja. Tatu and Dar were cross-fostered together with Moja in Reno, but only met Washoe and Loulis in Ellensburg. From May until December, Tatu and Dar lived next to Washoe, Loulis and Moja, but the two groups were separated by a wire mesh gate. In late December, 1981, the gate was opened and from then on the five chimpanzees lived together. (See Table 9.1 for a description of the early rearing conditions of the subjects).

METHOD

Daily Procedure

Throughout this study, a typical day in the life of Washoe, Loulis, Moja, Tatu, and Dar began around 8:00 A.M., when the human caregivers entered the laboratory, and greeted the chimpanzees. When greeting, the humans used both ASL signs and chimpanzee communicative gestures, such as head-bobs, pant-hoots, and bouncing (Goodall, 1986, pp. 114–145). Before breakfast, the chimpanzees were asked to help tidy their enclosure. They helped by returning their sleeping blankets as well as the feeding bowls, spoons, magazines, clothes, and branches they had received the night before. The chimpanzees were encouraged and thanked for helping. Here again, the humans used combinations of chimpanzee and human communicative gestures, for example, excited breathy pants, food-grunts, and big, showy THANK-YOU signs, when the cleaning task was nearly completed.

Table 9.1
Biographical Information for Each Chimpanzee

	Washoe	Moja	Tatu	Dar	Loulis
	female	female	female	male	male
Birth date:	9/65(est.)	11/18/72	12/30/75	8/2/76	5/10/78
Birthplace:	West Africa	LEMSIP, NY, USA	IPS, OK, USA	Holloman AFB, NM, USA	Yerkes Labs, GA, USA
Reared at: Univ. of Nevada, Reno*	6/66–10/70	11/72–12/79	1/76–5/81	8/76–5/81	------
Univ. of Oklahoma**	10/70–9/80	12/79–9/80	------	------	3/79–9/80
Central Washington Univ.***	9/80–	9/80–	5/81–	5/81–	9/80–
ASL Vocabulary (as of 10/87):	176	168	140	122	70

*Human cross-fostering; exposed to ASL only.
**Housed with other chimpanzees; exposed to ASL and spoken English. In the case of Loulis, ASL exposure was primarily from other chimpanzees.
***As above until 6/86; thereafter, exposed to ASL only.

For breakfast, each chimpanzee was offered a fruit drink called a "smoothie" and, depending on the season, fresh, frozen or dried fruit. The fruit smoothie consisted of various fruits and vitamins blended to make a thick, rich drink. Sometimes, the individual preparing breakfast selected an herbal tea, and offered that also. In the wild the chimpanzees eat over 140 different species of plants, as well as a variety of insects, birds' eggs, birds, and small mammals (Goodall, 1986, p. 232), and we tried to recreate this variety in the meals we provided. At the start of breakfast, all the chimpanzees came into one room and were served their smoothies in plastic beakers. During breakfast, the humans often gave the food-grunts that any good meal deserves. Washoe, as the eldest and most dominant member of the group, was usually served first. This was done out of respect for her social status in the group.

After breakfast, the humans cleaned the chimpanzees' compound. The chimpanzees had free access to the entire enclosure while cleaning took place and were free to do whatever they chose. They usually chose to interact with the humans who were cleaning. Interaction ranged from watching the humans at work, to elaborate attempts to engage them in chase games and other play. They frequently requested DRINK from the pistol-grip cleaning hose, and even asked to CLEAN. We responded by providing them with a pail of soapy water and scrub brushes. The chimpanzees worked on the inside of their enclosure, while the humans cleaned the outside area. Although cleaning was a required daily maintenance activity, it also provided excellent opportunities for the chimpanzees and the humans to interact, and some of the best observations of the chimpanzees as individuals and as a group took place during this task.

Typically after cleaning, a snack was served. Sometimes, the chimpanzees requested a treat, or several treats, during cleaning. At other times, we offered a SURPRISE treat, and they all responded with joyful and excited hooting. Along with dried fruits, fruit-leather, coffee, and gum, treat items included toothpaste on toothbrushes, flowers, snow, and water balloons (occasionally filled with fruit drinks). A special treat item was the raisin board—a six-inch-long board with several holes drilled in it, which were stuffed with raisins. This was offered together with a willow branch that served as a tool to extricate the food, as in termite fishing in the wild (Goodall, 1986, pp. 248–249).

In the period before lunch, play objects were brought out and handed to the chimpanzees: magazines, brushes, unbreakable mirrors, perfume samples, whistles, rubber bands, cardboard, cloth sacks, and so on. Some of the simplest objects were used the most, such as the empty paper or cloth sacks that were popular for games of chase. The chimpanzees covered the head with a sack and then engaged in a game similar to the children's game of "blind man's bluff."

At 12:00 lunch was served. Washoe, Loulis, Moja, Tatu and Dar were offered a choice of soups such as, bean, split pea, or lentil. These soups were flavored with different vegetables. We ground the soups in a mixer, otherwise the chimpanzees would pick out only their favorite vegetables and leave the rest. We served each of the chimpanzees a bowl of soup and served seconds to those who asked for MORE. Other proteins, such as tuna, beef, or chicken were offered occasionally for variety, but our chimpanzee group was not particularly fond of meat. We also gave them raw vegetables, yogurt, or peanuts at lunch. All meals were served in bowls or cups, with spoons for utensils. However, we also provided opportunities for foraging, by putting lettuce leaves heaped with some other vegetable on top of the chain link cover of the enclosure.

Lunch was followed by solitary play, quiet activities among the chimpanzees, or interactions with the human caregivers. For quiet activities, the chimpanzees were given drawing materials, as well as magazines or photo albums to look at alone or together with a human caregiver. The caregivers also played active games of tickle and chase with them. Because the humans always remained outside the enclosure, physical contact during these games was minimal, and hard plastic toys or long branches were used to tickle and poke the chimpanzees. But there are other ways of maintaining contact, and effective human play partners frequently produced chimpanzee gestures and vocalizations, such as the breathy laughter, play-faces, play-walking, foot stomping, and so on. Grooming and brushing was another interaction that helped to build good relations between the chimpanzees and their human caregivers. Caregivers could offer their own arms for grooming by placing an elbow or a forearm next to the chain link enclosure. The best indication of acceptance was when two or even three chimpanzees joined in a grooming session with the human caregiver. Such acceptance into the group was not only important in terms of social relations, but led to better opportunities to observe subtleties and individual differences in the behavior of these chimpanzees.

In the late afternoon, the compound was cleaned once more. Again, the chimpanzees were free to be passive observers or to take an active role as helper, or play partner. Dinner, served around 4:00 P.M. consisted of rice, cooked cereal, or steamed vegetables, or a combination of cooked grains and cooked vegetables. For variety, we also provided sandwiches, potato salad, pizza and on occasion, popcorn. After the dinner meal had been finished and the enclosure made tidy, each chimpanzee received a blanket for nesting and sleeping. At some seasons, we also provided willow branches, corn stalks and other vegetation as bedding material.

In these ways, we attempted to break the routine of an institution, to make each meal an interesting and enjoyable social event, and each day special, with many different activities and many opportunities for social interaction. We also celebrated the birthdays of Washoe, Loulis, Moja, Tatu, and Dar, as well as most of the holidays on the calendar, which made at least one, and usually more, days of each month extra special. Thus the Christmas celebration started sometime after Thanksgiving, when we set up a tree near the enclosure, and began to make garlands of edible ornaments for the tree and the hallways. By late December, the tree was covered with different edible treats such as nuts, dried fruit, popcorn, and gum. Throughout this period, the tree was a popular topic of conversation between the chimpanzees and their human caretakers. In 1986, the first snowstorm of the season came on the day after Thanksgiving. The following morning the laboratory seemed especially quiet and serene, with the sprinkle of snow on the ground visible from all the laboratory windows. As was usual during college vacations, the students were away, and only the

Foutses were in the lab. Perhaps all this reminded Tatu of Christmas, or perhaps she thought the Foutses needed to be reminded to set up a tree. During the cleaning routine, she followed them around, signing, SWEET SWEET SWEET TREE. Deborah Fouts assured Tatu, YOU MUST WAIT FOR SANTA.

Observer Training

There were strict prerequisites and requirements as well as a training regimen for prospective participants in this research. Before being admitted to the training program, prospective participants (usually, CWU students) completed at least one university level class in ASL. The training program began with a three-month introductory course, which included reading books and journal articles pertinent to this new field, as well as viewing films and video tapes of captive and wild chimpanzees.

Next, the participants were trained to recognize specific chimpanzee behaviors, both verbal and nonverbal, as well as the individual traits and habits of the chimpanzees in the group. Their training in ASL was extended to include the laboratory criteria of form and usage that had to be met for a gesture to be recorded as a sign and the PCM method of describing signs (Stokoe, 1965; Chapter 3 this volume). They had to master a manual of descriptive terms and abbreviations for nonverbal behavior as well. The majority of the 338 terms in this 40-page manual* are based on Goodall's (1968) classification of the facial expressions, vocalizations, postures and actions of wild chimpanzees. All of the participants had to pass a formal one-hour test on such terms as play-face, pant-hoot, and bipedal swagger.

After this, each trainee viewed video-taped interactions of the chimpanzees, together with an experienced observer. The experienced observer, a research participant who had at least two years experience with ASL and with these five chimpanzees, identified each behavior as specific examples appeared on the video screen. The trainees recorded observations of taped interactions in longhand, and then practiced identifying signs and transcribing nonverbal behavior into the abbreviations of the manual of nonverbal behavior (NVB).

Finally, each trainee recorded ongoing chimpanzee interactions together with the experienced research participant and their records were compared for interobserver reliability. Problem areas were discussed and there was further individualized instruction until the interobserver agreement was greater than 80%. Only then were the new research participants scheduled for data collection on their own.

---

*Copies of this manual of nonverbal behavior can be obtained from the authors on request.

Nonverbal behavior, such as the backhand thump or the bipedal swagger, was described with terms from the NVB manual which includes 49 terms that refer to facial expressions and vocalizations, 30 that refer to postures, and 117 that refer to actions. An English word gloss was used to describe each gesture that qualified as a sign. The specific word such as COME, HUG, or HURRY corresponds to a distinctive combination of place, hand configuration, and movement (cf. Chapter 3 this volume).

Sample

Daily Records

The chimpanzees' use of signs in the course of the daily routine was recorded over a period of 21 months (5/81–1/83). Comprehensive sampling sessions, 40-minutes in duration, were scheduled five times daily, five days per week (excluding weekends and school holidays). In each sampling session, the behavior and signs that occurred during interactions were recorded by an observer, sometimes by an observer and a trainee, standing just outside the enclosure. The observer assigned each interaction to a context, such as reassurance, play, feeding, mutual grooming, or discipline.

Of course, the chimpanzees also signed at other times and such observations of signing were recorded in the daily log that was kept for the individual chimpanzees. We will refer to records of interactions obtained outside of the systematic sampling sessions as *adventitious*. The systematic sampling sessions accounted for 76.4% of the reports that we analyzed, while the adventitious samples accounted for 23.6%.

Remote Video Recording

During a 15-day period at the end of July and the beginning of August, 1983, video cameras and remote video recorders monitored the chimpanzees' interactions, with no humans present (D. Fouts, 1984). There were three video cameras, each focused on a portion of the enclosure. There was some overlap of the areas covered by the three cameras, but only 75% of the total enclosure area was covered. The three cameras were connnected to video recorders located in a separate recording room. Every day during the 15-day period, the video cameras were turned on for three 20-minute recording periods between the hours of 9:00 A.M. and 5:00 P.M. Forty-five recording periods were scheduled so that each hour of the day was sampled randomly without replacement, either five or six times.

During these recording sessions no one entered the chimpanzee quarters, surrounding hallways, and adjacent rooms. Everyone stayed out of view and kept silent, and all activities in the laboratory that might be a distraction were stopped—even cooking of meals was forbidden, because the cooking odors might distract the chimpanzees from their interactions.

Parameters of Conversation

Initiator and Addresee

All interactions that included signing were classified as conversations, and the first chimpanzee to use signs within an interaction was classified as the initiator of that conversation. The addressee was determined on the basis of body and head orientation. Thus, if Loulis was signing while his body and his head, or his head alone was directed toward Dar, then Dar was considered to be Loulis' addressee.

Context

Interactions were classified into one of six behavior contexts, reassurance, grooming, play, discipline, eating/feeding, and social interaction, as follows.

In a reassurance context, the individual seeking reassurance beckons, crouches in a submissive posture or offers a pronated wrist, and may also whimper. The individual is calmed with a touch from the other chimpanzee. For example, after Loulis hit Moja, Moja whimpered as she approached Washoe and signed, HUG (soliciting reassurance). Washoe then signed COME HUG (offering reassurance), and when Moja approached, Washoe hugged her.

In a grooming context, one chimpanzee inspects the skin of another by parting the hair with one hand, and picking the skin with the free hand or lips. Grooming is often accompanied by lip smacking and clacking of the teeth. For example, Loulis approached Washoe as she sat on the bench, and then presented his back to be groomed. In another instance of a grooming interaction, Loulis took Tatu's foot while signing THAT GIMME, and then probed a sore on her foot.

In a play context, one chimpanzee tickles, wrestles, or chases another, or offers a play object such as a toy or his own foot. Play is often accompanied by breathy panting or laughter, and the "play-face" in which the lower teeth are exposed but the upper teeth are covered by the lip. For example, Dar signed CHASE to Loulis and then moved away as if in anticipation of being chased. Loulis approached and chased Dar, and then Dar and Loulis wrestled on the floor and began the breathy panting of laughter.

In a discipline context, one individual asserts dominance and enforces a change in the behavior of another chimpanzee. The disciplinarian uses gestures such as a backhand thump, a bipedal swagger, a bite, or a slap. For example, Tatu bit Loulis who responded by screaming. Next Washoe entered the room, swaggered bipedally at Tatu, thumped her with the back of the hand and signed GO to her. Tatu now screamed, and withdrew to an overhead tunnel.

In a feeding/eating context, food is present and some chimpanzees are eating. For example, Loulis, who had finished his meal, approached Washoe, who was still eating. Loulis whimpered and signed GIMME FOOD, and attempted to pull her bowl away. Washoe hugged Loulis, then took her bowl and moved away from him.

Finally, a social interaction context, encompasses soliciting objects or contact, and greetings and signs that do not fit into the other, more specific contexts described above. Undesignated affinitive and agonistic behaviors are included in this category.

Duration

Signed conversations consisted of one or more signed utterances and two or more turns. All of the signed conversations included some communicative behaviors in addition to signs (Fouts, Fouts, & Schoenfeld, 1984). For example, the following is a conversation that occurred during a play interaction between Loulis and Dar:

> Turn 1, Utterance 1: Loulis solicited a water balloon
> from Dar by signing HURRY HURRY while holding his
> hand toward the balloon.
> Turn 2: Dar moved away from Loulis.
> Turn 3, Utterance 2: Loulis signed WANT to Dar.
> Turn 4: Dar again moved away.
> Turn 5, Utterance 3: Loulis signed HURRY HURRY GIMME to
> Dar.
> Turn 6: Dar terminated the interaction by putting the
> balloon into his mouth and turning away from
> Loulis who also withdrew.
> (Later, in reference to the same piece of balloon, Loulis
> signed GUM GUM, placing the sign on Dar's cheek,
> and then signed GUM on his own cheek. Dar
> continued to chew on the balloon and Loulis did
> not get it.)

This conversation has six turns and three signed utterances, HURRY, WANT, and HURRY GIMME. Both in Turn 1 and in Turn 5, HURRY was counted as a reiterated sign and not as two separate HURRY signs, since reiteration is a way of modulating semantic meaning (Van Cantfort & Rimpau, 1982; Chapters 2 & 6 this volume).

RESULTS

Daily Records

Daily records showed that the introduction of Dar and Tatu to Washoe, Loulis and Moja produced a dramatic effect on the incidence of signing. In the eight-month period just prior to the introduction of Dar and Tatu (May, 1981–

Dec., 1981), the monthly totals of conversations between chimpanzees ranged from 12 to 85, with a mean of 37.75. However, during the 13-month period after Dar and Tatu were allowed physical contact with the other chimpanzees (Jan., 1982–Jan., 1983), the monthly totals for conversations ranged from 118 to 659 with a mean of 378.15.

Addressee. Before the introduction of Dar and Tatu, Loulis was the primary initiator of signing and he addressed 90% of his conversations to his adopted mother, Washoe. As he grew older and became more familiar with his new peers, Loulis addressed an increasing proportion of signs to Dar, his male peer, and a decreasing proportion to Washoe, his mother. During the final ten months of this sample (Apr., 1982–Jan., 1983), Loulis initiated 1,292 conversations and addressed 54% of these to Washoe, 27% to Dar, but only 10% to Tatu and 9% to Moja. Similarly, Tatu and Dar, closest in age to Loulis, initiated most of the signing addressed to Loulis during the same period.

Context. In this sample, 88% of the conversations occurred in just three contexts: social interaction (39%), reassurance (29%) and play (20%). Only 5% of the conversations occurred in a feeding context (Fouts et al., 1984).

Remote Video-Taped Records

To determine interobserver reliability, five of the 45 video-taped samples were scored independently by two experienced observers. Malcolm McClinton and Deborah H. Fouts had studied ASL, the NVB manual, and the chimpanzee subjects for two and a half years and five years respectively. An agreement was counted when these two observers agreed on all six aspects of the interactions: (1) context category; (2) initiator; (3) terminator; (4) gloss and form description of signs; (5) the number of signs; and (6) the number of turns. If any of these six aspects of an interaction was scored differently, it was counted as a disagreement. In the five segments, there were forty interactions, altogether. For 93% of the interactions, the two observers agreed in their reports for all aspects of the interaction. Disagreements were excluded from the final analysis of the data.

The 45 video-taped sessions randomly sampled each hour of the daily routine. The amount of signing varied from sample to sample. As many as 29 different conversations were recorded in a single 20-minute session, but in some sessions the chimpanzees rested or groomed during the entire 20 minutes. The 451 interactions that Loulis initiated accounted for 4 hours, 13 minutes or 28% of the total 15-hour video record. The 54 conversations (interactions containing signs) that Loulis initiated accounted for 43 minutes, 20 seconds.

Table 9.2 shows that the majority of the interactions (signed conversations and nonsigning interactions) that Loulis initiated were directed to Dar, his male peer. Of the 451 interactions, 40% (181) were addressed to Dar, while between 19% and 21% were addressed to each of the other three chimpanzees, Washoe, Moja, and Tatu. Loulis' preference for Dar as an addressee is even more marked when we consider the 54 conversations that he initiated: 50% were addressed to Dar, and between 5% and 22% were addressed to the other three chimpanzees.

Table 9.2
Contexts and Addressees for Interactions Initiated by Loulis

Context		Washoe	Moja	Tatu	Dar	Total
				Addressee		
Social	S	3	0	6	10	19
	NS	54	66	53	52	225
Play	S	1	3	0	16	20
	NS	20	6	1	85	112
Grooming	S	0	0	6	1	7
	NS	3	12	18	13	46
Reassurance	S	8	0	0	0	8
	NS	3	0	2	1	6
Discipline	S	0	0	0	0	0
	NS	0	0	0	0	0
Feed/Eat	S	0	0	0	0	0
	NS	3	2	0	3	8
Total	S	12	3	12	27	54
	NS	83	86	74	154	397
Total interactions		95	89	86	181	451

S = interactions with signing; NS = nonsigning interactions

Table 9.2 also shows that, in the context of play, Loulis initiated 4.8 times as many interactions with Dar as with his mother Washoe (101 vs. 21), and 11.2 times as many with Dar as with Moja, a female peer (101 vs. 9). He only initiated one play interaction with his other female peer, Tatu. In the social context, Loulis initiated a sizable and roughly equivalent number of interactions with each of the other chimpanzees. There were less than ten conversations in four of the six contexts (reassurance, grooming, discipline, and eating/feeding), too few to make comparisons of Loulis signing to his mother and to his three peers.

Table 9.3 shows that Loulis used more signs in his interactions with Dar

than with any other chimpanzee: 55% of the 206 signs Loulis used during interactions were addressed to Dar, 23% to Tatu, 17% to Washoe, and 4% to
Moja. When we compare these findings to earlier samples of conversations initiated by Loulis, it can be seen that the focus of his signing shifted from
Washoe to Dar. Goodall has described a similar shift from mother to peers in
the social development of wild chimpanzees (1971, pp. 156-157, 170 & 245;
1975, p. 137; 1986, pp. 81, 166).

Table 9.3
Number of Signs Used by Loulis as a Function of Context and Addressee

	Addressee				
Context	*Washoe*	*Moja*	*Tatu*	*Dar*	*Total*
Social	6	0	25	68	99
Play	2	9	0	43	54
Grooming	0	0	23	3	26
Reassurance	27	0	0	0	27
Discipline	0	0	0	0	0
Feed/Eat	0	0	0	0	0
Total	35	9	48	114	206

At the time of this video sample Loulis' total vocabulary consisted of 43
signs (see Table 8.1 this volume). Table 9.4 lists the signs that appeared in the
sample and the frequencies of each. Most of Loulis' signs were addressed to
one of the other chimpanzees, but in many cases his head and body were not
oriented toward his companions and he appeared to be signing to himself.
Table 9.4 lists these two cases separately as "interactions" and "private signing."

EXPANDING HORIZONS

At this writing we have video records for four consecutive years, and we
plan to add at least 15 hours of tape each year. These records provide a rich
sample of chimpanzee-to-chimpanzee signing that is currently under investigation. The following are examples of the topics in the ongoing investigation.

Modulation

Chapters 2 and 6 in this volume (see also Fant, 1972; Van Cantfort & Rimpau, 1982) take up the question of meaningful modulations of the shapes of
signs. Similar modulations appear in the remote video taping of chimpanzee-

to-chimpanzee signing. For example, during an interaction before lunch Tatu used repetition for emphasis together with questioning modulation. Tatu approached Washoe and signed TIME TIME TIME TIME EAT EAT. As she signed, Tatu looked steadily into Washoe's eyes while holding the last sign, EAT.

Table 9.4
Signs Used by Loulis During Interactions and When Signing to Himself

	Interactions	Private signing
HURRY	134	6
BALL	—	59
ME/MINE	17	24
HAT	—	16
GOOD	11	4
COME	13	—
MORE	7	—
DRINK	6	1
WANT	4	—
PEEKABOO	4	—
GUM	3	—
PERSON	3	—
GIMME	2	—
OUT	—	2
SHOE	1	1
FOOD	—	1
MASK	—	1
TICKLE	1	—
Total frequency	206	115

Signs for actions are placed on the addressee, to indicate agent-of-action (cf. Chapter 6 this volume). For example, we have recorded Dar making the TICKLE sign on Loulis' hand followed by a tickle game between the two young males (see Figure 3.4 this volume). Dar often uses yet another inflected form of TICKLE when he signs TICKLE on one of his toys, and then gives the toy to a human who is expected to tickle him with it. Incidentally, at this writing Dar's favorite toy to be tickled with is still a model of a Tyrannosaurus rex (see p. 257, Chapter 6 this volume).

Social Strategies

During a remote video-taping session Loulis used a social strategy that resembles one commonly used by human children. We recorded an instance of this, following a fight between Loulis and Dar. After the fight subsided, Dar moved away from Loulis, while continuing to scream. At the same time that Dar was screaming, Loulis approached and sat quietly behind Washoe and signed GOOD GOOD GOOD to her. Much like a human child, he seemed to be assuring his mother that he was good.

Signing and Aggression

In some interactions recorded by remote video tape, signing appeared to reduce aggression. There were several instances in which Loulis was harassing one of his female peers, Moja and Tatu, until either Washoe or Dar distracted Loulis by signing TICKLE, CHASE, GROOM or COME to him. This signed invitation to play or groom was often effective in distracting Loulis from further aggressive behavior.

In one such incident, Loulis harassed Moja and Tatu by rushing at them and hitting them both as they say grooming. Moja and Tatu moved away and began to resume grooming. When Loulis started to charge them again, Dar reached out and touched Loulis on the arm. Loulis ignored this touch, and continued his charge. Moja and Tatu moved away from Loulis once more. Now Washoe reached out and touched Loulis on the leg and Dar signed TICKLE on Loulis' arm. Loulis responded to Dar by turning toward him and wrestling with him. Washoe joined in this game by tickling Loulis with her hand, as Dar wrestled with him. Subsequently, Loulis withdrew from the area where Moja and Tatu were, and no further aggression occurred. Thus, these chimpanzees used signs to initiate a distraction which in turn served to inhibit aggression.

Tool Use

During the remote video-taping sessions we recorded three different instances of Loulis using a stick to groom Tatu's infected foot. In each case, Loulis held Tatu's foot and then picked up a willow branch from the floor. Next, Loulis used his teeth to break off a portion of the branch, and chewed the open end of the branch until it was pointed. He inserted the pointed end of the branch in the wound, and moved it around in the wound. If Tatu attempted to remove her foot Loulis sometimes signed GIMME, COME or HURRY to solicit the wounded foot, or merely grabbed the foot and began again. Washoe seemed to disapprove of this method of grooming. She was observed to remove the grooming stick from Loulis each time she saw him use it, or begin to fashion it with his teeth. On two occasions, after removing the stick, Washoe took Tatu's foot and groomed it with her lips and fingers, which is the standard method of grooming used by free-living chimpanzees in Africa. Tatu's wound was such an attractive target for grooming that the frequency of grooming interactions among all of the chimpanzees increased during the period in which we were video taping.

SUMMARY

In these studies we have demonstrated that chimpanzees used signs when conversing with each other, even when no humans were present. We have demonstrated that chimpanzee-to-chimpanzee signing was rich enough to provide texts that could be analyzed for context, initiator, addressee, number of signs and number of conversational turns. We have demonstrated that the signs used during interactions between chimpanzees were clear enough so that independent observers, fluent in ASL, agreed in their identification of more than 90% of the signs.

REFERENCES

Fant, L. (1972). *Ameslan: An introduction to American Sign Language*. Northridge, CA: Joyce Media, Inc.

Fouts, D.H. (1984). Remote video taping of a juvenile chimpanzee's sign language interactions within his social group. Unpublished master's thesis. Ellensburg, WA: Central Washington University.

Fouts, R.S., Fouts, D.H., & Schoenfeld, D. (1984). Sign language conversational interactions between chimpanzees. *Sign Language Studies, 34,* 1–12.

Gardner, R.A., & Gardner, B.T. (1978). Comparative psychology and language acquisition. *Annals of the New York Academy of Sciences, 309,* 37–76.

Goodall, J. van Lawick (1968). The behavior of free living chimpanzees in the Gombe Stream Reserve. *Animal Behavior Monographs, 1,* 163–311.

Goodall, J. van Lawick (1971). *In the shadow of man*. Boston, MA: Houghton Mifflin Company.

Goodall, J. van Lawick (1975). The chimpanzee. In V. Goodall (Ed.), *The quest for man*, (pp. 131–169). London: Phaidon Press.

Goodall, J. (1986). *The chimpanzees of Gombe*. Cambridge, MA: Harvard University Press.

Gorcyca, D., Garner, P., & Fouts, R. (December, 1975). Deaf children and chimpanzees: A comparative sociolinguistic investigation. Paper presented at the Speech Communication Association Meetings in Houston, TX.

Gorcyca, D., Garner, P., & Fouts, R. (1982). Deaf children and chimpanzees: A comparative sociolinguistic investigation. In M. R. Key (Ed.), *Nonverbal communication today*, (pp. 219–231). New York: Mouton Publishers.

Stokoe, W.C., Casterline, D., & Croneberg, C.G. (1965). *A dictionary of Ameri-

can Sign Language on linguistic principles. Washington, D.C.: Gallaudet College Press.

Van Cantfort, T.E., & Rimpau, J.B. (1982). Sign language studies with children and chimpanzees. *Sign Language Studies, 34,* 15–72.

10. Comparative and Developmental Sign Language Studies: A Review of Recent Advances

William C. Stokoe

I t must be clear to a reader of the nine preceding chapters that the term "sign language" is both too narrow and too broad to cover with precision all the behavior reported on in this volume. The cross-fostered chimpanzees herein described—as distinguished from those trained by operant conditioning—learned more than to respond to signed queries and to make their own appropriate use of lexical signs; they also learned to behave in ways comparable with the normal behavior of human children. Because anything that signifies something else is a sign in the strict semiotic sense of the term *sign*, the "sign languages" taught to great apes have varied from artificial codes using an assortment of plastic chips of different shapes and colors to the fully described interaction of a number of cross-fostered chimpanzees with their human companions.

In referring, therefore, to studies of sign languages, I would like to use the term *sign language* to stand only for a primary sign language, especially ASL; i.e., I would like to make use of Adam Kendon's classification of sign languages into primary and alternate (1986). *Primary* sign languages, as Kendon terms them, are those used by persons (for the most part deaf persons) as their chief or only linguistic system. *Alternate* sign languages are manually expressed systems used by persons who have complete competence in at least one spoken language. They usually have the free choice of using or not using the latter, a choice denied to most deaf persons.

What emerges from the studies and reviews of studies reported in this volume is a much broader enterprise than teaching manually produced signs to apes. The signs were selected for the most part from a primary sign language, ASL; but the subjects were given something even more important, the opportunity to develop generally and without restraint in a human environment. This is an environment, to be sure, quite foreign to their species but with patent similarities (e.g., the chimpanzee Dar's video-taped interaction with Tony McCorkle described in Chapter 6 by Rimpau and the Gardners is not unlike filmed interactions of a baby chimpanzee with its mother or an older sibling). These animals thus learned to interact more or less appropriately in encounters not untypical of those human infants experience. The behavior of Washoe, Moja, Pili, Tatu, and Dar in the situations described in Chapter 3 is unmistakably like that of human infants; but equally impressive is the care with which the observations of signing and the testing were done.

A few other experimenters have fostered chimpanzees, orangutans, or gorillas in more or less natural human environments. A smaller number, using the methods of strict behaviorism, have exercised varying degrees of care in the design and procedure of their experiments with caged animals. It seems difficult, in practice as well as in theory, to reconcile a natural or naturalistic setting with a rigorous, quantifiable experimental procedure. It has been done, however, as the descriptions and data in Chapters 3 and 4 demonstrate. Both the fostering care and the data-collecting the Gardners supervised stand out as examples of how such things ought to be done.

The chimpanzees reared in Reno were not overtly taught a sign language; they were engaged in constant interaction with human companions who used manual signs instead of words. It is not usual practice, either, to teach deaf children to use sign language. If the deaf children's parents can hear, and about ninety-five percent of them can, these children, in the recent past, were trained—not taught—by a specially trained therapist to produce language-like sounds modelled and monitored by that therapist, and to guess at language sounds the therapist and others made by inspecting their faces. Some changes have come about since all early teaching of deaf children of hearing parents was strictly oralist (i.e., limited only to artificial speech and lipreading). Some deaf children with hearing parents are now exposed not to a primary sign language but to a means of communicating in which manual signs stand for some of the words of the caretaker's language and are produced one after another in the normal order used in that language. Formal teaching of deaf children to communicate has thus evolved in the last half century from strict oralism to the use of manual signs as surrogates for spoken words, the latter in programs rather grandly called "total communication."

The exposure of the cross-fostered animals described in this volume is unlike either oralism or total communication. As described by those who began and carried it on for more than a decade (Chapter 3), it resembles instead the exposure of deaf children of deaf parents to the normal means of communication deaf people use among themselves. The human companions, or foster family members, of Washoe and the younger subjects were fully aware of the necessity of manual signs in the circumstances—earlier work had shown that a chimpanzee under the best of conditions did not learn to produce more than a handful of words. Some of these companions were native signers (i.e., persons born deaf of deaf signing parents), but all were or became familiar with the signs of

ASL and also with the literature on sign language linguistics and on deaf and hearing children's language acquisition.

Teaching Language

Whether a language is signed or spoken, it is still inappropriate for it to be taught overtly to young children. As long ago as 1976, Raymond Stevens explained why "Deaf children's language should be learned and not taught." Like other children, deaf children acquire their initial language by interacting with others. They use any sensory system or systems available to them, both for reading the messages of others and for expressing their own thoughts. Teaching a language, or any other system, in formal fashion to very young children is inappropriate (Krashen & Seliger, 1976). Before a child reaches the age (in psychologists' terms, the cognitive level) at which it is natural to ask, in effect, "What is the rule for that?" all overt teaching of anything as complex as language can be self-defeating. Nevertheless, a dozen years after the publication of the Stevens study, it is still common to find young deaf children being taught the rules for standard English grammar—often with manual signs substituting for words of a language quite opaque to the child.

Psycholinguists and sociolinguists disagree about what is essential for language acquisition. Is an innate language capacity in the human brain, a "language organ" carried by human genes, the *open sesame* of the whole system? Or is the real key constant interaction with other language-using human beings? Despite this fundamental disagreement, linguists of many persuasions can and do agree that overt teaching of a first language is at least unnecessary, and at worst pernicious. Unfortunately, in the teaching of deaf children, which has too long been overprotected against the penetration of linguistic knowledge, overt teaching of a language impenetrable to the working senses of deaf children continues. Ironically, this perverse clinging to failed and outdated procedures makes it easier to compare deaf children with those apes that were also overtly taught to use manual signs or chips or keyboards easier, while the real ends of teaching deaf children are lost.

The distinction between teaching sign language and teaching signs cannot be too much emphasized. Teaching a visual-gestural linguistic system, and teaching manual signs for words that stand for things and persons and actions, belong to two quite different logical types, even though the latter activity can be a sub-process of the former. As the authors in this volume make clear, their "teaching" of signs to cross-fostered chimpanzees has been deliberately modelled on the way language learning, not teaching, takes place. In an environment made as similar as possible to that of human infants the infant chimpanzees saw their caretakers signing; thus they received typically human, not narrowly behavioristic, reinforcement when their behavior, including the places, movements, and configurations they attempted, were appropriate in the context. The objects they were shown signs for naming were not arbitrarily introduced but were those commonly found in nurseries. The restraint and discipline used by these experimenters were also more typical of enlightened child rearing than of the procedures in laboratories where the experimental animals are kept in cages when not under treatment.

How It's Done

Critics of the experiment centered in Reno have often overlooked the fact that adult speech to very young children differs in many ways from the speech that adults use among themselves. In a study of both English-speaking and Spanish-speaking families, Blount and Kempton (1976) found thirty-four features in the speech of parents that marked it as appropriate for young children and usually inappropriate for adult speech—features that the adults were largely unaware of using. Clearly, whatever the nature of their "innate language organs" or "language acquisition devices" (or whether such things exist), human children are not exposed solely to adult speech from which they must use their internal language devices to decipher and infer a grammar. They are exposed instead to natural (i.e., unconscious) modifications of adult language that suit it to their status as learners of language. In this way, then, the cross-fostered chimpanzees fare much as those hearing children do, who hear speech unconsciously tailored to their needs—or as those deaf children do whose deaf parents sign to them.

What the chimpanzees experienced is even more similar to the experience of the exceptional deaf child who has deaf parents and who sees signs and signing modified (as in the parent language Blount and Kempton analyzed). In the early months of the child's life the purpose for all these unconscious modifications has been that of calling the infant's attention to what is going on (the speaking or signing). Later, as the child begins to attend to parental communication, their purpose is to call attention to the meaningfulness of the signing or speech. Julia Maestas y Moores (1980) gives a detailed description of the kinds of communicative behavior deaf parents do address to their infants—who may or may not turn out to be deaf. In the chapter by Rimpau and the Gardners (Chapter 6) it is clear that the same interactive modification of language behavior occurs between the human companion and the young chimpanzee. The chimpanzee signing an answer to WHAT? makes the sign GUM on the other's face and makes other changes in the citation form of the signs, and the video record will doubtless show that the human companion chooses signs and regulates the length and complexity of utterances just as do the parents Maestas writes about.

One might suppose, then, that appropriate data for comparing cross-fostered chimpanzees with human children who are acquiring language would be easy to find. What is found, instead, is that the circumstances of language acquisition in the real world vary much too widely to provide obvious parallels. The more the practitioners of theoretical language science agree in their postulation of universal rules of language, the more other, empirical, investigators observing what is there, find differences in all kinds of circumstances surrounding the infant's acquisition of the system. Theoreticians seeking universal rules for the way humans acquire language emphasize similarities and ignore or discount differences; and therefore much psycholinguistic study of young children's language development is intentionally species-specific and of little use to those who would compare it to what the apes have done.

This is painfully true for the comparative study of Washoe's accomplishments and those of other apes using manual signs. Obviously the better comparison for the chimpanzees' signing is not the accomplishment of hearing children in a speaking environment but that of deaf children developing language competence in a gestural-visual mode. When data on the language acquisition of deaf (or hearing) children exposed to signing is sought, however, the pertinent facts are still far from clear. Some of the signing children observed have been exposed to manual signs that stand for words (of signed English, signed Swedish, signed French, etc.); some exposed to hand and finger signs as cues to help them guess at the sounds that speakers are producing (Cued Speech); some exposed to signing by one parent but speaking by the other; some have siblings with whom they interact; others have none.

Few of the children studied, however, can confidently be said to have been exposed to a primary sign language. Recent studies make clear that it is not even possible to accept the claims of teachers and parents who say that they use ASL with their children (instead of some form of signed English)—not because the parents and teachers are untruthful but because individual signers cannot agree on definitions. Deaf signers from different backgrounds may not realize that they are in fundamental disagreement about the nature of the language they use. Erting (1982; 1985) found that these deaf signers themselves characterize ASL and signed English differently according to their family backgrounds, their expectations, and their self-image. Their sociocultural identities and notions of language are sharply defined by their own experience with signing, signers, deaf persons, and hearing persons. Only some of the deaf parents Erting studied claim to use ASL with their children. But 90 to 95% of deaf children have hearing parents, and so the number of children who acquire ASL as a primary language in the home cannot be large. Nor are they likely to acquire the language from teachers: Woodward and Allen (1987, pp. 1–10), in a survey of 1,888 teachers found 140 who stated they used ASL in the classroom, and by strict questioning determined that 25 of them maybe, and only 6 probably, were using ASL.

There is another reason that studies of language acquisition by deaf children in a primary sign language environment are not available for comparison with the huge corpus of data in this volume: No one to date has observed both the communicative behavior of a deaf child and its family, or foster family, members as has been done with chimpanzees and reported in the foregoing chapters. The studies here reported do more than reveal hitherto unknown capacities of apes for human-like communication (and show by the way that a primary sign language has sufficient linguistic power to bridge an inter-specific gap). These studies also point the way to far better studies of the acquisition of language by deaf children. Where oralists have assumed that the deaf child has no language at all until taught to form sounds and decipher lip and face changes, and where linguists have assumed that every child has all of language innately inside, studies of language acquisition have been impoverished by the constraints of their unwarranted assumptions. As more sign language studies of human children are conducted that break through these constraints to record and report as much as possible about what the young learners are doing, as the Gardners and their associates have done in this volume, then we shall have truly comparative data for human children.

Making Comparisons

As a first step in defining the rules for comparing what apes do with what children do as they acquire language, it is necessary to look at the similarities and differences between spoken languages and primary sign languages. Here the great disparity in trustworthy data and credible theories about each is at once apparent. Scientific study of spoken languages is of respectable age and has been carried out by many thousands of investigators. Studies of primary sign languages are not only new, engaged in by only a handful, but they are still tentative; it is possible to find both those who insist on the universality of language across sensory and motor channels and those who stress the differences at every level, from brain organization to finger use. At this time, the only safe advice to those who would compare ape and child as they communicate is to be aware of the sources of possible error. Experiments with nonhuman subjects done by empirically oriented investigators sort ill with descriptions of child language behavior presented by observers convinced that language is wholly innate in the human species alone, or that social interaction need not be attended to as a feature of language, or that a science of human behavior—or of any naturally occurring system—is simply a matter of rigorous logic.

Case studies of young deaf children or infants as they move from general interaction to intentionally communicative to genuinely linguistic behavior may provide the best material for comparison. Here the work of Volterra and associates (1985) comes to mind, for it not only distinguishes general communicative behavior from behavior that uses stable semiotic vehicles—i.e., they distinguish *vocalizations* and *gestures* from *words* and *signs*—but they also find an environmental factor crucial: though the deaf and the hearing children studied use both words and signs (language symbols), genuinely syntactic combination of either words or signs occurs in the child's behavior only if the parents of the child speak a particular spoken language or sign a particular primary sign language.

More generally, one who compares sign language acquisition or the development of communicative behavior across species needs to be aware of the important ways in which a child's sign language environment can vary. In the context of sign language, deafness is of course an important variable. Deafness, if present, may range from profound to slight, but because so much of speech requires very fine auditory discrimination, even a small loss of hearing acuity may have a severe effect on spoken language acquisition. Either or both of a deaf child's parents may be deaf or hard of hearing or may hear normally. Deaf parents may be fluent and relaxed signers, unselfconsciously using a primary sign language in most circumstances, or they may be reluctant to use signs at all with their offspring—a result of the conditioning that institutions and authorities in the past regularly imposed. Contrariwise, hearing parents may make the choice to sign with their deaf child, but their signing may slavishly follow one of the copyrighted systems for representing the words and grammatical particles of English (e.g., Anthony, 1971; Gustason, Pfetzing, & Zawolkow, 1975). Only a very few attempt, with more or less assistance from fluent signers, to use a primary sign language for interacting with the deaf child. Studies such as that by Woodward and Allen (1987) make it appear likely that even the most enlightened hearing parents sign and speak at the same time, and only produce manual signs for some of the key words that they are speaking.

Further, not only must the whole language environment of the sign-language-acquiring child be carefully described if valid comparison is to be made, but also it may be necessary to examine the sign language environment of the nonhuman experimental subject. That is, can it be determined what portion of the observed time the human companions' signing was in fact in a primary sign language and what portion used substitution of manual signs for the words of the language usually spoken?

Summing Up

Even though it is not yet possible, for the purpose of comparison, to point to definitive studies of the acquisition of sign language by children in ideal or well-defined circumstances, nor to define sign language itself completely and accurately (any more than spoken language can be so defined), it is very clear that studies of human-chimpanzee interaction have added to our knowledge of language and of our nearest nonhuman relatives. As with the chimpanzee, the human infant comes into the world with nothing resembling adult language. According to a once fashionable theory, the human infant is born with a language generating device able to construct a model of adult grammar (complete with its abstract rules) out of the various imprecise language performances in the surround; but there is no direct evidence that such is the case. Other theories may better explain what happens between infancy and the age at which the child is using adult language, but the work of the comparative psychologists in this volume is less concerned with theory building and theory validating than with facts. The facts are that like the newborn human infant, the infant chimpanzee demonstrates no competence in any language but that after months or years of interacting with signing human companions, chimpanzees can name objects, answer Wh-questions appropriately, and show by consistent and recurrent modification of signs that they appreciate the differences in the use of the signs in different contexts; etc.

These well-documented facts force a reconsideration of theory. The chimpanzees by definition can have no human language organ, and therefore their use of sign language signs in context and appropriately must result from the cognitive abilities of the chimpanzee plus consistent interaction with a human being using a linguistic system in the visual-gestural mode. The possibility then arises that there is a continuum in nature—even primate nature: what the human infant also experiences between birth and later childhood may result from human (and primate) cognitive abilities plus interaction with others, and not from a genetic "black box."

Another benefit conferred by these studies across species is more general: the investigations reported in this volume are models of scientific procedure. No claims are made that the animals think, joke, or lie like people; instead conditions and events are reported with copious and meticulous detail. No assumptions are made to form the basis for chains of inference: actions are described, and a careful record is compiled consistently over long periods. If only more investigations of children's development were as carefully conducted, we would know more about human language and human cognition.

References

Anthony, D. (1971). *Seeing Essential English*. Anaheim, CA: Union High School District.

Blount, B., & Kempton, W. (1976). Child language socialization: Parental speech and interactional strategies. *Sign Language Studies, 12*, 251–277.

Erting, C. (1982). *Deafness, communication and social identity: An anthropological analysis of interaction among parents, teachers and deaf children in a preschool*. Unpublished doctoral dissertation. Washington, D.C.: The American University.

Erting, C. (1985). Sociocultural dimensions of deaf education: Belief system and communicative interaction. *Sign Language Studies, 47*, 111–126.

Gustason, G., Pfetzing, D., & Zawolkow, E. (1975). *Signing Exact English*. Los Alamitos, CA: Modern Signs Press.

Kendon, A. (1986). Iconicity in Warlpiri sign language. In Bouissac et al. (Eds.), *Essays on the nature of culture, Festschrift for Thomas A. Sebeok on his 65th birthday.* Tubingen: Staffenburg Verlag.

Krashen, S., & Seliger, H. (1976). The role of formal and informal environments in 2nd language learning: A pilot study. *Linguistics, 172*, 15–21.

Maestas y Moores, J. (1980). Early linguistic environment: Interactions of deaf parents with their infants. *Sign Language Studies, 26*, 1–13.

Stevens, R. (1976). Children's language should be learned and not taught. *Sign Language Studies, 11*, 97–108. Also in W. Stokoe (Ed.), *Sign and culture: A reader for students of American Sign Language*, (pp. 206–216). Silver Spring, MD: Linstok Press.

Volterra, V. & Caselli, M. (1985). From gestures and vocalizations to signs and words. In V. Volterra and W. Stokoe (Eds.), *SLR '83: Sign Language Research*, (pp. 1–9). Silver Spring, MD: Linstok Press.

Woodward, J. & Allen, T. (1987). Classroom use of ASL by teachers. *Sign Language Studies, 54*, 1–10.

Contributors

Patrick Drumm, Department of Psychology, The Ohio State University, Columbus, OH 43210

Deborah H. Fouts, Department of Psychology, Central Washington University, Ellensburg, WA 98926

Roger S. Fouts, Department of Psychology, Central Washington University, Ellensburg, WA 98926

Beatrix T. Gardner, Department of Psychology, University of Nevada, Reno, NV 89557

R. Allen Gardner, Department of Psychology, University of Nevada, Reno, NV 89557

Susan G. Nichols, Department of Psychology, University of Nevada, Reno, NV 89557

Chris O'Sullivan, Department of Psychology, University of Kentucky, Lexington, KY 40506

James B. Rimpau, Department of Psychology, University of Nevada, Reno, NV 89557

William C. Stokoe, Department of Linguistics, Gallaudet College, Washington, DC 20002; Linstok Press, 9306 Mintwood Street, Silver Spring, MD 20901

Thomas E. Van Cantfort, Department of Psychology, University of Nevada, Reno, NV 89557

Carey Page Yeager, Department of Psychology, University of California, Davis, CA 95616

BIOGRAPHICAL INFORMATION FOR CHIMPANZEE SUBJECTS

WASHOE, female. b about September, 1965, West Africa. Reared 6/66-10/70, Univ. of Nevada, Reno; 10/70-9/80, Univ. of Oklahoma; 9/80-   Central Washington Univ.

MOJA, female. b November 18, 1972, Laboratory for Experimental Medicine and Surgery in Primates, New York. Reared 11/72-12/79, Univ. of Nevada, Reno; 12/79-9/80, Univ. of Oklahoma; 9/80-   Central Washington Univ.

PILI, male. b October 30, 1973, Yerkes Regional Primate Research Center, Georgia. Reared 11/73-10/75, Univ. of Nevada, Reno. Died of leukemia, 10/20/75.

TATU, female. b December 30, 1975, Institute for Primate Studies, Oklahoma. Reared 11/76-5/81, Univ. of Nevada, Reno; 5/81-   Central Washington Univ.

DAR, male. b August 2, 1976, Albany Medical College, Holloman AFB, New Mexico. Reared 8/76-5/81, Univ. of Nevada, Reno; 5/81-   Central Washington Univ.

LOULIS, male. b May 10, 1978, Yerkes Regional Primate Research Center, Georgia. Reared 3/79-9/80, Univ. of Oklahoma; 9/80-   Central Washington Univ.

Index

Italicized page numbers refer to figures and tables.